Handy DIY

HANDY

DIY

a complete A to Z guide

First published in 2003 by Collins,
an imprint of HarperCollins Publishers
77–85 Fulham Palace Road, London, W6 8JB

www.collins.co.uk

Text copyright © HarperCollins Publishers
Photography, artworks and design © HarperCollins Publishers
Based on material from the *Collins Complete DIY Manual* by
Inklink, and *Tommy Walsh's DIY Survival*

Created by: Focus Publishing,
11a St Botolph's Road, Sevenoaks, Kent, TN13 3AJ

e
ed in any
copying,
mission

A CIP catalogue record for this book is available from the
British Library

ISBN 000714668X

Colour reproduction in Singapore, by Colourscan
Printed and bound in Spain

Please note: Always take care when embarking on any DIY
project. Read the instructions for tools before you commence,
and take appropriate safety precautions. Great care has been
taken to ensure that the information contained in this book is
accurate and correct. However, the publishers can accept no
responsibility or liability for any loss or damage.

Contents

How to use this book

Handy DIY is a uniquely user-friendly guide to do-it-yourself. The pocket-sized format makes it quick and easy to use and the contents are arranged in a convenient A–Z style. Sound advice, numerous tips and special projects are accompanied by clearly presented illustrations throughout.

Clear, quick-reference folios

Handy tip tables

Alphabetical organisation

Easy-reference corner tabs

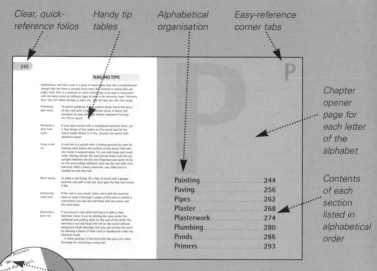

Chapter opener page for each letter of the alphabet

Contents of each section listed in alphabetical order

Coloured 'hand' symbols

▲ Coloured 'hand' symbols accompanied by page numbers throughout the book indicate cross-references to other parts of the book which are relevant and may be useful

PROJECT LEVEL

BEGINNER

INTERMEDIATE

ADVANCED

Handy DIY features numerous practical projects, all graded by degree of difficulty. There is something for everyone, from the novice to the experienced DIYer.

Introduction

'Do-It-Yourself' today is a very different proposition from the haphazard, amateurish pastime it was once widely derided as being. More and more people are discovering the pleasures of making home improvements themselves, while enjoying the benefits of a highly sophisticated market that reflects the way that DIY has developed in recent years. Householders have become used to a ready supply of well-made products and materials that are easy to use. With these, the competent DIY-er can produce first-class results that many a professional would be proud of.

In addition to improved materials and products, those interested in DIY can choose from countless home improvement television series, videos, books, magazines and websites. For the beginner, the range of DIY information and ideas now available must sometimes seem utterly bewildering – where do you start, and what is the best source of easy, quick-reference information to get a basic grip on the job in question?

Handy DIY is designed to answer these questions and to provide an easy-to-use introduction to DIY for the enthusiastic novice. However, it is also a pocket-sized reference point for the experienced DIY-er who needs to brush up on techniques, or perhaps a few new tips to complete a job to a better standard.

Arranged in a convenient A–Z style, this little book comprises numerous practical tips and special projects. There is advice on tools, equipment, materials and techniques, all described with the paramount consideration of safety firmly in mind.

Designed for dipping in and out of rather than for reading from cover to cover, *Handy DIY* features detailed, colour-coded cross-referencing that refers you to other information related to the task in hand.

Whether you want to learn how to change a fuse, un-block a drain or lay a ceramic floor, this book provides all the basic information you need in a straightforward, no-nonsense manner. With *Handy DIY* at your side, you can get your career as a home improver off to the best possible start.

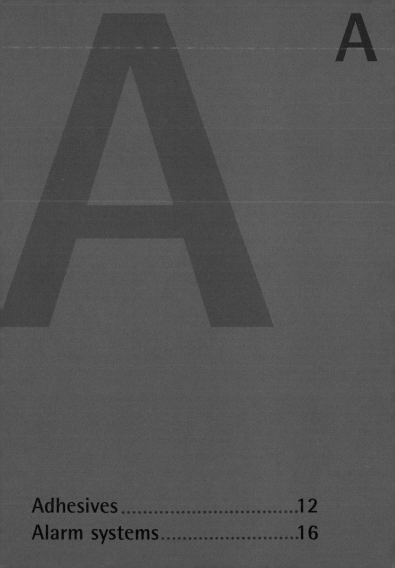

A

Adhesives

There are so many general-purpose and specific-purpose glues on the market today that it can be confusing as to which one is best for the job you are doing. Although there is no true 'universal glue' that will stick anything to anything, you can bond most materials if you use the appropriate adhesive. Those discussed here relate to many of the procedures dealt with in this book.

Fixing ceiling tiles

Expanded-polystyrene ceiling tiles and coving can be glued to plaster and plasterboard surfaces using a synthetic latex-based 'non-flamm' adhesive. These adhesives haves gap-filling properties that allow the material to be fixed effectively to rough or uneven surfaces. They also allow some degree of movement so that the tiles can be adjusted after they have been stuck in place.

Fixing ceramic tiles

Ceramic wall tiles are fixed in place with adhesive that is available ready-mixed or in powder form. Some are dual-purpose, to be used as either adhesive or grout. Ordinary 'thin-bed' adhesives are for tiling on fairly flat surfaces; there are 'thick-bed' ones available for

use on rough and uneven surfaces.

Use a water-resistant version for kitchens and bathrooms. Epoxy-based grouts resist mould growth and help keep kitchens and bathrooms germ-free.

Ceramic floor tiles are usually laid with a cement-based tile adhesive. Thick quarry tiles are sometimes laid on a sand-and-cement mortar – to which a special builder's adhesive, PVA bonding agent, can be added to improve adhesion (a method also used for repairing sand-and-cement renderings and concrete). 🖙

Gluing metals

Metals can be glued with epoxy-resin adhesives, which produce a powerful bond. The adhesives come in two parts, a resin and a hardener, supplied in separate tubes or

▼ Multipurpose adhesive

a special twin dispenser. Both parts are mixed together, then used within a prescribed time after mixing.

Cyanoacrylates

The cyanoacrylates, or 'super glues', come close to being universal adhesives that will stick anything. They rapidly bond a great many materials, including human skin – so take great care when handling them (see Adhesive solvents, page 14).

Usually supplied in tubes with fine nozzles, super glues must be used sparingly. Most are thin liquids, but a gel type is also available. They are commonly used for joining small objects made of metal, glass, ceramic, glass fibre or rigid plastic.

Acrylic polymer adhesive

This is a solvent-free adhesive, sold in cartridges, which is used in place of mechanical fixings, such as nails and screws, to secure wooden mouldings and boards.

Polyurethane-foam adhesive

Available in pressurized cans, this glue is used for fast and clean application when bonding a range of building materials such as ceiling tiles to masonry, plaster, man-made boards or stone. Some expand rapidly for use as gap fillers.

▼ Use this chart as a guide for gluing the materials on the left to those across the top.

	Wood and man-made boards	Masonry	Plaster	Metal	Stone	Glass	Ceramic	Rigid plastic/fibre glass
Wood/man-made boards	1,2,3,5,8	5,8,10	5,8,10	4,8	5,8	4,8	4,8	4,8,10
Metal	4,8			4,7,8	4,7,8	4,7,8	4,7,8	4,7,8
Synthetic laminates	3	3	3		3			3
Floor coverings	5,6	5,6	5,6		5,6		5,6	
Ceiling tiles/panels	6,9,10	6,9,10	6,9,10		6,9,10			
Ceramic	4,8,9	9	9	4,8	9	4,7,8	4,7,8	4,8
Stone	4	4		4	4	4		
Glass	3,4	4	4	4,7,8	4	4,7,8	4,7,8	4,8
Rigid plastics/glass fibre	4,8,10			4,8	8,10	4,8	4,8	4,7,8

KEY **1.** PVA woodworking adhesive **2.** Synthetic-resin/Resorcinol and urea **3.** Rubber based contact **4.** Epoxy-resin **5.** Rubber-resin **6.** Synthetic latex **7.** Cyanoacrylates **8.** Acrylic polymer **9.** PVA/Acrylic tile adhesive **10.** Polyurethane foam

SEE ALSO
383–96

Glue guns

An electric 'hot-melt' glue gun is loaded with a rod of solid glue that melts under heat; the glue is then discharged as a liquid when the gun is activated onto whatever it is you are fixing. The components are pressed or clamped together and the glue bonds as it cools.

Glue guns are useful for accurate spot-gluing or where you have to get the adhesive into an awkward, fiddly spot. There is a choice of glue rods for use with various materials. The glues are able to cool and set within 20 to 90 seconds.

Cold gun-applied adhesive for fixing wallboards and ceiling tiles is supplied in cartridges fitted with nozzles. When you squeeze the gun's trigger, a ram pushes on the base of the cartridge and forces out the glue.

◄ Glue gun

Adhesive solvents

When using an adhesive, you will inevitably end up putting some of it where you don't want it. So have the right solvent handy for the glue in question and use it promptly. The more the glue has set, the harder it is to remove; and once the glue has set hard, it may be impossible to dissolve it. The table below shows which solvent to use for which type of adhesive.

ADHESIVE	SOLVENT
PVA woodworking glue	Water
Synthetic-resin	Water
Rubber-based contact glue	Acetone
Rubber-resin	Petrol
Synthetic-latex	Water
Epoxy-resin	Acetone or methylated spirit; liquid paint stripper if hard (not on skin)
Cyanoacrylates (super glues)	Special manufacturer's solvent
Acrylic adhesive	Water
Polyurethane foam	Special manufacturer's solvent

Woodworking

To glue wood and man-made boards for use indoors, apply a polyvinyl (PVA) woodworking glue to one or both surfaces. Clamp and wipe off any excess glue squeezed from the joint with a damp cloth. The bond will be complete in 24 hours.

When gluing wall panels to furring strips (battens of sawn timber), use a synthetic rubber-based contact adhesive or a gun-applied acrylic adhesive. Apply to both surfaces, and allow to become touch-dry. Press surfaces together for an almost instantaneous bond.

Outdoors, use waterproof exterior PVA glue or powdered

▶ *Wood glue*

synthetic-resin glue. Or use a two-part resorcinol or urea adhesive. The two parts – resin and hardener – are either mixed or applied separately to the faces being glued. In the latter case, the adhesive begins to set only when the faces are joined. For all these glues, clamp during setting period. ☞

Wallpaper paste

Most pastes come as powder or flakes for mixing with water. Some come ready-mixed.

All-purpose paste
Standard wallpaper paste is suitable for most lightweight to medium-weight papers.

Heavy-duty paste
Specially prepared for hanging embossed papers and other heavyweight wallcoverings.

Fungicidal paste
Pastes often contain a

fungicide to prevent mould developing under impervious wallcoverings.

Ready-mixed paste
Thixotropic paste specially made for heavyweight papers.

Stain-free paste
For delicate papers easily stained by conventional paste.

Repair adhesive
Sticks down peeling edges and corners. Glues vinyl to vinyl, so is suitable for applying decorative border rolls. ☞

☞ SEE ALSO 194–6

☞ SEE ALSO 416–20

Alarm systems

Although they are no substitute for good locks, an alarm system provides extra security and may deter intruders if there are less well-protected premises nearby. The system must be reliable, and you need to be disciplined in its use. If neighbours are constantly subjected to false alarms, they are less likely to call the police in a genuine break-in.

Alarm systems differ greatly, but there are two basic categories: passive systems, which detect the presence of an intruder inside the house, and perimeter systems, which guard all likely means of entry. The best systems incorporate a combination of these features, in case perimeter detectors are bypassed.

Control unit

Where fitted, the control unit is the heart of the system, connecting all the detectors. From it, the signal is passed to a bell or siren. The control unit has to be set to allow sufficient time for legitimate entry and exit. If it has a zone-monitoring option, you can activate door contacts or sensors in selected parts of the house – to permit freedom of movement upstairs at night, for example, while entry doors and downstairs areas remain fully guarded.

The control unit must be tamper-proof, so that it will trigger the alarm if disarming is attempted by any means other than a key or the correct digital code. It is usually wired directly to the mains-power consumer unit – but it should also have a rechargeable battery in case of power failure.

Detectors

Entrances can be fitted with magnetic contacts that trigger the alarm when broken by someone opening a door or window. Other types of detector sense vibrations caused by an attempted entry, including breaking glass. They must be accurately placed and set to distinguish between an intrusion and vibration from external sources.

Scanning devices

Infra-red sensors can be strategically positioned so they scan a wide area. The height of

INFRASONIC ALARMS

Some alarm systems can detect the ultra-low noise levels created by the displacement of air when doors or windows are opened or closed. Even when the alarm is set, neither you nor your pets will trigger it unless you open a door or window. Infrasonic alarms are particularly easy to install.

the beam can be adjusted to ignore small pets. Detectors of this type are usually connected to a central control unit, but there are independent battery-operated sensors for protecting a single room.

The alarm

Most burglar alarms have a bell or siren mounted on an outside wall. These have to switch off automatically after a set period, but some alarms are designed to continue signalling with a flashing light and others will automatically rearm themselves. Many systems transmit a warning directly to a monitoring centre for swift and reliable response to a break-in. Whichever type you choose, it is important that the alarm is triggered by any attempt to tamper with it, either by dismantling or by cutting wires.

Personal-attack button

With most systems you can have a 'panic button' installed beside entry doors or elsewhere in the house to press in the event of an attack. Pressing a personal-attack button trips the alarm even when the system is switched off. ☞

DIY systems

If you want to avoid the expense of professional installation, there are several DIY alarm systems that are quick and easy to install. However, you may need advice from the supplier of the equipment on the choice and siting of sensors and detectors. Consult your insurance company to check whether your choice of alarm affects your policy in any way.

Make sure the system will enable you to select the type and number of detectors you require, and that it

BRITISH STANDARDS FOR BURGLAR ALARMS

Professionally installed alarm systems should comply with BS 4737 for wired systems and BS 6799 for wireless ones. If you install a DIY wireless system, ensure it complies with BS 6707. Check that a wireless alarm has the DTI's approval (MPT 1340) and operates on an approved frequency.

incorporates a reliable tamper-proof control unit.

Wireless systems – which use secure coded radio signals to trigger the alarm – avoid the need for extensive wiring and can be extended to monitor sheds and garages.

☞
SEE ALSO
432

Installing external security lighting

Security lighting covers a wide range of products. With some simple but clever designing, they can be effective but unobtrusive. Your choice will depend on how you want your lighting to work – whether it is low voltage background lighting or high-powered sensor floodlights.

Mains operated systems

The two popular systems of security lighting are dusk-to-dawn lighting, which is triggered automatically by the ambient light levels, or the passive infra-red sensor system, which only comes on if something crosses the remote detector, avoiding unnecessary wastage of electricity.

It is fairly simple to fit these, by either linking into the existing lighting circuit, or via a 13-amp plug to an electrical socket. All lights are normally supplied with instructions – read them thoroughly before beginning work.

Unscrew the rear light cover to reveal the connection terminals [A], attach the flex [B] and secure the rear cover. After selecting the light position, secure the mounting brackets to the wall by

hammer drilling, and fixing with plugs and screws [C] that usually come with the security light. Attach the light unit to the bracket [D], ensuring you do not touch the lamp inside. Next, secure the flex to the wall or the weatherboarding beneath the eaves of the house as shown [E]. Alternatively, drill a hole through the wall directly behind the lamp and feed the cable directly inside.

This is where you decide to connect the light to the house electrical supply, or simply connect to a 13-amp plug into a socket. You may have to

adjust the pre-set timer of the security light to suit your personal requirements [F].

Individual sensors can be installed independently to the light fitting to enlarge the catchment area or create an early warning system [H].

BATTERY OPERATED SENSOR LIGHTS

Sensor light systems that are purely battery powered are not readily available as an off-the-shelf stock item. However, specialist electrical retailers and wholesalers can obtain kits by special order.

Smoke detectors

A smoke detector will identify the presence of smoke and fumes, even before flames start, and sound a shrill warning. Although detectors can be incorporated into an alarm system, self-contained battery-operated units are easier to fit yourself.

There are two basic types of smoke detector. Photoelectric devices detect smoke from smouldering or slow-burning fires. Ionization detectors are more attuned to small particles of smoke produced by blazing fires, such as a burning chip pan. Some detectors also combine both systems to give good, all round performance.

Siting a smoke detector

The best place for a smoke detector is on the ceiling, at least 300mm (1ft) away from any wall or light fitting. If it has to be wall mounted, then make sure it is 150 to 300mm (6in to 1ft) below the ceiling. Don't install a smoke detector

▲ **Smoke detectors**
A detector provides an early fire warning. Choose only those that comply with BS 5446 Part 1

in a kitchen or bathroom, as steam can trigger the alarm; and don't fix one directly above a heater.

If you live in a bungalow, fit a smoke detector in the hallway between the bedrooms and living area(s). For a two-storey home, fit at least one detector in the hallway, directly above the bottom of the stairs. Some alarms can be linked with bell wire – if one detects smoke, they are all triggered at once.

Gas detectors

These devices warn you before escaping gas reaches a dangerous concentration. They are normally designed to detect natural gas, so are usually screwed to a wall no more than 300mm (1ft) below the ceiling of the kitchen or the room where the main gas appliance is installed. Make sure that any gas detector you install for natural gas complies with BS 7348.

If the alarm sounds, extinguish naked flames, including cigarettes, and don't operate electrical switches. Turn off the gas supply at the meter, and open doors and windows. Then call the Gas Emergency Service.

B

Bathrooms

If the bathroom does not provide the amenities you require, estimate whether there is space for extra appliances, even if this means rearranging the existing layout. For example, is there room for a shower cubicle as well as a bath? What about installing a bidet?

Planning

If the bathroom isn't accessible to all the bedrooms, it's worth investigating the possibility of installing a second bathroom or a shower cubicle elsewhere. Alternatively, consider plumbing a basin in some of the bedrooms.

Make a note of electrical installations in the bathroom. If they do not comply with accepted recommendations, they must be replaced with new units. ☞

Bathroom zones

IEE Wiring Regulations define areas – zones – in bathrooms where specific safety precautions apply. Regulations also describe what type of electrical appliances can be installed in each zone, and the routes cables must take. There are special considerations for

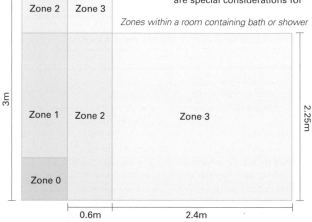

Zones within a room containing bath or shower

Zone 2 | Zone 3

Zone 1 | Zone 2 | Zone 3

Zone 0

3m

2.25m

0.6m | 2.4m

ZONE	LOCATION	PERMITTED
Zone 0	Interior of the bathtub or shower tray.	No electrical installation.
Zone 1	Directly above the bathtub or shower tray, up to a height of 2.25m (7ft 5in) from the floor.	Instantaneous water heater. Instantaneous shower. All-in-one power shower, with a suitably waterproofed integral pump. The wiring that serves appliances within the zone.
Zone 2	Area within 0.6m (2ft) horizontally from the bathtub or shower tray in any direction, up to a height of 2.25m (7ft 5in) from the floor. The area above zone 1, up to a height of 3m (9ft 11in) from the floor.	Appliances permitted in zone 1. Light fittings. Extractor fan. Space heater Whirlpool unit for the bathtub. Shaver socket to BS EN 60742 Chapter 2, Section 1. The wiring that serves appliances within the zone and any appliances in zone 1.
Zone 3	Up to 2.4m (7ft 11in) outside zone 2, up to a height of 2.25m (7ft 5in) from the floor. The area above zone 2 next to the bathtub or shower, up to a height of 3m (9ft 11in) from the floor.	Appliances permitted in zones 1 and 2. Any fixed electrical appliance (a heated towel rail, for example) that is protected by a 30 milliamp RCD. The wiring that serves appliances within the zone and any appliances in zones 1 and 2.

extra-low-voltage equipment with separated earth – best left to a qualified electrician.

The four zones
Any room containing a bathtub or shower is divided into four zones. Zone 0 is the interior of the bathtub or shower tray – not including the space beneath the tub, which is covered by other regulations. Zones 1 to 3 are specific areas above and all round the bath or shower, where only specified electrical appliances and their cables may be installed. Wiring outside these areas must conform to the IEE Wiring Regulations, but no specific 'zone' regulations apply.

SEE ALSO
122–4

Changing the taps on a bath

INTERMEDIATE

An easy and inexpensive way of giving an old bath or sink a makeover is to just change the taps. If you live in a period property, then why not restore an old pair of taps that is more in keeping with the era of the house? Even an old stainless steel sink will benefit from new taps.

Changing a tap

Turn off the isolator valve (if you have one) with a slotted screwdriver [A]; otherwise, turn off your mains stopcock and drain down the system by opening the taps.

Undo the pipework and waste connections beneath the bath or sink's taps [B]. Unscrew the back nut using a wrench [C] and lift out the old taps [D]. Clean the area thoroughly around the taps before refitting the new taps or mixer unit.

Insert the new taps or mixer into position onto

plastic or rubber washers to protect the sink and seal from leaks [E], press the unit firmly home [F], and then connect the pipes to the base of the taps beneath the bath [G]. The distance between the centres of tap

Tools

Slotted screwdriver
Wrench

holes on sinks and baths is generally between 175–180mm (7–7¼in). There are swivel union attachments that can be added to allow a lot more tolerance.

Make sure you fit the flat rubber washer and hand-tighten the shower hose [H], if there is one. If you want to give the hose a half turn with the wrench, use a cloth to avoid any scratching.

Take this opportunity to fit some flexible copper pipe to the tap tails to enable easier fitting and

maintenance – this will mean some small adjustments to the pipe work.

The procedure for a sink mixer is as above, but you might be able to remove the sink for ease of fitting as you change the taps.

Bathrooms: heaters

Installing electrical heating in bathrooms is covered by stringent regulations, and unless you have had considerable experience in home wiring you would be advised to get a professional to undertake the installation of bathroom heaters. Make sure that your existing bathroom or new installation is up to scratch.

HEATED TOWEL RAIL

The Wiring Regulations covering other kinds of heater also apply to a heated towel rail situated in a bathroom. As the towel rail is mounted near the floor, run a flex from it to a flexible-cord outlet, which must in turn be wired to a fused connection unit outside the bathroom.

For a towel rail of 1kW or less, fit a 5amp fuse; otherwise, fit a 13amp fuse.

If a heated towel rail is installed in a bedroom, the fused connection unit can be mounted alongside it.

Fused connection units

A fused connection unit is a device for joining the flex (or sometimes cable) of an appliance to circuit wiring. The connection unit incorporates the added protection of a cartridge fuse similar to that found in a 13amp plug. If the appliance is connected by a flex, choose a unit that has a cord outlet in the faceplate.

Fused connection units
1 Unswitched connection unit.
2 Switched unit with cord outlet and indicator.
3 Connection unit and socket outlet in a dual mounting box.

Radiant wall heaters

These must be fixed high on the wall, outside zones 0 to 2, in order to conform with safety regulations. A fused connection unit fitted with a 13amp fuse (or 5amp fuse for a heater of 1kW or less) must be mounted at a high level outside the zones, and the heater controlled by a double-pole pull-cord switch.

Many heaters have a built-in double-pole switch. However, if this is not fitted, you would need a 15 amp pull-cord switch screwed to the ceiling.

If it is not possible to run a spur to the FCU from a socket outside the bathroom, there must be a separate radial circuit from the connection unit to a 15amp fuseway in the consumer unit, connected by 2.5mm² cable. In either case, the circuit should be protected by a 30 milliamp RCD. It is vital that these stipulations are observed in order for the installation to be fully safe.

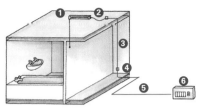

Wall-heater circuit
1. Heater
2. Connection unit
3. Spur cable
4. Socket
5. Power circuit
6. Consumer unit with a 30mA RCD

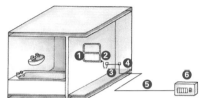

Towel-rail circuit
1. Towel rail
2. Flex outlet
3. Spur cable
4. Connection unit
5. Power circuit
6. Consumer unit with a 30mA RCD

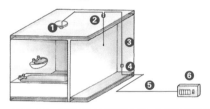

Heat/light circuit
1. Heat/light unit
2. Ceiling switch
3. Spur cable
4. Connection unit
5. Power circuit
6. Consumer unit with a 30mA RCD

Heat/light unit

Heat/light units incorporate a radiant heater and a light fitting in the one appliance. These units must never be connected to lighting circuits.

When he installs such a unit, your electrician should identify the lighting cables, remove the rose and withdraw the cables into the ceiling void. A junction box should then be fitted to a nearby joist and the lighting cables terminated at that point.

The switch cable should not be connected, as it won't be needed.

A ceiling-mounted 15amp double-pole switch should be connected by 2.5mm² two-core-and-earth spur cable to an unswitched FCU mounted outside the bathroom. A similar cable should connect the switch to the heat/light unit. The electrician should then wire the heat/light unit according to the manufacturer's supplied instructions.

SEE ALSO
22–3

SEE ALSO
176–7

Blocks: concrete blocks

Cast-concrete blocks are used in a variety of situations – from foundations to soundproof internal partitions. Having been introduced as a cheap substitute for bricks that were just to be covered with plaster or render, modern concrete blocks are superior to clay bricks in terms of both acoustic and thermal insulation.

Density

Lightweight-concrete blocks

Made from aerated or foamed concrete, these blocks can be carried easily in one hand, which enables bricklayers to build walls quickly and safely. Aerated blocks can be drilled, cut to shape, and chased for electric cables, using hand-tools or power tools. They are used extensively in the building trade for the construction of both internal and external walls.

Dense-concrete blocks

Made from relatively heavy concrete, these are also known as dense-aggregate or medium-density blocks.

Nowadays, with the availability of lightweight loadbearing blocks, dense-concrete blocks are used less frequently, even though they are slightly cheaper than equivalent building blocks made of aerated concrete.

Varieties of Block

Construction

Most building blocks are rectangular blocks of cement-grey or white concrete.

The larger ones, especially if made from dense concrete, are in hollow-block form with enclosed supporting ribs between the outer skins. Having voids not only reduces the weight, but allows for metal rods to be inserted to reinforce retaining walls. With cellular blocks, the voids are open at the bottom only.

Grades

Standard-grade blocks have no aesthetic qualities whatsoever. They are used for the structural core of a wall to be either rendered or plastered, and so are usually made with zigzag 'keying' on both faces.

Fair-face building blocks, which are intended to be visible, usually have smooth faces. However, some blocks are shot-blasted to create a hard-wearing finely textured surface finish.

Paint-quality concrete blocks are ideal for walls decorated directly with masonry paint.

Qualities

Loadbearing

Lightweight and dense-concrete blocks are produced for either loadbearing or non-loadbearing applications. Dense-concrete blocks are made in a greater range of high compressive strengths. It is possible, though, to buy lightweight blocks that are perfectly suited to building loadbearing foundations and multistorey dwellings.

Insulating

Aerated blocks greatly reduce heat and sound transmission. Blocks with superior acoustic-insulation properties are made for partitions and party walls. Those with a high degree of thermal insulation reduce the need for secondary insulation. ☛

Moisture and frost resistance

Like bricks, most concrete blocks are weatherproof. Frost-resistant and moisture-proof blocks are for foundations and walling below ground.

▼ *Paint-quality blocks decorated with smooth masonry paint make a welcome change from the usual monotonous grey concrete* ☛

☛
SEE ALSO
183

☛
SEE ALSO
250–1

Blocks: different uses

When you are getting blocks delivered, make sure they are unloaded as near as possible to where they are needed to save time and reduce the possibility of damage in transit – they are quite brittle and chip easily. Stack them on a flat, dry base and protect them from rain and frost with a tarpaulin or a polythene sheet.

Available sizes

The average concrete block measures 450 x 225mm (1ft 6in x 9in) and ranges in thickness from 75 to 230mm (3 to 9in). Specials, such as foundation blocks, may be similar in length and height but will differ in thickness (check your supplier's catalogue). Brick-size concrete blocks, known as coursing bricks, are made for infilling above door and window lintels.

Estimating quantities

To calculate the number of blocks required, divide a chosen area of walling by the dimensions of a specific block. The dimensions given above are actual sizes, but some manufacturers may specify nominal sizes (known as 'co-ordinating sizes'), which include a 10mm (3/8in) allowance for mortar on the length and height. Since block walls are often constructed with one skin of masonry, the thickness of a block is normally given as the actual size. ☞

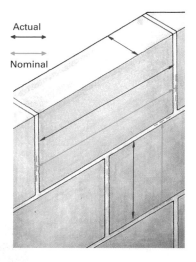

Actual

Nominal

◀ *Sizes of structural blocks*
The nominal size of a block refers to the length and height only. Thicknesses are always specified as the actual size

Screen blocks

Pierced concrete blocks are most often used for building decorative screens in the garden. The blocks are not bonded like brickwork or structural blocks, and therefore require supporting piers that are made from matching pilaster blocks. These are constructed with locating channels that take the pierced blocks. Coping slabs finish the tops of the screen and piers.

Screen blocks should not be used in the construction of loadbearing walls. However, they can support a light-weight structure, such as a wood-and-plastic carport roof.

▲ Decorative screen blocks are normally 300mm (1ft) square and about 90mm (about 3½in) thick.

Artificial stone blocks

Artificial-stone blocks, which are made from poured concrete, can look very convincing once they have weathered outside for a few months. Depending on where you live, these blocks may be easier to obtain than natural building stone, and are probably cheaper. Aesthetically, however, nothing can surpass quarried stone, such as granite or sandstone.

The stretcher faces (a bricklaying term for the long sides of a brick) of concrete blocks made specifically for garden walling are textured to resemble natural stone. Single blocks are laid in mortar and bonded like real stonework; and there are larger blocks that look like two or three courses of squared rubble or dressed stone. Coping slabs add the finishing touch.

SEE ALSO
300–2

Block laying: building with concrete blocks

Don't dampen concrete blocks before you lay them – wet blocks may shrink and crack the mortar joints as the wall dries out. Block walls need the same type of concrete footings and mortar mixes as brickwork. Ensure mortar joints are flush with the wall to be rendered or plastered.

Building a partition wall

It is usual to divide up large interior spaces with non-loadbearing stud partitions; but if your house is built on a concrete pad, a practical alternative is to use concrete blocks.

If you're going to install a doorway in the partition, plan its position to avoid cutting too many blocks. You will need to allow for the wooden doorframe and lining, as well as a precast lintel to support the masonry above the opening. Fill the space above the lintel with concrete coursing bricks.

Bolt metal connectors to the existing structure in order to support each end of the new

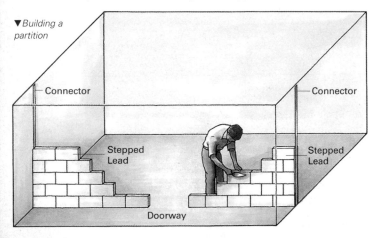

▼ *Building a partition*

Connector

Connector

Stepped Lead

Stepped Lead

Doorway

partition wall. Make sure you plumb the connectors accurately to make sure the new wall is built perfectly upright.

Lay the first course of blocks without mortar across the room to check the spacing and to determine the position of a doorway, if one is to be included. Mark the positions of the blocks before building

stepped leads at each end, as for brickwork (see Bricks). Check for accuracy with a spirit level, and then fill in between the leads with blocks.

Build another three courses, anchoring the end blocks to the connectors with wall ties in every joint. Leave the mortar to harden overnight before you continue with the wall. ☞

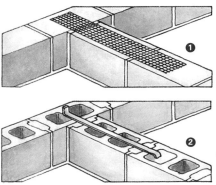

1. Wire-mesh wall ties for solid blocks
2. Metal tie bar for hollow blocks

Building intersecting walls

Butt intersecting garden walls together with a continuous vertical joint between them, but anchor the structure as for brickwork with wire-mesh wall ties (1). This will strengthen the structure of the two adjoining walls.

If you build a wall with heavyweight hollow blocks, use stout metal tie bars with a bend at each end. Fill the block voids with mortar to embed the ends of the bars (2). It is important to install a metal tie bar in every course to add to its stability.

☞
SEE ALSO
74–5

Block laying: screen building

Basic bricklaying techniques and tools are used to build a pierced concrete screen, but the blocks are stack-bonded – with continuous vertical joints. If a screen wall is to be built higher than 600mm (2ft), it must be reinforced vertically with 16mm (5/8in) steel bars and horizontally with galvanized-mesh strips. 🖝

Constructing a screen

Set out and fill the footings, making them twice the width of the pilaster blocks. Embed pier-reinforcing bars in the concrete, and support them with guy ropes until the concrete sets. 🖝

Lower a pilaster block over the first bar, setting it onto a bed of mortar laid around the base of the bar. Check that the block is vertical and level. Pack mortar or concrete into its core, then proceed with two more blocks so that the pier

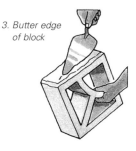

3. Butter edge of block

corresponds to the height of two mortared screen blocks (1).

Allow the mortar to harden overnight, then lay a mortar bed for two screen blocks next to the first pier. Butter the vertical edge of a screen block with mortar and press it into the pier- locating channel (2). Mortar the next block and place it alongside the first. When buttering screen blocks with mortar, keep the faces clean by making a neat chamfered bed of mortar (3).

Lay two more blocks against the next pier. Stretch a bricklayer's line to gauge the

1. Build the piers

2. Fit block to pier

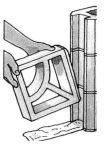

4. *Lay a wire reinforcing strips into the mortar*

alternate courses. Finally, lay coping slabs on top of each pier and along the top of the screen (5).

If you don't like the look of ordinary mortar joints, rake out some of the mortar and repoint with mortar made with silver sand. A concave rubbed joint looks good with decorative screening.

top edge of the first course, then lay the rest of the blocks towards the centre. Before building any higher, embed a wire reinforcing strip running from pier to pier in the next mortar bed (4).

Continue to build the piers and screen up to a maximum height of 2m (6ft 6in), inserting a wire strip into

5. *Lay coping slabs along the wall*

▼ *Use a bolster and club hammer to cut a block.*

Cutting concrete blocks

If you don't have a masonry saw, don't worry. Score a line around the block using a bolster chisel and straightedge. Deepen the line into a groove by striking the chisel with a club hammer, working around the block until it eventually fractures along the groove.

SEE ALSO
48–9

SEE ALSO
87

Boards

Nowadays, five types of man-made board are widely used by woodworkers – plywood, chipboard, block-board, hardboard and fibreboard.

Plywood

Plywood is a sheet material made by bonding a number of thin wood veneers, or plies, together under high pressure. For stability, the plies are laid in an odd number with their grain direction alternating.

The type of glue used in its manufacture determines whether plywood is suitable for interior or exterior use. Best-quality plywood is used for manufacturing furniture, while the cheaper grades are mostly used for building work such as shuttering for concrete.

Typical thicknesses range from 3 to 18mm (⅛ to ¾in). A common standard sheet size is 2440 x 1220mm (8 x 4ft).

Chipboard

Chipboard is a relatively cheap material commonly used to make modern cabinet furniture. The board is made by gluing small softwood chips together under pressure.

Standard chipboard, which is sanded smooth on both sides, can be filled and primed for painting. Extra-thick melamine-faced boards are made for kitchen worktops.

Standard chipboard sheets measure 2440 x 1220mm (8 x 4ft) and are either 9, 12, 15 or 18mm (⅜, ½, ⅝ or ¾in) thick.

Melamine-faced and veneered chipboard come in planks 15mm (⅝in) thick. These range from 150 to 600mm (6in to 2ft) wide and are either 1820 or 2440mm (6 or 8ft) long. They are used for shelving and DIY cabinet-making. ☛

Blockboard

Blockboard consists of a core of rectangular-section wood battens sandwiched between two double layers of pressure-bonded veneer. It is used where structural strength and stability are needed: for example, an unsupported span of worktop or heavy-duty shelving. Blockboard is an excellent material for veneering – but where appearance is important, exposed edges need to be covered with strips of solid wood known as lipping.

For painting, the surface veneers need only light sanding.

Blockboard is sold as 2440 x 1220mm (8 x 4ft) sheets, 12, 18 or 25mm (½, ¾ or 1in) thick.

Hardboard

Hardboard is a dense, thin sheet material made from compressed softwood pulp. Structurally not as strong as other man-made boards, it is fairly cheap and very stable.

Standard hardboard is brown in colour and 3.2mm (⅛in) thick, with one smooth shiny side and one textured. Other types include duo-faced; perforated; textured; oil-tempered ; flame-retardant; prefinished.

Standard hardboard is relatively light, easy to cut, and ideal for small sliding doors, cabinet backs and and as an underlay for floorcoverings.

Standard hardboard sheets are 2440 x 1220mm (8 x 4ft).

Fibreboards

Like hardboard, these are made from compressed wood fibre in various densities. Soft types are used for insulation, pinboard and wall sheathing.

Medium-density fibreboard (MDF) is a dense material with smooth surfaces on both sides. MDF is 3 to 25mm (⅛ to 1in) or more in thickness; sheet size is 2440 x 1220mm (8 x 4ft). A grooved board, 6mm (¼in) thick, is made for bending into curved shapes.

1. *Plywood*
2. *Blockboard*
3. *Chipboard*
4. *Medium-density fibreboard (MDF)*
5. *Hardboard back*
6. *Hardboard face*
7. *Soft fibreboard*

SEE ALSO
150–1

Boards: floorboards

The boarding laid over a floor's structural elements – timber floor joists or concrete slab – is known generally as flooring. It may consist of hardwood or softwood planks, or take the form of man-made boards.

1. Quarter-sawn boards
Shrinkage does not distort these boards.

2. Tangentially sawn boards
Shrinkage can cause these boards to 'cup'.

Floorboards are usually made from softwoods and are sold planed all round, with square or tongue-and-groove edges.

Narrow boards produce superior floors, as any movement due to shrinkage is less noticeable. However, they cost a lot to lay and so tend to be used in the more expensive houses only. Hardwoods such as oak or maple are also used for high-grade flooring, but add even more to the cost.

The best floorboards are quarter-sawn (1) from the log, a method that diminishes distortion due to shrinkage. However, since this method wastes timber, floorboards are more often cut tangentially (2) to reduce costs. Yet boards cut in this way tend to 'cup' (bow) across their width and should be fixed with the concave side facing upwards, as there is a tendency for the grain on the other side to splinter.

The joint on T & G boards is not at the centre of the edges but closer to one face, and these boards should be laid with the offset joint nearer to the joist. Although T & G boards are nominally the same sizes as square-edged boards, the edge joint reduces their floor coverage by about 12mm (½in) per board.

▶ Types of flooring

1. Square-edged softwood board
2. T & G softwood board
3. Square-edged chipboard
4. T & G chipboard
5. Square-edged plywood
6. T & G plywood
7. Square-edged MDF

Boards: interior panelling

Walls that are in poor condition – except those that are damp – can be covered with panelling to conceal them and to provide a decorative surface.

Tongue-and-groove boards

Solid-wood panelling is made from planks with a tongue along one edge and a matching groove on the other. The main function of this joint is to provide room for movement resulting from atmospheric changes, but it also allows for 'secret nailing' when fixing planks to the wall.

The meeting edges of tongued, grooved and V-jointed (TGV) boards are machined to produce a decorative V-shaped profile, accentuating the junction between boards. Other types of T & G boards have more decorative profiles.

Make sure you buy enough TGV boards to complete the work. Boards from another batch may not be compatible, because the machine used to shape their edge joints may have been set to slightly different tolerances.

Wallboards

Manufactured sheet wallboards are made to various sizes ranging from 4 to 6mm (³⁄₁₆ to ¼in) thick. Plywood or hardboard panels are faced with real-timber veneers or paper to simulate wood grain, and there are plastic-faced boards in a range of colours. Typical surfaces include V-grooving, embossed- brick, stone, plaster and tiled effects.

Wall panels made from wood-fibre board are 12mm (½in) thick and can have cork, grass and fabric surfaces; they reduce sound penetration and are heat-insulating.

◀ *Solid-wood T & G planks are sold by timber merchants in various lengths up to 3m (10ft); usual dimensions are 100 x 12mm (4 x ½in). Prepacked kits of TGV boards are available from specialists. Various profiles are made: tongued, grooved and V-jointed (1), rebated shiplap (2), moulded TGV (3).*

SEE ALSO
156–7

Boilers: central heating

Central-heating boilers today are much smaller than their predecessors, though no less efficient. Gas and oil are the most popular fuels for central-heating, although solid fuel can still be found heating homes.

▲ *Gas installers*
Gas boilers must be installed by competent fitters registered with CORGI (Council for Registered Gas Installers). Make sure as well that your installer has the relevant public-liability insurance for working with gas.

The capacity (heat output) of the boiler needed to satisfy your requirements can be calculated by adding up the manufacturer's specified heat output of all the radiators, plus a 3kW allowance for a hot-water cylinder. Ten per cent is added to allow for exceptionally cold weather. The overall calculation is affected by the heat lost through the walls and ceiling, and also by the number of air changes caused by ventilation.

Some plumbers' merchants will make the relevant calculations for you, if you provide them with the dimensions of each room. Alternatively, you can calculate your requirements yourself, using a software package produced for use with a home computer. There are also purpose-made calculators known as Mears wheels, which can be hired, complete with instructions, from a supplier of central-heating equipment. ☞

Ideal room temperatures

A central-heating installer normally aims at providing a system that will heat rooms to the temperatures shown below, assuming an outdoor temperature of -1°C (30°F).

ROOM TEMPERATURE	
Living room	21°C (70°F)
Dining room	21°C (70°F)
Kitchen	16°C (60°F)
Hall/landing	18°C (65°F)
Bedroom	16°C (60°F)
Bathroom	23°C (72°F)

Gas-fired boilers

Many gas-fired boilers have pilot lights that burn constantly to ignite the burners whenever heat is required. Burners may be operated manually or by a timer set to switch the heating on and off at selected times. The boiler can be linked to a room thermostat, so the heating is switched on and off to keep heat at the required level throughout the house.

An increasing number of boilers have electronic ignition; the pilot is not ignited until the room thermostat demands heat – once the boiler reaches the right temperature, valves to the burner and pilot light close, shutting off the fuel supply until heat is next called for.

Oil-fired boilers

Pressure-jet oil-fired boilers are fitted with controls similar to the ones for gas boilers. Oil boilers can be floor-standing or wall-mounted. To run oil-fired central heating, you need a large oil-storage tank outside, with easy access for delivery.

Solid-fuel boilers

Solid-fuel boilers are invariably floor-standing and require a conventional flue. Back boilers are small enough to be built into a fireplace.

Instant control of heat isn't possible with a solid-fuel boiler – the rate at which the fuel is burnt is usually controlled by a thermostatic damper and sometimes by a fan.

The system must allow heat to escape in the event of the circulation pump failing. This is usually by means of a natural-convection circuit (pipe) that leads from the boiler and heat exchanger in the domestic hot-water cylinder to a radiator in the bathroom.

Combination boilers

Combination boilers provide both hot water to a sealed heating system and a separate supply of instant hot water directly to taps and showers. The advantages are ease of installation (no tanks or pipes in the loft), space-saving (no hot-water storage cylinder) and economy (you heat only the water you use).

The main drawback is a fairly slow flow rate – so it takes longer to fill a bath and it's not usually possible to use

▼ *Combination boilers provide an instant supply of hot water without the need for a tank.*

SEE ALSO
319

two hot taps at the same time. Combination boilers are therefore best suited to small households or flats. However, to overcome these problems, the newer generation of combination boilers have a small built-in hot-water storage tank.

Condensing boilers

Condensing boilers extract more heat from the fuel than other types of boiler. This is achieved either by passing the water through a highly efficient heat exchanger or by having a secondary heat

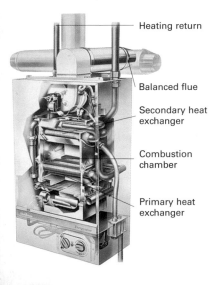

▼ *Condensing boiler*

Heating return

Balanced flue

Secondary heat exchanger

Combustion chamber

Primary heat exchanger

BOILER FLUES

All boilers need some means of expelling the combustion gases that result from burning fuel. This is often done by connecting the boiler to a conventional flue or chimney that takes the gases directly to the outside.

Some boilers, known as room-sealed balanced-flue boilers, are mounted on an external wall and the flue gases are passed to the outside through a horizontal duct. Balanced-flue ducts are divided into two passages – one for the outgoing flue gases, and the other for the incoming air needed for efficient combustion.

exchanger that uses heat from the flue to 'preheat' cool water returning from the radiators.

With a conventional boiler, moisture within the exhaust gases passes through the flue as steam. Since a condensing boiler extracts more heat from the gases, much of the moisture condenses within the boiler. The water produced is collected at the bottom of the combustion chamber and drained through a small pipe.

Another by-product on a cold damp day is a light cloud of water vapour at the flue outlet, where the relatively cool exhaust gases meet the outside air. There are regulations governing the siting of balanced flues – check the requirements with your Building Control Officer.

Ventilating a boiler

A boiler that takes its combustion air from within the house and expels fumes through a conventional open flue (see box) must have access to a permanent ventilator fitted in an outside wall. The ventilator has to be of the correct size – as recommended by the boiler manufacturer – and must not contain a fly-screen mesh, which could become blocked. Refer to Building Regulations F1 – 1.8 for specific guidance. A boiler starved of air will create carbon monoxide – a lethal invisible gas with no smell.

A cupboard that houses a balanced-flue room-sealed boiler must be fitted with ventilators at the top and bottom to prevent the boiler overheating. 👉

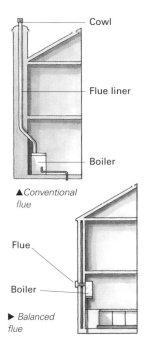

▲ *Conventional flue*

▶ *Balanced flue*

▲ *Pressure-jet oil boiler*

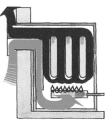

▲ *Balanced flue for gas*

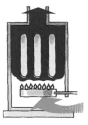

▲ *Conventional gas flue*

SEE ALSO
405

Bricks

At one time, bricks were named after their district of origin, where a particular clay had a distinctive colour. Nowadays names are often chosen by manufacturers to suggest the continuation of that tradition, such as London stocks, Leicester reds and Blue Staffs.

Choosing bricks

Facings

Facings are made as much for their look as their structural qualities and come in a wide range of colours and textures. Used for exposed brickwork.

Commons

Commons are cheap, general-purpose bricks for plastered or rendered brickwork, the inner leaf of cavity walls and foundations. Concrete building blocks have all but replaced commons for cavity walling and internal partition walls.

Engineering bricks

Engineering bricks are very dense and strong. You are unlikely to need them for the average wall, but, because they are impervious to water, they are sometimes used to construct damp-proof courses.

Buying bricks

Bricks are usually sold in pallets of about 450, but builders'

▲ *Weathered antique bricks are much sought after*

merchants can sell them in smaller quantities. It can be cheaper straight from the manufacturer, provided a load is large enough to make the delivery charge economical.

Estimating quantities

The dimensions of a standard brick are 215 x 102.5 x 65mm (8½ x 4 x 2½in), but these can vary by a few millimetres.

To calculate how many bricks you need, allow roughly 60 bricks for every sq m (50 per sq yd) of single-skin walling. Add an extra 5 per cent for cutting and breakages. ☛

Brick colour and texture

The popularity of brick as a building material stems largely from its range of subtle colours and textures, which actually improve with weathering. Weathered brick can be difficult to match by using a manufacturer's catalogue, so try to borrow samples from your supplier's stock – or if you have spare bricks, take one to the supplier to compare it with new bricks.

Colour

The colour of bricks is largely determined by the type of clay used in their manufacture, although the colour is modified by the addition of certain minerals and the temperature of the firing. Large manufacturers supply a wide variety of colours; and you can also buy brindled (multicoloured or mottled) bricks, which are useful for blending with existing masonry.

Texture

Texture is as important to the appearance of a brick wall as colour. Simple rough or smooth textures are created by the choice of

materials. Others are imposed upon the clay by scratching, rolling, brushing and so on. A brick may be textured all over or on the sides and ends only.

▼ Brick colours and textures

A small selection from the wide range of colours and textures.
1. Smooth blended
2. Handmade
3. Sandfaced yellow
4. Smooth blue engineering
5. Sandfaced grey
6. Smooth red stock
7. Wirecut brindle
8. Textured buff multi
9. London stock (second)
10. Wirecut blue
11. Red common
12. Coarse fletton
13. Moulded fletton
14. Dragfaced red multi

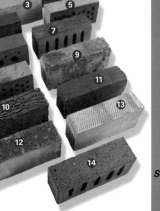

SEE ALSO
301

Bricks: durability and spalled

There are a number of different types of brick with different purposes, and durability can vary accordingly. It is important to choose the right kind.

Solid bricks

The majority of bricks are solid, either flat on all surfaces or with a depression known as a 'frog' on one face. When filled with mortar, the frog keys the bricks.

Cored or perforated bricks

Cored bricks have holes running through them, performing the same function as the frog. A wall made with cored bricks must be finished with a solid-brick or slab coping.

Special shapes

Specially shaped bricks are made for decorative brickwork. Master bricklayers draw upon the full range when building structures such as arches and chamfered or rounded corners. Shaped bricks are made for coping walls.

Frost resistance

Freezing can damage bricks. Bricks are made with different degrees of frost resistance.

F-category bricks are totally frost resistant, even when a saturated wall is exposed to freezing.

M-category bricks are moderately frost resistant. Though suitable for most external uses, these bricks may suffer if they are subjected to extreme weathering.

O-category bricks are likely to be damaged by frost and should be used for building internal walls only. Make sure that these bricks are always stored under cover.

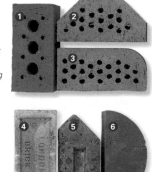

1. Standard cored brick
2. Double-cant coping
3. Bullnose brick
4. Standard brick with frog
5. Squint for shaped corner
6. Half-round coping

Spalled masonry

Moisture that has penetrated soft masonry will expand in icy weather, flaking off the outer face of brickwork and stonework. The result, known as spalling, not only looks unattractive but also allows water to seep into the wall.

If spalling is localized, cut out the bricks or stones and replace them with matching ones. The sequence below describes how to repair spalled brickwork, but the process is similar for a stone wall. ☞

▲ *Spalled bricks caused by frost damage*

Replacing a spalled brick

Use a cold chisel and club hammer to rake out the pointing surrounding the brick, then chop out the brick itself. If the brick is difficult to remove, drill numerous holes in it with a large-diameter masonry bit, then slice up the brick with a cold chisel and hammer. It should crumble, enabling you to remove the pieces easily.

To fit the replacement brick, first dampen the opening and spread mortar on the base and one side. Then dampen the replacement brick, butter the top and one end with mortar, and slot the brick into the hole (see below left).

If you can't find a replacement brick of a suitable colour, remove the spalled brick carefully, turn it round to reveal its undamaged face, and reinsert it.

◄ *Having mortared the top and one end, slip the new brick into the hole you have cut*

☞ SEE ALSO 294–5

Bricklaying

As with most techniques, bricklaying demands practice before you can do it at speed, so first concentrate on the basics and then accuracy. Using mortar of exactly the right consistency helps to keep the visible faces of the bricks clean. In hot, dry weather dampen the footings and bricks before you begin, but let any surface water evaporate before you lay the bricks.

Basic bricklaying techniques

First, make sure that your initial course of bricks is completely straight by stretching a bricklayer's line (a taut piece of nylon or string) along the intended length of the wall. Hold the trowel with your thumb in line with the handle and pointing towards the tip of the blade (1).

Mix up the mortar according to instructions; scoop a measure and shape it roughly to match the dimensions of the trowel blade. To pick up the mortar, slide the blade under the pile, settling the mortar

▲ 3. Stretch the bed of mortar along the course

▲ 4. Furrow the mortar with the point of the trowel

▼ 1. The correct way to hold a brick trowel

▶ 2. Scoop a measure of mortar onto the trowel

onto the trowel with a slight jerk of the wrist (2). ☞

Spread the mortar along the top course by aligning the edge of the trowel with the centre line of the bricks. As you tip the blade to deposit the mortar, draw the trowel

▲ 5. Pick up a brick with your thumb on the edge

▲ 6. Push the brick down and remove excess mortar

▲ 7. Spread mortar onto the head of the next brick

back towards you to stretch the bed over at least two to three bricks (3). Furrow the mortar by pressing the point of the trowel along the centre (4) of the bed.

Pick up a brick with your other hand (5). Press the brick into the bed, picking up excess mortar squeezed from the joint by sliding the edge of the trowel along the face of the wall (6).

Spread mortar onto the header of the next brick, making a neat 10mm (⅜in) bed for the header joint (7). Press

the brick against its neighbour, scooping off any excess mortar with the trowel.

Having laid three bricks, use a spirit level to check that they are horizontal. Make any adjustments by tapping them down with the trowel handle (8).

Hold the spirit level along the outer edge of the bricks to check that they are in line. To move a brick sideways without knocking it off its mortar bed, tap the upper edge with the trowel at about 45 degrees (9).

▲ 8. Level the course of bricks with the trowel handle

▲ 9. Tap the bricks sideways to align them

SEE ALSO
74–5

Bricklaying: blocking doors

If you are creating a new opening in a wall, you may also have to block off an existing one. Obviously you will want the patch to be invisible, so take care when plastering or filling plasterboard joints and refitting skirtings.

Choosing the right materials

It's generally best to block in the opening with the type of materials that were used in the construction of the wall. This prevents cracks forming from differential movements in the structure (for this purpose, consider bricks and blocks to be the same). It is possible to fill an opening in a brick wall with a wooden stud frame and plasterboard, but it will not have the same acoustic properties as a solid infill, and cracks are difficult to prevent or disguise. ▀

Removing the door lining

Remove the architraves, then saw through the side door-jamb linings close to the top, prising them away from the brickwork with a wrecking bar. If the linings were fitted before the flooring, the ends may be trapped; in which case, cut them flush with the floor. Next, prise the soffit board away from the top.

Bricking up the opening

Cut back the plaster about 150mm (6in) all round the opening. There's no need to cut straight or neat edges; an irregular outline helps disguise the shape of the doorway.

To bond the new brickwork into the old, cut out a half-

1. Nail ties

2. Frame cramp

3. Wall connector system

brick on each side of the opening at every fourth course, using a power drill or a club hammer and bolster chisel. If the wall is made from concrete blocks, remove a quarter block from alternate courses.

However, if you don't want to cut blocks or bricks to fit, tie new and old masonry together by using 100mm (4in) cut clasp nails driven dovetail fashion into the bed joints of the side brickwork (1). If you prefer, use metal frame cramps (2) or a wall connector system (3) – fix them to the side walls, resting on every fourth brick.

Lay the bricks or blocks in mortar, following the original courses. If a wooden suspended floor runs through the doorway, lay the bricks on a timber sill nailed across the opening. When the mortar has set, spread on a basecoat of plaster, then follow it with a finishing top coat.

Fit two complete new lengths of skirting – or, if you are able to match the original, replace the skirting using shorter pieces. To help disguise the opening, make sure the joints in the skirting boards do not align with the original doorway.

▲ Cut out half-bricks

▲ Lay bricks into the courses

▲ Cut blocks to match bonding

SEE ALSO
33–4

Bricklaying: bonding/coping

If bricks were laid one on top of each other, with continuous vertical joints, the structure would be very weak. Bonding simply staggers the vertical joints to strengthen the structure. Coping – on the top course of the wall – protects the brickwork from weathering.

Stretcher bond

The stretcher bond is the simplest form of bonding. It is used for single-thickness walls – including the two leaves of a cavity wall used in constructing modern buildings. Half-bats are used to complete the bond at the end of a straight wall, while a corner is formed by alternating headers and stretchers.

▶ Flemish bond

English bond

If you were to build a wall 215mm (8½in) thick by laying courses of stretcher-bonded bricks side by side, there would be a weak vertical joint running centrally down the wall. An English bond strengthens the wall by using alternate courses of headers.

▼ Stretcher bond

Staggered joints are kept at right-angle corners by inserting a queen closer before the last header.

Flemish bond

The Flemish bond is another method used for building a solid wall 215mm (8½in) thick. Every course is laid with alternate headers and stretchers. Stagger the joint at the end of a course and at corners by laying a queen closer before the header.

Decorative bonds

Stretcher, English and Flemish bonds are designed to construct strong walls;

decorative qualities are incidental. Other bonds, used mainly for their visual effect, are suitable for low non-loadbearing walls only.

Stack bonding
Laying bricks in groups of three creates a basket-weave effect. Strengthen the continuous vertical joints with wall ties.

Honeycomb bond
Build an open decorative screen by using a stretcher-like bond with a quarter-bat-size space between each brick. This type of screen has to be built with care, in order to keep the bond regular. Cut quarter-bats to fill the gaps in the top course. Very attractive but not particularly strong.

Coping brick walls
Finish a wall with a coping of matching bricks, or create a contrast with engineering bricks, which also offer superior water resistance. Special coping bricks are designed to shed rainwater.

Stone or cast-concrete slabs are popular for coping garden walls. Both are quick to lay and are usually wide enough to form low bench-type seating.

On an exposed site, install a damp-proof course under the coping to reduce the risk of frost attack. You could use a standard bituminous-felt DPC, or lay two courses of plain roof tiles with staggered joints and a brick coping above. Let the tiles project from the face of the wall, but run a sloping mortar joint along the top of the projection to shed water.

Brick coping
Specially shaped coping bricks are designed to shed rainwater

Slab coping
Choose a stone or concrete slab that is wider than the wall itself

Tile-and-brick coping
Lay flat roof tiles or creasing tiles beneath a coping of bricks

SEE ALSO
138

Building a barbecue

INTERMEDIATE

Once you've learnt the basics of bricklaying, test out your skills with this fairly small, but extremely useful, project. Choose the position – and direction – well.

Wherever you decide to build your barbecue, it must be on a solid hardstand (an area of concrete or paving). The site chosen here was a paved utility area. The garden is large, so the barbecue doesn't suddenly become the dominant feature.

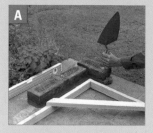

Make a wooden frame to act as a template guide to the dimensions of the grill kit. Lay the bricks out dry (without mortar) to enable the correct brickwork bond to be determined. Bed the bricks on a bed of mortar made up of five parts soft building sand to one part cement, with plasticizer added [A].

Use a spirit level to ensure the brickwork is level and

plumb. Consider using a paving slab to act as a tabletop. Lay the slab down as a guide to the independent leg position [B], all the time chacking to see that your first layer is completely level.

To get the brickwork bond correct, it's necessary to cut half bricks. Cut these on a soft surface with a bolster chisel and club hammer [C]. Don't

Tools

Spirit level
Trowel
Club hammer
Bolster chisel
Jointer
Safety glasses
Protective gloves

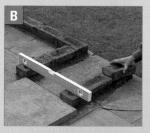

forget your protective gloves and safety glasses.

When you've built the brickwork to the correct height for the slab table, turn some of the bricks as shown [D], so that they act as corbels (supports) for the table and barbecue grate.

The corbels are repeated again two courses up to support the cooking griddle. Two more courses of bricks are required to complete the barbecue. Push four metal pins into the mortar below the top course of brickwork to support the warming griddle shelf [E]. You could lay a flat coping or brick-on-edge course to finish off and really enhance its appearance.

Bed the paving slab on mortar to make your table top to the side of the main barbecue structure [F]. Leave the brickwork to cure (dry off and set) for a couple of hours.

Then, using a jointer (a bent copper pipe or garden hose will suffice), rake out the mortar, to make a tidy job. Finally, take a soft hand brush and carefully brush over the brickwork to complete the job [G].

Bricklaying: pointing

Pointing the mortar between the bricks makes for packed, watertight joints as well as enhancing the appearance of the wall. Well-struck joints and clean brickwork are essential if the wall is to look professionally built; for best results, the mortar must be shaped when it has just the right consistency.

▲ *Flush joint*

▲ *Rubbed joint*

▲ *V-joint*

▲ *Raked joint*

▲ *Weatherstruck joint*

Consistency of the mortar

If the mortar is still too wet, the joint will not be crisp and you may drag mortar out from between the bricks. On the other hand, if it's left to harden too long, pointing will be hard work and you may leave dark marks on the joint.

Test the consistency of the mortar by pressing your thumb into a joint. If it holds a clear impression without sticking to your thumb, the mortar is just right for pointing. You may have to point the work in stages before you can complete the wall. ☞

Shaping the mortar joints

Flush joint

Use the edge of your trowel to scrape the mortar flush; stipple joints with a stiff-bristle brush to expose the sand aggregate.

Rubbed (concave) joint

Buy a shaped jointing tool or improvise with a length of bent tubing. Scrape the mortar flush, then drag the tool along the joints. Finish the vertical joints, then shape the horizontal ones. This joint is ideal for a wall with second-hand bricks that are not good enough to take a crisp joint.

V-joint

Similar to the rubbed joint, the V-joint gives a smart finish to brickwork and sheds rainwater.

Raked joint

Use a piece of wood or metal to rake out the joints to a depth of about 6mm (¼in), then compress them again by smoothing the mortar lightly with a lath or piece of rounded dowel rod.

Weatherstruck joint

The angled weatherstruck joint will withstand harsh conditions. Use a small pointing trowel to shape the vertical joints (1).

▲ *Shape the mortar with a jointing tool*

▲ *1. Shape a weatherstruck joint with a trowel*

Shape the horizontal joints, allowing the mortar to spill out at the base of each joint. Finish the joint by cutting off excess mortar with a tool called a Frenchman, rather like a table knife with its tip bent at 90 degrees. You can improvise by bending a strip of metal. Make a neat straight edge to the mortar, using a batten

▲ *2. Remove excess mortar with a Frenchman*

aligned with the bottom of each joint to guide the Frenchman (2).

Building regulations and planning permission

If you live in a single-family house, you may undertake certain developments without planning permission. The chart on page 58 is intended to help you decide whether you need to seek planning permission or Building Regulations approval before starting work.

Loft conversion
No planning permission is required for a loft conversion, provided the actual volume of the house remains unchanged and the highest part of the roof is not raised.

Extensions
There's a strong possibility you will need permission to extend your home. This is due to additional volume and other factors. Check the chart on the following page.

SEE ALSO
74–5

WILL YOU NEED APPROVAL?

Type of work	Planning permission		Building reg. approval	
Decorations or repairs inside and outside	No	Unless listed building	No	
Replacing windows and doors	No	Unless beyond wall of house facing highway	No	Consult your Building Control Officer
Electrical work	No		No	IEE Regs must apply
Plumbing	No		Maybe	Consult BCO
Central heating	No		No	
Oil-storage tank	No	Check local authority	No	
Structural alterations inside	No Yes	If use is unchanged If listed building	Yes	
Loft conversion	Maybe	Check regulations	Yes	
Building a garden wall or fence	Yes	If more than 1m high, adjoining highway	No	
Planting a hedge	No	Unless hindering traffic	No	
Laying a path or driveway	No	Unless access to road	No	
Felling or lopping trees	No	Unless protected	No	
Installing a satellite-TV dish	No	Unless dimensions exceed limits	No	
Constructing a small outbuilding	Maybe	Depends on location and height; check	Yes	Consult BCO
Building a porch	No	Size/position important	No	Consult BCO
Building a conservatory	Maybe	Treat as extension	No	Consult BCO
Building a garage	Maybe	Treat as extension	Maybe	Consult BCO
Hardstanding for a car	No	If within your boundary	No	
Building an extension	Maybe	Check local authority	Yes	
Demolition	Maybe	If listed; seek advice	Maybe	Consult BCO
Converting a house to flats or business premises	Yes	Includes conversion to bedsitters or partial business use	Yes	If alterations are structural and for conversion to flats
Wall cladding	Yes	If in conservation area	No	

C

Cables and flexes

You can carry out many repairs without worrying about the wiring system in your home. Provided light fittings and appliances have been disconnected, there is no risk of getting an electric shock while working on them. ☞

Flexible cord (flex)

All portable appliances and some of the smaller fixed ones are connected to your home's permanent wiring system by means of conductors in the form of flexible cord, normally called 'flex'.

Each of the conductors is made up of numerous fine wires twisted together and are insulated from the others by a covering of plastic insulation. So that the conductors can be identified easily, the insulation is usually colour-coded (brown = live; blue = neutral; and green-and-yellow = earth).

There is added protection on most flexible cords in the form of an outer sheathing of insulating material enclosing the inner conductors.

▼ *Electrical flex comes in various forms and colours*

TYPES OF ELECTRICAL FLEX

Parallel twin flex has two conductors, insulated with PVC, running side by side. This kind of flex should only be used for wiring audio-equipment speakers. One of the conductors will be colour-coded.

Flat twin sheathed flex has colour-coded live and neutral conductors inside a PVC sheathing. This flex is used for double-insulated light fittings and small appliances.

Two core circular sheathed has colour-coded live and neutral conductors inside a PVC sheathing. It is used for wiring certain pendant lights and some double-insulated appliances.

Three-core circular sheathed This is like two-core circular sheathed flex, but it also contains an insulated and colour-coded earth wire. This flex is used for all kinds of appliances.

Unkinkable braided This flex is used for appliances such as kettles and irons, which are of a high wattage and whose flex must stand up to wear.

Coiled flex A coiled flex that stretches and retracts can be a convenient way of connecting a portable lamp or appliance.

Two-core and earth cables

Cable for the fixed wiring of electrical systems normally has three conductors: the insulated live and neutral ones and the earth conductor lying between them. The live conductor is insulated with red PVC, and the neutral one with black. If an earth conductor is exposed, as in a socket outlet, it should be covered with a green-and-yellow sleeve.

Heat-resistant sleeving is available for the conductors in an enclosed light fitting, where the temperature could adversely affect the normal PVC insulation.

Three-core-and-earth cable

This type of cable is used for a two-way lighting system, which can be turned on and off at different switches. It contains three insulated conductors – with red, yellow and blue coverings – and a bare earth wire.

Single-core cable

Insulated single-core cable is used where the electrical wiring is run in metal or plastic conduit – rarely found in domestic buildings. The cable is colour-coded in the normal way: red for live, black for neutral, and green-and-yellow for earth.

Single-core 16mm² cable in a green-and-yellow PVC covering is used for connecting the consumer unit to the earth.

▼ *Cable sizes* The chart below gives the basic sizes of cables used for wiring domestic circuits. If the company fuse is larger than 60amps, 25mm² meter leads are required – but consult your local electricity company

CIRCUIT-CABLE SIZES

Circuit	Size	Type
Fixed lighting	1.0mm² & 1.5mm²	Two-core-and-earth
Bell or chime transformer	1.0mm²	Two-core-and-earth
Immersion heater	2.5mm²	Two-core-and-earth
Storage heater	2.5mm² & 4.0mm²	Two-core-and-earth
Ring circuit	2.5mm²	Two-core-and-earth
Spurs	2.5mm²	Two-core-and-earth
Radial – 20amp	2.5mm²	Two-core-and-earth
Radial – 30amp	4.0mm²	Two-core-and-earth
Shower unit	10.0mm²	Two-core-and-earth
Cooker	4.0mm² & 6.0mm²	Two-core-and-earth
Consumer earth cable	16.0mm²	Single core
Meter leads	16.0mm²	Single core

SEE ALSO
176–7

Choosing a flex

Not only is the right type of flex for the job important; the size of its conductors must suit the amount of current that will be used by the appliance.

Flex is rated according to the area of the cross section of its conductors, $0.5mm^2$ being the smallest for normal domestic wiring. The flex size required is determined by the flow of current that it can handle safely. Excessive current will make a conductor overheat – so the size of the flex must be matched to the power (wattage) of the appliance that it is feeding.

Conductor	Current rating	Appliance
$0.5mm^2$	3amp	Light fittings up to 720W
$0.75mm^2$	6amp	Light fittings and appliances up to 1440W
$1.0mm^2$	10amp	Appliances up to 2400W
$1.25mm^2$	13amp	Appliances up to 3120W
$1.5mm^2$	15amp	Appliances up to 3600W
$2.5mm^2$	20amp	Appliances up to 4800W

▼ Multi-purpose tool. This tool will crop and strip any size of cable or flex

Manufacturers often fit $1.25mm^2$ flex to appliances of less than 3000W (3kW), since it is safer to use a larger conductor than necessary if a smaller flex might be easily damaged. It is advisable to adopt the same procedure when replacing flex. ☞

Connecting flexible cord

Although the spacing of terminals in plugs and appliances varies, the method of stripping and connecting the flex is the same.

Stripping the flex

Crop the flex to length (1). Slit the sheath lengthwise with a sharp knife (2), being careful not to cut into the insulation covering the individual conductors. Peel the sheathing away from the conductors, then fold it back over the knife blade and cut it off (3).

Separate the conductors, crop them to length and, using wire strippers, remove about 12mm (½in) of insulation from the end of each one (4).

Divide the conductors of parallel twin flex by pulling them apart before exposing their ends with wire strippers.

1. Crop the flex to length

2. Slit sheathing lengthwise

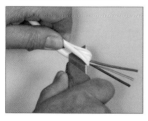

3. Fold sheathing over the blade and cut it off

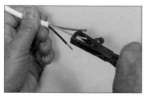

4. Strip insulation from conductors

Connecting conductors

Twist together the individual filaments of each conductor to make them neat.

If the plug or appliance has post-type terminals, fold the bared end of wire (1) before pushing it into the hole. Make sure the insulation butts against the post and that all the wire filaments are enclosed within the terminal. Then tighten the clamping screw and pull gently on the wire to make sure it is held quite firmly.

When you're connecting to clamp-type terminals, wrap the bared wire round the threaded post clockwise (2), then screw the clamping nut down tight onto the conductor. After tightening the nut, check that the conductor is held securely.

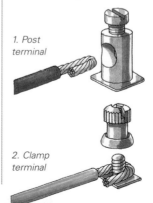

1. Post terminal

2. Clamp terminal

SEE ALSO
126–7

Cables/flexes: extending cord

If you find that a table lamp or other appliance will not reach a socket without the flex being stretched taut, leading to an accident, try extending the flex. Do not, however, be tempted to join two lengths of flex by twisting the bared ends of wires together – this can have fatal consequences.

Flex connectors

If possible, fit a longer flex, wiring it into the appliance itself. But if you don't want to dismantle the appliance, use a flex connector. There are two-terminal and three-terminal connectors, which you should match to the type of flex you are using. Never join two-core flex to three-core flex.

Strip off just enough sheathing for the conductors to reach the terminals, and make sure the sheathed part of each cord can be secured under the cord clamp at each end of the connector.

Cut the conductors to length, then strip and connect the conductors – connecting the live conductor to one of the outer terminals, the neutral to the other, and the earth wire (if present) to the central terminal. Make sure that matching conductors from both cords are connected to the same terminals. ☞

In-line switches

If you plan to fit a longer continuous length of flex you can install an in-line switch that will allow you to control the appliance or light fitting from some distance away – a great advantage for the elderly and people confined to bed. Some in-line switches are luminous.

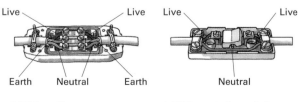

Live　　　　　　　Live　　　　Live　　　　　　　Live

Earth　　Neutral　　Earth　　　　　　Neutral

▲ *Wiring a flex connector*　　　　▲ *Wiring an in-line switch*

Extension leads

If you fit a long flex to a power tool, it will inevitably become tangled and one of the conductors will eventually break. The solution is to buy an extension lead or make one.

The best type of extension lead is wound on a drum. There are 5amp ones – but it's safer to buy one with a 13amp rating. If you use such a lead while it is wound on the drum it may overheat, so unwind it fully each time you use it.

You can make an extension lead from a length of 1.5mm² three-core flex with a standard 13amp plug on one end and a trailing socket on the other. Use unbreakable rubber casings.

'Multi-way' trailing sockets will take several plugs and are ideal for hi-fi systems or computers with individual

Multi-way trailing socket

Two-part flex connector

components that need to be connected to the mains supply.

You can also extend a lead by using a lightweight two-part flex connector. One half has three pins that fit into the other half of the connector.

Drum-type extension lead

13amp plug and trailing socket

SEE ALSO
128–9

Carpets

Carpet is an extremely versatile floorcovering and offers a wide range of choice for virtually all areas of the house, from the bathroom to the kitchen.

Originally, piled carpets were made by knotting strands of wool or other natural fibres into a woven foundation; but gradually, with the introduction of machine-made carpets and synthetic fibres, a very wide variety of different types has been developed. There is a good choice available, whether the need is for something luxurious or simply practical and hardwearing.

▼
1. Cut pile
2. Velvet pile
3. Looped pile
4. Cord pile
5. Twisted pile
6. Woven jute
7. Saxony pile
8. Underlays

Choosing a carpet

When shopping for carpet there are various factors to consider, including fibre content, type of pile and durability. Although wool carpet is luxurious, synthetic-fibre carpets also have a lot to offer in terms of finish, texture, comfort underfoot and value for money. ☞

Fibre content

The best carpets are made from wool or a mixture of wool plus a percentage of man-made fibre. Wool carpets are expensive, so manufacturers have experimented with a variety of fibres to produce cheaper but durable carpets. Materials such as nylon, polypropylene, acrylic, rayon and polyester are all used for carpet making – singly or combined.

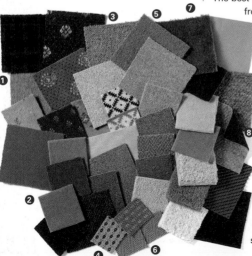

Synthetic-fibre carpets were once inferior substitutes, often with an unattractive shiny pile and a reputation for a build-up of static electricity. Today, manufacturers have largely solved the problem of static, but you should seek the advice of the supplier before you buy.

As far as its appearance, a modern carpet made from good-quality blended fibres is hard to distinguish from one made from wool.

Rush, sisal, coir and jute are natural vegetable fibres used to make coarsely woven rugs or strips.

Which type of pile?
The nature of the pile is even more important to the feel and appearance of a carpet than the fibre content. Piled carpets are either woven or tufted. Axminster and Wilton are two traditional methods of weaving the pile simultaneously with the foundation, so the strands are wrapped around and through the warp and weft threads. With tufted carpets, continuous strands are pushed between the threads of a pre-woven foundation. Although secured with an adhesive backing, tufted pile isn't as permanent as a woven pile.

DURABILITY RATING	
Classification	**Application**
Light domestic	Bedrooms
Medium domestic	Light traffic only – dining room, well-used bedroom
General domestic	Living rooms
Heavy domestic	Hallways/stairs

The importance of underlay
A carpet undoubtedly benefits from having a resilient cushion laid between it and the floor – it is more comfortable to walk on and the carpet lasts longer.

An underlay can be either a thick felt or a layer of foamed rubber or plastic. When you purchase a foam-backed or rubber-backed carpet, the underlay is an integral part of the floorcovering.

Choosing a durable carpet
Whether woven, tufted or bonded, a hardwearing carpet must have a dense pile. When you fold the carpet and part the pile, you should not be able to see the backing to which it is attached.

The British Carpet Classification Scheme categorizes floorcoverings according to their ability to withstand wear.

SEE ALSO
383

Carpets: laying

Fixing carpet
Use one of three ways

A properly stretched and fixed carpet beats loose-laying – and, provided you are carpeting a fairly simple rectangular room, it isn't very difficult to accomplish.

Fold tacked to the floor

Double-sided tape

Gripper strip

Joining at a doorway
Use one of the bars below

Double threshold bar

Single threshold bar

Methods of fixing

There are different methods for holding a carpet in place, depending on the carpet type.

Carpet tacks

A 50mm (2in) strip can be folded under along each edge and nailed to a wooden floor with improved cut tacks about every 200mm (8in). Underlay should be laid 50mm (2in) short of the skirting to allow carpet to lie flat along the edge.

Double-sided tape

Use adhesive tape for rubber-backed carpets only. Stick 50mm (2in) tape around the perimeter of the room; then peel off the protective paper layer from the tape.

Gripper strips

These wooden or metal strips have fine metal teeth that grip the weave. Nail strips to the floor, 6mm (¼in) from the skirting, with the teeth pointing towards the wall. Glue strips to a concrete floor. Cut underlay up to the edge of each strip.

Laying standard–width carpet

If you are laying separate underlay, join neighbouring sections with short strips of carpet tape or secure them with a few tacks.

Roll out the carpet, butting one machine-cut edge against a wall: fix that edge to the floor.

Stretch the carpet to the wall directly opposite and temporarily fix it with tacks or onto gripper strips. Don't cut the carpet yet. Work from the centre towards each corner, stretching and fixing the

▼ *The only special tool required for laying carpet is a knee kicker for stretching it. Hire a knee kicker from a tool-hire company.*

carpet; then do the same at the other sides of the room.

Cut a triangular notch at each corner, so the carpet will lie flat. Adjust the carpet until it is stretched evenly, then fix to the floor. When using tape or gripper strips, press the carpet into the angle between skirting and floor with a bolster chisel; trim with a knife held at 45 degrees to the skirting. Tuck the cut edge behind a gripper strip with the bolster.

Cutting to fit
Cut and fit carpet into doorways and around obstacles, as for sheet vinyl (page 412). Join carpets at a doorway with a single- or double-sided threshold bar.

Joining carpet
Glue straight seams with latex adhesive or adhesive tape. Expensive woven carpets should be sewn by a professional. 🐘

Carpeting a staircase
If possible, use standard-width narrow carpet on a staircase. Order an extra 450mm (1ft 6in), so that the carpet can be moved at a later date to even out the wear. This allowance is turned under onto the bottom step.

Fit carpeting across the width of the treads, or stop short to reveal a border of polished wood; you can then use traditional stair rods to hold the carpet against the risers.

▶ Straight stairs
1. Tack underlay pads.
2. Tack carpet face down on first tread.
3. Pull over nosing and tack to base of riser.
4. Run carpet upstairs, fixing to grippers

Alternatively, tack the carpet to the stairs every 75mm (3in) across the treads. Push the carpet firmly into the angle between riser and tread with a bolster chisel while you tack the centre, then work outwards.

Unless it's rubber-backed, use gripper strip to fix in place.

▼ Winding stairs
Don't cut the carpet, but fold the excess under (1) and fix to the risers with stair rods or long carpet tacks.

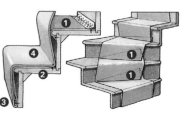

SEE ALSO
12–15

Cement: exterior render

Rendering is the application of a relatively thin layer of cement or cement-and-lime mortar to the surface of exterior walls on a house to provide a decorative and weather-resistant finish.

Planning ahead

Except for listed buildings or ones in a conservation area, there are no official regulations controlling change of colour or texture for exterior walls. As a result, houses are often made conspicuous by individualistic decorative treatment.

If you want to rerender a wall, that is always acceptable, as it is simply a case of renewing what is already there.

Rendering old brickwork is a more questionable practice. It might improve the weather-resistance of the wall, but at the cost of spoiling the overall appearance. To improve weather-resistance, it is better to rake out crumbling mortar joints and repoint them with

fresh mortar – then, if necessary, treat the porous brickwork with a clear sealant. ☞

Rendering techniques

The technique used for rendering is virtually the same as for plastering. It generally involves using the same tools, though a wooden float is better than a plasterer's trowel for finishing cement render – as the wood leaves a finely textured surface that looks better than the very smooth one produced with a metal trowel.

Rendering the walls of a house is really a job for a professional, as it not only involves covering a large area but also requires the ability to colour-match the batches of mortar to avoid a patchy appearance. Before attempting to render a large wall, practise on a smaller project, such as a garden wall. Divide the wall into manageable panels with screed battens, as for plastering.

▼ *Rendering can be kept in character*

Binders for exterior render

Mortar

Mortar is a mixture of sand, cement and clean water. The sand bulks out the mix, and the cement binds the particles together. A good cement mix will bond to any masonry. Mortars of different strengths are produced by adjusting the proportions of sand and cement or by adding lime.

A cement-and-sand mix is best for a wall of dense hard bricks, whereas a weaker mix of cement, sand and lime is more suitable for soft bricks.

Cement does not need to dry out in order to set; the more slowly it dries, the stronger it will be.

Hot weather reduces workable time, and can affect the set of the mortar by making it dry out too fast. When the weather is hot, keep the work damp by lightly spraying it with water or cover it with polythene sheeting.

Cement

Cement made from limestone or chalk and clay is generally called Portland cement. Various types are made by adding other materials or by modifying the production methods, for example, ordinary

▲ Sympathetic rendering

Portland cement (OPC), white Portland cement, quick-setting cement and masonry cement.

Lime

Lime is made from limestone or chalk. When it leaves the kiln it is called quicklime, and may be non-hydraulic or hydraulic. Non-hydraulic lime sets by combining with carbon dioxide from the air as the water mixed with it dries out. Hydraulic lime has similar properties to cement; it sets when water is added and so can be used in wet conditions. When quicklime (the non-hydraulic type, especially) is 'slaked' (mixed with water), it expands and gives off heat.

Hydraulic lime is less active and, like cement powder, is dry-mixed with sand.

SEE ALSO
225

Cement: mixing mortar

Mix only as much mortar as you can use in an hour – and if the weather is very hot and dry, shorten this to half an hour. Keep all your mixing tools and equipment thoroughly washed, so that no mortar sets on them.

Measure the required amount of sand onto a mortar board or a smooth, level base, such as a concrete drive. Using a dry bucket and shovel – kept only for cement powder – measure out the cement.

Tip the cement over the heaped-up sand, and mix together by shovelling from one heap to another and back again (1). Continue to turn this dry mix (the sand will actually be damp) until the whole takes on a uniform grey colour.

Form a well in the centre of the heap and pour in some water (2), but not too much at this stage.

Shovel the dry mix from the sides of the heap into the water until the water is

2. Form a well in the heap and pour in water

3. Shovel dry material into the water

absorbed (3). Add more water as you go, until you achieve the right firm, plastic consistency in the mortar, turning it repeatedly to mix it to an even colour. If, after turning, the mix is still quite dry, sprinkle it with water (4) – too much water, however, will weaken the mix, so go easy.

1. Shovel dry mix from one heap to another

Draw the back of your shovel across the mortar with a sawing action to test its consistency (5). The back of the shovel should leave a smooth texture on the surface of the mortar.

Make a note of the amount of water used and the proportions of the dry materials, so that further mixes will be consistent.

4. Sprinkle mix with water if it's too dry

For cement-lime-sand mixes, the lime powder can be added with the cement and dry-mixed as above. When you have finished, hose down the work area – especially if it is a driveway, as any cement slurry will stain the surface.

5. Test the mix's consistency with a shovel

Machine mixing

A small electric-powered or diesel-driven cement mixer can save a great deal of time and effort, especially on big

jobs, and is quite easy to use. Unless you plan to use a mixer regularly, hire one by the day rather than buy one outright.

A few tips: set the machine as close as possible to the work area; place a board under the drum to catch any spilt materials; dry-mix materials first by running the mixer, then add some water; run the mixer for a couple of minutes to test for consistency; wash out the mixer drum after each mix.

◀ *Hire a mixer for large batches*

SEE ALSO
300–1

Cement: mortar for walls

When building a wall, mortar is used to bind together the bricks, concrete blocks or stones. The durability of the wall depends to a certain extent upon the quality of the mortar used and whether it is mixed correctly.

The ingredients of mortar

General-purpose mortar is made from cement, hydrated lime and sand, mixed together with enough water to make a workable paste.

Cement is the hardening agent that binds the other ingredients together. The lime slows down the drying process and prevents the mortar setting too quickly. It also makes the mix flow well, so that it fills gaps in the masonry and sticks to the texture of blocks or bricks. Sand acts as an aggregate, adding body to the mortar, and reduces the possibility of shrinkage.

For general-purpose mortar, fine builder's sand is ideal – but if you want a pale mortar for bonding white screen blocks, use silver sand instead.

▲ *Correct consistency*
The mortar mix should be firm enough to hold its shape when you make a depression in the mix

Plasticizers

If you're laying masonry in a period of cold weather, substitute a proprietary plasticizer for the lime. Plasticizer produces an aerated mortar in which the tiny air bubbles allow water to expand in freezing conditions, reducing the risk of cracking. Pre-mixed masonry cement, which has an aerating agent, is ready for mixing with sand.

Ready-mixed mortar

This type of mortar contains all the ingredients mixed to the correct proportions – you simply add water. It is a more expensive way of buying mortar, but it's convenient and available in small quantities.

Mixing mortar

Mortar should be discarded if it isn't used within two hours of being mixed; make only as much as you can use within that time. An average of about two minutes for laying each brick is a reasonable estimate.

Choose a flat site on which to mix the materials – a sheet of plywood is fine – and dampen it slightly to prevent it absorbing water from the mortar. Make a pile of half the amount of sand to be used, then add the other ingredients. Put the rest of the sand on top and mix the dry materials thoroughly.

Scoop a depression in the pile and add clean tap water – never use contaminated water. Push the dry mix from around the edge of the pile into the water until it has absorbed enough for you to blend the mix with a shovel, using a chopping action. Add more water, little by little, until the mortar has a butter-like consistency – slipping easily from the shovel, but firm enough to hold its shape if you make a hollow in the mix. If the sides of the hollow collapse, add more dry ingredients until the mortar

firms up. Make sure the mortar is sufficiently moist – dry mortar won't form a strong bond with the masonry.

If the mortar stiffens while you are working, add more water to restore consistency.

Proportions for mixing mortars

Mix the materials according to the conditions at the building site. Use a general-purpose mortar for where the wall is reasonably sheltered. A stronger mix is required where the wall will be exposed to wind and driving rain or if the site is elevated or near the coast. If you are using plasticizer rather than lime, follow the manufacturer's instructions regarding the quantity you should add to the sand. 🠚

▼ *Masonry cement*
A ready-mixed cement that is used without adding lime or plasticizer.

	❶	❷	❸
General-purpose mortar (Moderate conditions)	1 part cement 1 part lime 6 parts sand	1 part cement 6 parts sand/ plasticizer	1 part masonry cement 5 parts sand
Strong mortar (Severe conditions)	1 part cement ½ part lime 4 parts sand	1 part cement 4 parts sand/ plasticizer	1 part masonry cement 3 parts sand

KEY **Mortar mixing proportions 1.** Cement/lime mortar
2. Plasticized mortar **3.** Masonry-cement mortar

SEE ALSO
48–9

Chimneys

Although most homes are nowadays equipped with central heating, many still boast an open fireplace. Whether you decide to block it up or have an open fire, you will still need to tend to the chimney.

Capping the chimney

When you close off a fireplace opening, you need to cap the chimney to keep the rain out – while allowing enough of an outlet to draw air through the vent in the room below. Either replace the chimney pot with a half-round ridge tile bedded in cement (below, top), or fit a proprietary cowl or cap (below, bottom).

Half-round ridge tile

Commercial cowl

Cleaning chimneys

All solid fuels give off dust, ash, acids and tarry substances as they burn; and this combination of materials is carried up the chimney, where some of them are deposited as soot. If too much soot collects in a chimney, its size is effectively reduced internally, restricting the flow of gases and stopping the fire burning properly. A build-up of soot can even create a complete blockage, particularly at a bend in the chimney, and cause the more serious hazard of a chimney fire.

To prevent soot building up, have your chimney swept

VACUUM SWEEPING

You can have a chimney swept with a special vacuum cleaner. Its nozzle is inserted through a cover over the fire opening and sucks the soot out of the chimney. Although this is a relatively clean method, it may not remove heavy soot deposits or other obstructions which you really need cleared for efficient combustion of your fire.

▲ Sweeping a chimney
Seal off the fireplace with an old sheet and feed the canes up under it

annually – if it is left unswept for too long, smoke begins to billow into the room and soot occasionally drops into the fire.

Though it seems a dirty job, a chimney can be swept without making a great deal of mess. If you want to clean the chimney yourself, you can hire sets of brushes and canes.

Remove any loose items from the hearth. If the room has a large rug or a carpet that isn't fitted, roll it back and cover it with a dust sheet. Drape an old sheet or blanket over the fire surround and weight it down along the mantle shelf. Lean something heavy against each side to form a seal.

Screw a brush head to the first cane and place it inside the flue above the fireplace, then gather the sheet around the cane and weight down its edges securely on the hearth. Now screw on the next cane and begin to push the brush up the flue.

Continue screwing on lengths of cane and push the brush upwards until you feel resistance cease as the brush emerges from the top of the chimney pot. Be careful not to push the cowl off the chimney if you have one fitted.

If the brush meets an obstruction in the flue, pull it back slightly, then push upwards again until you clear the blockage. Don't twist the canes as this may unscrew a joint and leave the brush stuck up the chimney.

Pull the brush back down, unscrewing the canes as they appear; then pull out the brush and shovel the heap of soot out of the grate or use a hired industrial vacuum cleaner. ☞

CHEMICAL CLEANING

There are chemicals that will remove light deposits of soot and help prevent sooting in the future. In liquid or powder form, they are sprinkled onto a hot fire, producing a non-toxic gas that causes soot to crumble away from inside the chimney.

☞
SEE ALSO
143

Chimney flashing

Flashings are used to weatherproof the junctions between the roof and other parts of a building.

On a chimney, an apron flashing is fitted at the front. The upstand is folded round onto the sides of the stack, and its top edge set in a joint in the brickwork.

Stepped single-lap or double-lap flashings are fitted to the sides of the chimney. At the back, there's a timber-supported gutter. The front edge of the lead is turned up the face of the brickwork; and its ends are folded over the side flashings. A separate cover flashing is dressed over the upstand at the rear of the chimney. The back of the gutter follows the roof slope and is lapped by the tiles, which are fitted last. ☞

1. Engage the hook of the ladder over the ridge

2. A roof ladder spreads the load

Working safely

Working on a roof can be hazardous; if you feel insecure working at that height, you should hire a contractor.

If you decide to do it yourself, don't use ladders alone to reach the roof. Hire a sectional scaffold tower and scaffold boards to provide a safe working platform (see page 81).

Roof coverings are fragile and may not bear your weight – hire special roof ladders to gain access. Wheel the ladder up the slope (1) and then turn it over to engage the hook.

Roof ladders are made with rails that keep the treads clear of the roof surface and spread the load (2); but you can use padding in the form of paper-stuffed or sand-filled sacks to help spread the load further. ☞

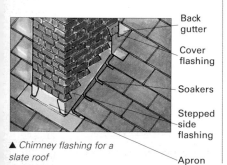

Back gutter

Cover flashing

Soakers

Stepped side flashing

Apron

▲ Chimney flashing for a slate roof

Chimneys: flue liners

If your house was built before 1965, there's a good chance that its chimneys are unlined. Over the years, the corrosive elements in the smoke from the fire eat into a chimney's mortar and brickwork, eroding them and allowing condensation to pass through.

Choosing a flue liner

You can deal with these problems by installing a flue liner, which protects the brickwork from the corrosive elements. A liner also reduces the 'bore' of the flue. This speeds up the flow of gases, preventing them from cooling and condensing, and the increased draught of air through the fire encourages more efficient combustion.

It's important to fit a liner that's suitable for the kind of heating appliance you're using, and it pays to have the liner installed by a professional.

Flue liners take the form of tubes, either one-piece or in sections, and are made of metal or some other rigid non-combustible material, such as pumice.

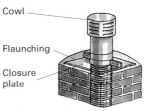

Cowl

Flaunching

Closure plate

▲ *An approved cowl for a gas heater*

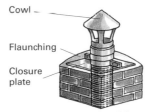

Cowl

Flaunching

Closure plate

▲ *An approved cowl for oil-fired heaters*

CASTING A FLUE LINER

Professional installers can cast a flue liner in situ. A deflated tube is lowered into the chimney. It is inflated and a lightweight concrete infill is poured into the gap between the tube and the flue. When the infill has set, the tube is deflated and removed, leaving a smooth-bore flue liner.

SEE ALSO
320–1

Flexible flue liners

A popular type of liner is a one-piece flexible corrugated tube of stainless steel that's fed easily into the flue. Thin-wall tubes are sufficient for gas appliances, but they burn through in next to no time if they are connected to solid-fuel or wood-burning stoves. For a solid-fuel or wood stove, install a double-skinned liner with a smooth inner surface. Some installers recommend filling around the liner with lightweight insulation.

As you have to get onto the roof to install most liners, you must expect to have secure scaffolding erected round the chimney (see next page). Before the work begins, it's advisable to have the chimney swept (see page 76).

The installer will feed the liner into the chimney from the top. A weighted cord lowered down the chimney (1) is attached to the conical endpiece of the flue liner. An assistant pulls gently on the cord from below while the liner is fed down the chimney (2). When the conical endpiece emerges in the fireplace, it is removed and either the liner is connected to a closure plate set across the base of the chimney or it is attached to the heating appliance's flue outlet. Once the joint has been sealed with fire cement and fibreglass-rope packing, the chimney pot is replaced and additional mortar is shaped to match the original flaunching.

If the liner is connected to a gas or oil-fired appliance, a top closure plate is bedded on mortar laid on the top of the chimney and a cowl is fitted (3).

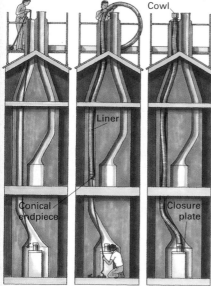

1. A weighted cord is lowered   *2. Liner is fed into chimney*   *3. Top closure fitted with cowl*

Installing a sectional flue liner

A lightweight-concrete liner is very durable, and suitable for any type of fuel. It's made in short sections, which are mortared together inside the flue. This type of liner is ideal for straight flues, although it can be adapted with standard elbow sections to fit offset flues.

The installer will have to remove the chimney pot, and may also need to make holes at key points in the chimney to gain access to the flue.

Liner sections are lowered down the flue one at a time – with the top joint of each section mortared to receive the next one. Once the liner is complete, the void around the liner is usually filled with lightweight concrete. Finally, the chimney pot is put back.

Remove pot and flaunching to access chimney

Join sections with steel collars or interlocking joints

Access holes at bends to feed sections to lower flue

Offset flues have ready-made elbows

Fill void with lightweight concrete

Register plate or adaptor seals opening

▶ *Cross-section of a typical installation*

▲ *Erect a safe platform when installing a liner*

Safe Access

Never try and tackle any job on the roof without first ensuring you have the correct equipment, such as roof ladders and scaffolding, to keep you up there safely. Two units of scaffolding will make a half platform for a central or side chimney. Four units will provide an all-round platform. ☞

SEE ALSO
179

Clothing

The maxim 'the right tools for the right job' also holds true for what you wear when you carry out certain tasks. Safety gear, which includes clothing, is vital for any job that puts your physical safety at risk, so plan ahead and make sure you're well covered up.

▼ *Whatever the task you are attempting, don't neglect the proper clothing or safety equipment*

Workwear and protective clothing

It is important that when using certain tools in particular, safety precautions should always be observed. Equally important is the care that should be taken for wearing the right clothes when using these tools. An obvious – but often ignored – example is that baggy shirts and loose ties should never be worn near moving parts.

It is vital that the operator should fully acquaint themselves with the range of protective clothing available and wear whatever is appropriate. It is no longer just a case of wearing overalls to keep clothes clean.

Head protection

Helmets or hard-hats should be worn whenever you are working overhead and whenever working on a building site or anywhere there is a danger of falling materials. They should also be used with power tools that may throw up wooden chips or material such as metals, or where there may be a risk of the tool or material kicking upwards.

Eye protection

The comprehensive range of eye protection extends from simple goggles to a full face mask, for a number of varying applications from protection against dust particles to flying chips, sparks and liquid splashes.

Within this range, particular care should be taken to select the right type of protection (for example, if you are undertaking welding, special Grade 1 or 2 impact goggles are required, which may not be needed for simply sanding the floor).

Goggles should also be worn when you are stripping paint and varnish off with a blowtorch. Electrically heated hot air strippers do the work just as quickly but with less risk of fire than a blowtorch, so you may prefer to use one of these tools. However, these also operate at extremely high temperatures, demanding full body protection. 🠖

Household rubber gloves

Industrial rubber gloves

Hardwearing protective gloves

▶ Various types of protective gloves

SEE ALSO
179–80

Ear defenders

Protection is needed against damage which can be caused to the ears, particularly when using certain power tools. Ear defenders are readily available in various types from the simple plug to the full and comfortable covers and pads for the whole ear.

Respiratory protection

If you need any convincing of the amount of dust particles in 'clean' air, then look at a shaft of sunlight to see how many there are. Consider some of the simplest DIY jobs – such as sanding a floor, sawing timber or man-made boards, or insulating the loft – and you will understand why protection with a mask or even respirator is vital.

Many of the solvents in paint (volatile organic compounds – VOCs) contribute to atmospheric pollution and can exacerbate conditions such as asthma. It is important not only to ventilate the room in which you are working, but to definitely wear a mask or a respirator if you suffer from breathing disorders.

Hands

The expression 'working gloves' covers a wide range of hand protection, from simple twill gloves that keep hands

Head protection

Safety goggles

Respirator mask

Fully covered ear protectors

◄ Many jobs require basic safety protection

► *Protective gloves are vital when using any tool that puts your hands in danger*

clean to special armoured gloves for hard wear.

Rubber gloves are extremely useful items to have around, not only to keep hands clean when tackling blocked drains or WCs, but also when handling cleaning solutions or liquid sanders that are applied by hand.

When using any tool that is in close contact with your hands, hard-wearing protective gloves are vital. This is definitely the case when using a blowtorch or hot air stripper, chiselling out old ceramic or quarry tiles, or rolling out loft insulation.

Overalls

It is important to make the distinction between protective clothing – such as lightweight overalls for decorating and for protecting clothes in the home – with more substantial protective clothing which is designed quite specifically for a purpose such as protecting against chemicals or from damage by certain tools. Make sure you follow the manufacturer's guidelines for clothing.

Accessories

Certain clothing accessories can help make the DIY job easier. Among these are nail bags that you wear around the waist, to hold your nails conveniently while you are working. Tool holders and pouches – which are also worn around the waist, either on a belt or complete with their own belt – are available for many tools, such as hammers and screwdrivers. ☞

SEE ALSO
184–5

Concrete

Concrete is a more versatile material than some people imagine. It may appear to be a rather drab, utilitarian material for the garden, but you can add texture and colour to ordinary concrete, or use one of the many types of cast-concrete slabs and bricks to add unusual textures to patios, paths and driveways.

Ingredients of concrete

Concrete consists of cement and fine particles of stone known as aggregate. The dry ingredients are mixed with water to create a chemical reaction with the cement, which binds the aggregate into a hard, dense material.

Cement

Standard Portland cement, sold in 50kg (110lb) bags, is used in the manufacture of concrete.

Sand

Sharp sand constitutes part of the aggregate of a concrete mix. Don't buy fine builder's sand and avoid unwashed or beach sand, which can affect the quality of the concrete.

Coarse aggregate

Coarse aggregate is gravel or crushed stone composed of particles large enough to be retained by a 5mm (¼in) sieve, up to a maximum size of 20mm (¾in) for normal use.

Pigments

Special pigments can be added to a concrete mix to colour it, but it's difficult to guarantee an even colour from one batch to another.

Combined aggregate

Naturally-occurring sand-and-gravel mix, known as ballast, is sold as a combined aggregate for concreting.

Dry-packed concrete

You can buy dry cement, sand and aggregate mixed to the correct proportions for concrete.

Water

Use ordinary tap water.

PVA admixture

You can buy a PVA admixture to make a smoother concrete mix that is less susceptible to frost damage.

Footings for garden walls

Building Regulations govern the size and reinforcement of the footings required to support high walls, especially loadbearing walls. However, most garden walls can be built upon concrete footings laid in a straight-sided trench.

Size of footings

Footings must be substantial to support the weight of the wall. The surrounding soil must be firm and well drained to avoid subsidence. Do not set footings in ground that has been infilled recently, such as a new building site; also avoid tree roots and drainpipes. If the trench begins to fill with water as you dig, seek professional advice before proceeding.

Dig the trench deeper than the footing itself, so that the first one or two courses of brick are below ground level. This will allow for an adequate depth of soil for planting right up to the wall.

If the soil is not firmly packed when you reach the required depth, dig deeper until you reach a firm level; then fill the bottom of the trench with compacted hardcore up to the lowest level of the proposed footing.

Concrete and steel lintels

A lintel bridges the gap above an opening. Modern lintels are made from reinforced concrete, galvanized steel or a combination of both. These strong lintels can support masonry over a wide span.

Lintel construction

In most cases, a damp-proof course is installed above the window opening to prevent any moisture within the cavity permeating the inner leaf of masonry or the window frame.

The front face of some concrete lintels is visible. Where a brick facing is required, a steel lintel is installed, and the bricks laid on the lintel's thin metal ledge.

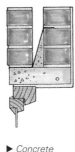

◀ Through-the-wall concrete lintel

▶ Concrete boot lintel

SEE ALSO
48–9

Concrete: assessing and mixing

Hire small mixing machines if you have a large volume of concrete, but for the average job it's easier to mix by hand. It isn't necessary to weigh the ingredients – mix by volume, choosing the proportions that suit the job.

Mixing by hand

Use two buckets to measure the ingredients, one for the cement and (to keep the cement dry) another identical bucket for the sand and coarse aggregate. Using two shovels is also a good idea.

Measure the materials accurately, levelling them with the rim of the bucket. Tap the side of the bucket with the shovel, so that the loose particles are shaken down.

Mix the sand and coarse aggregate first, on a hard, flat surface. Scoop a depression in the pile for the cement and mix all the ingredients until they form an even colour.

Form another depression and add water. Push the dry ingredients into the water until the surface water has been absorbed, then mix the batch by chopping the concrete with the shovel (1). Add more water, then turn the concrete from the bottom of the pile and chop as before until it has an even consistency.

To test the workability of the mix, form a series of ridges by dragging the back of the shovel across the pile (2). The surface of the concrete should be flat and even in texture, and the ridges should hold their shape without slumping.

1. Mix the ingredients by chopping the concrete mix with the shovel. Turn the mix over, and chop again

2. Make ridges with the back of the shovel to test the workability of the mix

Mixing by machine

Set up the mixer on a hard, level surface and ensure the drum is upright before you start the motor. Use a bucket to pour half the measure of coarse aggregate into the drum and add water. Add the sand and cement alternately in small batches, plus the rest of the aggregate. Keep adding water little by little along with the other ingredients.

Let the batch mix for a few minutes. Tilt the drum while it is still rotating and turn out some of the concrete into a wheelbarrow so you can test its consistency. If necessary, return the concrete to the mixer to adjust.

Machine safety

When you hire a concrete mixer, read the safety advice that comes with the machine.

- Read operating instructions before you turn machine on.
- Prop the mixer with blocks of woods until level and stable.
- Never put your hands or a shovel into drum while mixer is running.
- Don't lean over a rotating drum to inspect contents.
- Wear goggles when mixing concrete.

Ready-mixed concrete

If you need a lot of concrete for a driveway or large patio, it may be worth ordering a delivery of ready-mixed concrete from a local supplier.

Always contact the supplier to discuss your particular requirements. Specify the proportions of the ingredients, and say whether you require a retarding agent to slow down the setting time. (Once a normal mix of concrete is delivered, you will have about two hours to finish the job. A retarding agent can add a couple of hours to the setting time.) Tell the supplier exactly what you need the concrete for.

In order to avoid moving the concrete too far by wheelbarrow, you will want it discharged as close to the site as possible. A single cubic metre of concrete will fill 25 to 30 large wheelbarrows. ☛

PROFESSIONAL MIXING

There are companies who will deliver concrete ingredients and mix them to your specifications on the spot. All you have to do is barrow the concrete and pour it into place. There's no waste, as you pay only for the concrete you use. Telephone a local company for details on price and minimum quantity.

SEE ALSO
300-1

Concrete: finishes and reinforcing rods

The surface finishes produced by tamping or striking off with a sawing action are adequate for a workmanlike, skid-proof surface for a pad, drive or pathway.

Float finishes

You can smooth the tamped concrete by sweeping a wooden float across the surface or make an even finer texture with a trowel (steel float). Let the concrete dry out a little before using a float or you will bring water to the top and weaken it. Bridge the formwork with a stout plank so that you can reach the centre.

Brush finishes

To produce a finely textured surface, draw a yard broom across the setting concrete. Flatten the concrete initially with a wooden float and then make parallel passes with the broom, held at a low angle to avoid 'tearing' the surface.

Exposed-aggregate finish

Embedding small stones or pebbles in the surface makes an attractive finish.

Scatter dampened pebbles onto the freshly laid concrete. Tamp them firmly with a length of timber till they are flush with the surface (1). Place a plank across the formwork and apply your weight to ensure the surface is even. Leave to harden until all the surface water has evaporated, then use a fine spray and brush to wash away the cement from around the pebbles until they protrude (2). Cover for about 24 hours, then lightly wash the surface again to clean any sediment off the pebbles. Cover the concrete again, and leave it to harden.

Reinforcing rods

To add a narrow strip to a pad of concrete (for example, if you want to erect a larger garden shed which is bigger than the existing concrete base), drill holes in the edge of the original concrete pad and use epoxy adhesive to glue onto short, reinforcing rods before pouring in the fresh concrete.

1. Tamp pebbles into fresh concrete

2. Wash the cement from around the pebbles

Concrete: laying a floor

Before replacing a damaged suspended timber floor with a solid concrete floor, consult your local Building Control Officer. Converting one floor can affect the ventilation of another – insulation may also be required.

Preparing the ground

Strip out the infected timbers and burn them. Also remove the door. Treat the ground and surrounding masonry with a strong fungicide. Fill in any recesses left in the walls, as a result of removing timber, with bricks and mortar.

Mark the walls with a levelled chalk line indicating the level of the finished floor, allowing for the floorcovering if you intend to use a thick material such as quarry tiles or wood blocks.

About 50mm (2in) below this line, mark another one, the space between them representing the thickness of the screed. Then mark a third chalk line 100mm (4in) further down, indicating the thickness of the concrete slab. Mark a fourth line, 50mm (2in) below that, to indicate a layer of insulation board.

The infill

Lay the infill material in layers of no more than 225mm (9in), compacting each layer and breaking up larger pieces with a sledgehammer (1). You can use brick and tile rubble for the infill or gravel rejects (coarse stones from quarry waste).

Bring the surface up to within 25mm (1in) of the chalk line for the insulation, then

1. Preparing the ground
Mark the walls with chalk lines indicating the level of the finished floor, the thickness of the screed and the thickness of both the concrete slab and insulation

SEE ALSO
258–60

2. Laying the concrete

Working towards the doorway, lay concrete in bands not more than 600mm (2ft) wide. Tamp down the concrete. Bring it level with the chalked line

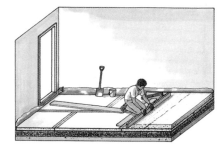

▼ 3. Laying the screed

Apply a band of cement grout to the concrete base and set levelled screed battens in mortar at each end. Lay the screed in bands not more than 600mm (2ft) wide

'blind' the surface with a layer of sand, tamped or rolled flat.

Laying the damp-proof membrane

Spread a polythene damp-proof membrane (DPM) of 1000 or 1200 gauge thickness over the surface of the sand, turning its edges up all round and lapping it up the walls to form a tray.

Make neat folds at the corners and hold temporarily in place with paperclips. If the floor needs more than one sheet of polythene to cover it, the sheets must overlap by at least 200mm (8in) and the joints should be sealed with special waterproof tape.

Including insulation

Lay closely butted polystyrene board on the DPM and tape the joints. As the work progresses, place strips of insulant between the concrete and the walls.

Laying the concrete

Mix a medium-strength concrete, with 1 part cement, 2½ parts sand, 4 parts aggregate. Don't add too much water – the mix should be a relatively stiff one.

Lay concrete progressively, in bands about 600mm (2ft) wide, working towards the doorway. Tamp the concrete with a length of 100 x 50mm (4 x 2in) timber to compact it,

and finish level with the chalk line (2). Slight unevenness will be taken up by screed, but check the surface using a spirit level and straightedge, and fill in any hollows. Leave the concrete to cure for at least three days under polythene to prevent shrinkage. 🔻

Laying the screed

Mix a screed mortar from 3 parts sharp sand, 1 part Portland cement. Dampen the floor and prime with a cement grout mixed to a creamy consistency with water and bonding agent in equal parts. Working from one wall, apply a 600mm (2ft) band of grout with a stiff brush.

Apply a bedding of screed mortar at each end of the grouted area to take 38 x 38mm (1½ x 1½in) 'screed battens'. Check with a spirit level and straightedge, so that they are flush with the surface-level lines on the walls.

Lay mortar between the battens and tamp down well (3). Level the mortar with a straightedge, then smooth it with a wooden float. Lift out the battens carefully, fill the hollows with mortar, and level again with the float.

Repeat the procedure, working your way across the floor in bands 600mm (2ft) wide. When the screed is firm, cover the finished floor with polythene and leave to cure for about a week. As soon as the floor is hard enough to walk on, trim the damp-proof membrane to within 25mm (1in) of the floor and fit the skirtings to cover its edges (4).

The floor will not be fully dry for about six months. Allow one month for every 25mm (1in) of thickness – don't lay an impermeable floorcovering.

4. Finishing the edges
Allow the floor to cure before using the room. Trim the edges of the DPM to within 25mm (1in) of the surface, and cover it with skirtings nailed or bonded to the wall

SEE ALSO
72–3

Concrete: laying a pad

Laying a simple pad as a base for a small shed or similar structure involves the basic principles of concreting.

Excavating the site

First, mark out the area of the pad with string lines attached to pegs driven into the ground outside the work area (1).

Remove topsoil down to a level to allow for the thickness of concrete and subbase. Extend the area of excavation about 150mm (6in) outside the space for the pad. Level the bottom by dragging a board across it (2); compact the soil. ☞

Erecting the formwork

Until the concrete sets, it must be supported by formwork. Construct this from softwood planks, 25mm (1in) thick. The planks need to be held in place with 50 x 50mm (2 x 2in) wooden stakes. To join planks, butt them end to end, nailing a cleat on the outside (3).

Using string lines as a guide, erect one board at the 'high' end of the pad and drive stakes behind it at about 1m (3ft) intervals, one for each corner. Nail the board to the stakes (4).

Tape a shim of timber to one end of the straightedge and, with the shim resting on the 'low' stakes, place the other end on the opposite board (5).

Erect the ends of the formwork. Allow the boards to overshoot at the corners to make it easier to dismantle when the concrete has set (6).

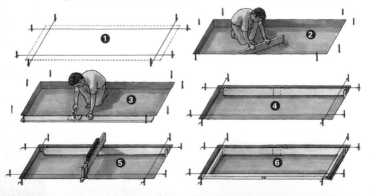

Laying the subbase

Hoggin, a natural mixture of gravel and sand, is ideal for a subbase – but you can use crushed stone or brick. Pour hardcore into the formwork and rake it level before tamping it down with a heavy balk of timber (7). Fill in low spots with more hardcore or sharp sand until the subbase comes up to the underside of the formwork boards.

Filling with concrete

Mix the concrete and transport to the formwork in a wheelbarrow. Set up firm runways of scaffold boards if the ground is soft.

Dampen the subbase with a fine spray, and let surface water evaporate before tipping the concrete in place. Push firmly into the corners (8). Rake level until the concrete stands about 18mm (¾in) above the level of the boards.

Tamp down with the edge of a plank 50mm (2in) thick that is long enough to reach across the formwork. Starting at one end of the site, compact the concrete with steady blows of the plank, moving it along by about half its thickness each time (9). Repeat, then remove excess concrete, using the plank with a sawing action (10).

Cover the pad with sheets of polythene, taped at the joints and weighted down with bricks around the edge (11).

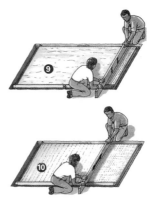

SEE ALSO
258–60

Concrete: repairing

Concrete suffers from the effects of damp and related defects, such as cracking and crumbling. Repairs can usually be made in the same way as for brickwork and render, although be aware of special considerations.

Sealing concrete

New concrete has a high alkali content, so efflorescence can develop on the surface as it dries out. Use only water-thinnable paint until the concrete is completely dry. When treating efflorescence on concrete, follow the procedure recommended for brickwork.

Cleaning dirty concrete

You can scrub dirty concrete with water (as described for brickwork); but when a concrete drive or garage floor is stained with patches of oil or grease, you will need to apply a proprietary oil-and-grease remover. This is a detergent that is normally diluted with an equal amount of water, but can be used neat on heavy staining. Brush on the solution liberally, then scrub the surface with a stiff-bristle brush. Rinse off with clean water.

▼ Before you fill a narrow crack, open it up and undercut the edges, using a cold chisel

Binding dusty concrete

If trowelling is overdone, cement is brought to the surface; and when the concrete dries out, this thin layer begins to break up, producing a loose, dusty surface. Treat a dusty concrete wall with stabilizing primer.

Repairing cracks and holes

Rake out and brush away loose debris. If the crack is less than 6mm (¼in) wide, open it up with a cold chisel (see left). Add a fine aggregate such as gravel to a sand-and-cement mix. Make sure the fresh concrete sticks in shallow depressions by priming the damaged surface with 3 parts bonding agent, 1 part water.

Treating spalled concrete

When concrete breaks up or spalls due to frost, the process is accelerated as steel reinforcement is exposed and corrodes. Fill as above, but paint the metalwork first with a rust-inhibitive primer.

D

Damp

Try to locate and eliminate damp as quickly as possible. This is sometimes easier said than done – as one form of damp may be obscured by another. The three main types are penetrating damp, rising damp and condensation.

Penetrating damp

Penetrating damp is the result of water permeating the house's structure from outside. The symptoms only occur during wet weather. After a few dry days, damp patches dry out, often leaving stains.

As isolated patches are caused by a heavy deposit of water in one area, you should be able to pinpoint their source fairly accurately. General dampness usually indicates that the wall itself has become porous but equally it could well be caused by some other problem.

Penetrating damp most often occurs in older homes with solid walls. Relatively modern houses, built with a cavity between two thinner brick skins, are less likely to suffer from penetrating damp, unless the cavity is bridged in one of several ways.

Principal causes of penetrating damp
1. Broken gutter
2. Leaking downpipe
3. Missing roof tiles
4. Damaged flashing
5. Faulty pointing
6. Porous bricks
7. Cracked masonry
8. Cracked render
9. Blocked drip groove
10. Defective seals around frames
11. Missing weatherboard
12. Bridged cavity

Rising damp

Rising damp is caused by water soaking up from the ground into the floors and walls. Most houses are protected by an impervious barrier built into the walls and under concrete floors, so water can't permeate above a certain level.

DPC in a solid wall
A layer of impervious material is built into a joint between brick courses, roughly 150mm (6in) above the ground.

DPC and DPM in a cavity-wall
The DPM in a concrete floor is linked to the DPC protecting the inner leaf of the cavity wall. The wall's outer leaf has its own DPC.

If either the damp-proof course (DPC) in the walls or the membrane (DPM) in a floor breaks down, water can seep into the upper structure. Some older houses were built without a DPC.

This type of damp is confined to the lower sections of walls and to solid floors. It is a constant problem and becomes worse with prolonged wet weather.

Condensation

Air carries moisture in the form of water vapour. As air warms, it absorbs more water, like a sponge. When water-laden air comes into contact with a surface that is colder, the air cools until it can no longer hold the water it has absorbed and

condenses, depositing the water on the cold surface.

Conditions for condensation
Most moisture vapour is produced by cooking, using baths and showers, and even breathing. In cold weather the low temperature outside cools external walls and windows below the temperature of the heated air inside. This leads to moisture in the air condensing, running down windowpanes and soaking into the wallpaper and plaster. It is often worse in winter when windows and doors are kept closed, so fresh air is unable to replace humid air before it condenses.

Damp in a fairly new house in good condition is invariably due to condensation.

SEE ALSO
47

PENETRATING DAMP: PRINCIPAL CAUSES

Cause	Symptoms	Remedy
Broken or blocked gutter. Rainwater overflows, saturates wall, preventing it drying out normally	Damp patches near ceiling in upstairs rooms; mould forms immediately behind the leak	Clear leaves and silt; repair damaged gutters or replace with maintenance-free plastic guttering
Broken or blocked downpipes. Cracked or rusted downpipes, or leaves packed behind downpipe	Isolated damp patch, often appearing halfway up wall; mould growth behind the downpipe	Repair cracked or corroded downpipe or replace with plastic version; clear the blockage
Loose or broken roof tiles. Defective tiles allow rainwater to penetrate roof	Damp patches appear on upstairs ceilings, usually during a heavy downpour	Replace the faulty tiles, renewing any damaged roofing felt
Damaged flashing. If flashing cracks or parts from masonry, water trickles down inside building ☞	Damp patch on ceiling extending from wall or chimney breast, maybe on chimney breast itself	If existing flashing is intact, refit securely; otherwise, replace with similar material or self-adhesive strip
Faulty pointing. Ageing mortar between bricks in wall is likely to fall out and let water in	Isolated damp patches or sometimes even widespread dampness, depends on deterioration	Repoint joints between the bricks, then treat the entire wall with water-repellent fluid
Porous bricks. Old soft bricks become porous and so entire wall is eventually saturated	Widespread damp on inner face of exterior walls; increase in damp during a downpour	Repair bricks that have spalled; waterproof exterior with a clear water-repellent fluid
Cracked brickwork. Cracks in a brick wall allow rainwater to seep through to the inside face	Isolated damp patch – on a chimney breast, for example, due to a cracked chimney stack	Fill cracked mortar and replace any damaged bricks
Defective render. Cracked/blown render encourages rain to seep between render and brickwork behind	Isolated damp patch; can become widespread, persisting for a time after the rain ceases	Fill and reinforce crack. Hack off large areas of blown render and patch with new sand-cement render
Damaged coping. If coping stones on roof fall off, rain penetrates	Damp patches on ceiling near to wall right below parapet	Bed new stones on fresh mortar and make good the joints

	PENETRATING DAMP: PRINCIPAL CAUSES	
Cause	Symptoms	Remedy
Blocked drip groove. Rain runs under windowsill and off at the groove; if full of moss, rain soaks wall	Damp on underside of window frame; rotting wooden sill; mould on inside face of wall below window	Rake out the drip groove. Nail a batten to the underside of a wooden sill to deflect drips
Failed seals. Timber frames shrink, pulling pointing from edges so rainwater gets in	Rotting woodwork, damp patches around frame; gap where mortar has fallen out	Repair the window or door frame and seal around the edges with mastic
No weatherboard. Angled weatherboard should shed water clear of threshold	Damp floorboards just inside the door; rotting at the base of the doorframe	Fit a weatherboard, even if no obvious signs of damage; repair any rotten wood
Bridged wall cavity. If mortar drops between inner/outer leaves, water can bridge gap	Isolated damp patch anywhere on wall, particularly after a heavy downpour	Open up wall and remove mortar bridge, then waterproof wall externally

	RISING DAMP: PRINCIPAL CAUSES	
Cause	Symptoms	Remedy
No DPC or DPM. If house was built without either, walls are able to soak up water from ground	Widespread damp up to about 1m above skirting level; damp concrete floor surface	Fit a new DPC or DPM
Damaged DPC/DPM. If either deteriorates, water will penetrate at that point	Damp at skirting level (possibly isolated but spreading)	Repair or replace the DPC or DPM
DPC is too low. If DPC is lower than 150mm above ground, heavy rain can splash wall	Damp at skirting level, but only where the ground is too high	Lower level of ground outside; or cut a 150mm wide trench and fill with gravel
Bridged DPC. If exterior render covers DPC, moisture can cross to inside	Widespread damp appearing at and just above the skirting level	Hack of render to expose DPC; remove several bricks and rake out debris
Debris against wall. Flower beds or paving and garden refuse can all bridge the DPC	Damp at skirting level in area of bridge only or spreading from that point	Remove earth, paving or debris and allow wall to dry out naturally

SEE ALSO
320–1

CONDENSATION: PRINCIPAL CAUSES

Cause	Symptoms	Remedy
Insufficient heat. In cold weather, air in an unheated room may become saturated with moisture	General condensation	Heat room to increase ability of air to absorb moisture without condensing – NOT with a paraffin heater
Paraffin heaters. These produce a lot of water vapour, causing condensation on windows and walls	General condensation in rooms where paraffin heaters are used	Substitute another form of heating
Uninsulated walls and ceilings. Moist air condenses on cold ceilings/walls	Widespread damp or mould; not along ceiling joists, which remain fairly warm	Install efficient loft insulation; line ceiling with insulating tiles or polystyrene lining
Cold bridge. Even with cavity insulation, there can be a cold bridge across lintel over windows	Damp patches or mould surrounding the window frames	Line the walls and window reveals with expanded-polystyrene sheeting
Unlagged pipes. Cold-water pipes attract condensation; water collects and drips from pipe	Line of damp on ceiling/wall following pipework; beads of moisture on pipe's underside	Insulate cold-water pipes with plastic foam lagging tubes or mineral-fibre wrapping ☞
Cold windows. Often first feature to show condensation, as glass is thin and exposed to elements	Misted windowpanes or water collecting in pools at the bottom of the glass	Install double-glazing. If secondary system is used, place silica-gel crystals in the cavity between panes
Sealed fireplace. Air trapped inside flue cannot circulate and eventually condenses on the inside	Damp patches appearing anywhere on the chimney breast	Ventilate chimney with grille or air brick at low level; treat chimney breast with damp-proofing liquid
Loft insulation blocking airways. If air cannot circulate around eaves, leads to condensation	Widespread mould affecting the timbers in the roof space	Unblock airways; if possible, fit a ventilator grille in the soffit or install tile/slate vents
After building work. New plaster/mortar can exude moisture	General condensation on walls, ceiling, windows, solid floors	Wait for work to dry out, then review situation

Damp: treatments

Remedies for different forms of damp are suggested in the charts on the previous pages. The information below supplements these suggestions by providing advice on measures relating solely to the eradication of damp.

Eradicating mould

In damp conditions mould can develop, usually in the form of black specks. It is vitally important to locate and remedy the cause of the damp before you begin to redecorate the walls or ceiling, otherwise you will find all your efforts to be in vain.

If the mould is growing on wallpaper, soak the area in a solution made from 1 part household bleach to 16 parts water, then scrape off the contaminated paper and burn it. Wash the wall with a fresh bleach solution to remove paste residue.

Apply a liberal wash of similar solution to sterilize the wall and leave it for at least three days, but preferably a week, to make sure no further growth develops.

When the wall is completely dry, apply a stabilizing primer

thinned with white spirit, followed by a coat of size containing a fungicide solution if you are planning to repaper the wall.

Alternatively, you could try painting the wall with an emulsion that contains a fungicide.

If mould growth is affecting a bare-plaster or painted wall

▶ *Mould, typified by black specks, will grow on damp plaster or wallpaper*

SEE ALSO
188–9

or ceiling, apply a liberal wash of the bleach solution.

Wait for at least four hours, and then scrape off the mould, wipe it onto old newspaper and by burn it outside.

Wash the wall or ceiling once more with the solution, then leave it for three days in order to sterilize the wall completely before finally redecorating.

Waterproofing walls

Applying a repellent to the outside of a wall not only prevents rainwater soaking into the masonry but also reduces the possibility of interstitial condensation. This means that water vapour from inside the house penetrates the wall until it reaches the damp, colder interior of the masonry, where the vapour condenses. The moisture migrates back to the inner surface of the wall, causing stains and mould.

There are also damp-proofing liquids for painting onto the inside of walls, but these should be considered a temporary measure only, as they do not treat the source of the problem. Remove wall-coverings and make sure that

2. A bridged groove

3. Drip moulding

1. Water drips to ground

the wall surfaces are sound and clean. Treat any mould growth with a fungicide. Apply two full brushcoats of waterproofer over an area appreciably larger than the present extent of the damp. Once the wall is dry, you can decorate it with paint or a wallcovering.

If any of your walls show signs of efflorescence, apply the appropriate treatment, then paint with heavy-duty moisture-curing polyurethane.

Providing a drip moulding.

Because water cannot flow uphill, a drip groove on the underside of an external windowsill forces rainwater to drip to the ground before it reaches the wall behind (1). When redecorating, scrape out old paint or moss from drip grooves before it forms a bridge (2).

If an external wooden windowsill does not have a pre-cut drip groove, it is worth adding a drip moulding by pinning and gluing a hardwood strip, 6mm (¼in) square, 35mm (1½in) from the front edge of the sill (3). Paint or varnish the drip moulding to match the colour of the sill itself.

▲ *Apply mastic with an applicator gun*

Sealing around window frames

Scrape out old or loose mortar from around the frame, and fill deep gaps with expanding-foam filler; then seal all around the frame with a flexible mastic. Mastic is available in cartridges, some designed for use with an applicator gun. Cut the end off the cartridge nozzle and run it along the side of the frame to form an even, continuous bead. If the gap's very wide, fill it with a second bead once the first has set. ☞

Most sealants form a skin and can be overpainted after a few hours, although they are waterproof without painting.

Bridged cavity

A bridged wall cavity allows water to cross over to the inner leaf. The easiest way to deal with it is simply to apply a water repellent to the outer surface.

However, this does not address the cause, which may lead to further dampness in the future. When convenient (during repointing, perhaps), remove two or three bricks from the outside, in the vicinity of the damp patch, by chopping out the mortar around them. Use a small mirror and a torch to inspect the cavity. If you find mortar lying on a wall tie, rake or chip it off with an opened wire coat hanger or a metal rod, then replace the bricks.

▼ **Exposing a bridged wall tie**
Remove a few bricks in order to rake or chip the mortar from the wall tie

SEE ALSO
433–5

Doors: architraves

An architrave moulding provides a decorative frame to a door, as well as concealing the joint between door lining and wall. You can buy standard architrave mouldings or more elaborate ones can be made by specialist suppliers.

Fitting a classical-style architrave

A classical-style architrave comprises a fluted moulding with decorative top and bottom blocks that avoid the need to cut mitre joints in the moulding. Some are made as kits for fixing with hidden plastic clips, but you can make your own from separate components and nail them in place. It's not always necessary to fit skirting blocks.

However, if you are using skirting blocks, they should be fitted first (1). The upright architrave mouldings are then centred on them and fixed with nails. Fix the top blocks in place (2). When both sides of the doorway are complete, measure the distance between the top blocks and cut the horizontal architrave moulding to fit, then nail it in place.

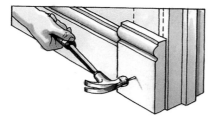

1. Nail the skirting block in place first

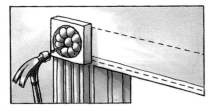

2. Pin the corner block, centred on the upright

Fixing standard architraves

Hold a short length of the architrave moulding about 6mm (¼in) above the door opening; after checking it is level, mark its width on the wall and on the front face of the door lining. Next, hold one slightly overlength upright in position, roughly 6mm (¼in) from the face of the door jamb. Transfer the marks previously made on the wall above to it (1, *right*).

1. Mark the length of the upright

2. Mark the length of the top moulding

Cut a 45 deg mitre on the marked end; then, using a spirit level, nail it to the door jamb, inserting 500mm (2in) lost-head nails every 300mm (1ft) or so. Don't drive the nails in fully, in case you need to move the architrave. Cut and fix the second upright on the other side.

Rest the top section of architrave upside down on the ends of the uprights and mark its length (2). Cut a mitre at each end and nail the moulding between the uprights (3). Drive a nail through the top edge into the mitred joint at each end (4). Drive all the nails below the surface, then fill the holes and joints before priming and painting the woodwork. ☞

3. Nail the moulding to the door lining

4 Drive a nail into the mitred joint

SEE ALSO
192–6

Doors: furniture

Exterior door furniture traditionally comprises a letter plate, a door knob and a knocker. Interior doors can also have finger plates fitted to protect the paintwork.

Fitting a door pull (knob)

A period-style iron door knob or a well polished brass one can be attractive features on a panelled door. Such knobs are reproduced in many traditional styles and patterns.

An external door knob is usually fitted on the centre line of a panel door. If a letter plate occupies the middle rail, place the knob just above it.

Drill a counterbored hole from the inside of the door to take the head of the screw used for fixing the knob; the clearance hole for the threaded shank passes through the door.

Reproduction door furniture

1. Brass 'Georgian' letter plate
2. Brass 'Georgian' knocker
3. Brass 'Georgian' door knob
4. Black-iron door knob
5. Black-iron knocker
6. Black-iron letter plate

▲ *Counterbore the hole for the fixing screw*

The backplate of the knob has a locating peg on the reverse that stops the knob turning when the screw is tightened. Drill a shallow recess for the peg; fit the knob and tighten the screw. To finish, plug the counterbored hole on the inside to conceal the screw head. ☞

Fitting a door knocker

Being the most ornate item in the set, a door knocker is more often regarded as an optional decorative feature rather than an essential item – especially since, from the functional point of view, electric door bells have made door knockers virtually obsolete.

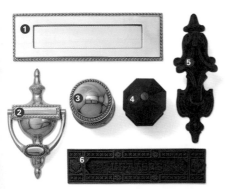

On a panel door, fit a knocker to the muntin (central vertical piece) at about shoulder height. Mark a vertical centre line at the required height and drill a counterbored clearance hole for the fixing screw (as for fixing a door pull). Plug the counterbored hole on the inside after fixing the backplate.

Reproduction brass fittings are usually finished at the factory with a clear lacquer to prevent tarnishing. If not, you can always apply a water-clear acrylic lacquer yourself.

Fitting a letter plate

Letter plates are available in a variety of styles and materials – solid brass, stainless steel, plated, cast iron and aluminium. They are designed either for horizontal or vertical fitting. Fitting a horizontal letter plate is described here, but the same method is applicable to the vertical type.

Mark out the rectangular opening on the centre of the cross rail. The slot must be only slightly larger than the hinged flap on the letter plate (1). Drill a 12mm (½in) access hole in each corner of the rectangle for the blade of a padsaw or power jigsaw. After cutting out the slot, trim the corners with a chisel and clean up the edges.

Mark and drill the fixing holes, then attach the letter plate (2). You may have to shorten the screws if the door is thin. Plug or fill the counterbored holes that house the screw heads.

Better still, fit an internal flap cover. Made from metal or plastic, these are held in place with small woodscrews. A flap cover reduces draughts, looks neat and allows the letter plate to be removed for machine-polishing from time to time.

▲ 1. Take dimensions from the flap and make the opening slightly larger

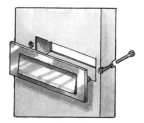

▲ 2. Counterbore the door for the plate and bolts

SEE ALSO
332–5

Replacing door furniture

INTERMEDIATE

There has always been a vast range to choose from, but the golden rule is to always buy good-quality fittings. It is advisable not to opt for cheap, poor-quality door furniture because it just won't last – or look as good.

Replacing a door handle

The first thing to do is to remove the old handle. Using a screwdriver, remove the four screws holding the handle plate [A]. Remember to remove only one side of the handle plate at a time. Then, place the new handle over the square spindle [B] to check if you need to cut the spindle shorter, in order to allow the new handle plate to sit flat against the door when it has been fitted.

Use a spirit level to check if your new handle plate is level by holding it vertically against the edge of the fitting. Then

mark your fixing holes with a bradawl [C] and drill small pilot holes for the screws [D]. Make sure the holes are just big enough to accept the screw provided with the new handles. Screw the first handle to the door, checking with the spirit level [E] and

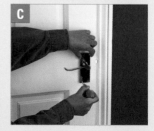

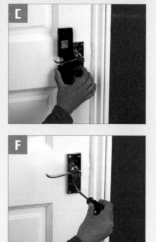

adjusting as you go [F].

Now go to the other side of the door and do exactly the same to fix the other handle.

Oiling the latch mechanism

It is always a good idea to oil the latch mechanism in the door handle while you are undoing the mechanism. To do this, remove both door handles and the spindle, remembering to place something on the floor between the door and the jamb to keep the door ajar. Use a cushion or something soft to wedge the door open.

Place a long bladed screwdriver through the hole where the spindle goes, and remove the two holding screws on the edge of the door.

Holding the screwdriver either side of the door, give it a firm pull towards the forward edge to free the latch [G]. Having oiled the latch, push it back into position and replace the two fixing screws. Replace the handles as mentioned above. You can now close and open the door with your new handles perfectly attached.

Doors: fitting locks and draughtproofing

It is worth fitting strong locks on your front and back doors for your own security. Throughout the home, doors should also help exclude draughts and keep in warmth.

Fitting a mortise lock

Scribe a line centrally on the edge of the door with a marking gauge; use the lock body to mark the top and bottom of the mortise (1). Drill out most of the waste wood between the marked lines.

Square up the edges of the mortise with a chisel (2) until the lock fits snugly. Mark around the edge of the faceplate with a knife (3); chop shallow cuts across the waste with a chisel. Pare out the recess until the faceplate is flush with the edge of the door.

Hold the lock against the face of the door and mark the centre of the keyhole with a bradawl (4). Clamp a block of scrap timber to the other side of the door, over the keyhole position, then drill through on the centre mark – the block prevents splintering the face of the door on the other side. Cut out the keyhole slot on both sides with a padsaw or jigsaw.

Screw the lock into its recess

and check its operation; screw on the coverplate and then the escutcheons over the holes on each side (5). With the door shut, operate the bolt to mark the position of the striking plate on the door frame. If the bolt has no built-in marking device, shoot the bolt fully out, then push the door to, so you can draw round the bolt on the face of the frame (6).

Mark out and cut the mortise and shallow recess for the striking plate (7), as above.

1. Mark the mortise

2. Chop out the waste

3. Mark the faceplate

4. Mark the keyhole

5. Screw the escutcheons on to cover the keyhole

6. Mark bolt on frame

7. Fit striking plate

Fitting a cylinder rim lock

Although fitting instructions vary, the following method applies to most. Using the templates provided, mark then drill holes for the cylinder (1). Hold the lock body against the door, so that you can mark and cut a recess for its flange (2).

Pass the cylinder into the hole from the outside and check the required length of the flat connecting bar. Cut to size with a hacksaw (3). Bolt the cylinder to the door.

Screw the mounting plate for the lock on the inside of the door (4) and attach the lock body to it.

1. Mark cylinder centre

2. Draw round flange

3. Cut connecting bar

4. Fit mounting plate

Use the fitted lock as a guide for positioning the staple on the doorframe.

Draughtproofing doors

A certain amount of ventilation is desirable for a healthy environment and to keep condensation at bay.

But using uncontrolled draughts is hardly an efficient way to ventilate a house. It is therefore worth spending a little money and effort on draughtproofing your doors.

If the gap between the bottom of the door and the floor is very large, it's bound to admit fierce draughts, so use a threshold excluder to seal the gap.

These come in various forms and designs, including flexible-strip excluders (a strip of plastic or rubber that sweeps across the floorcovering to form a seal); brush seals (a long nylon-bristle brush to exclude draughts); automatic excluders (spring loaded to lift from the floor when door is opened); flexible arch excluders (a vinyl insert that presses against the underside of the door); and door kits, with an aluminium weather trim and weather bar for exterior doors. ☛

SEE ALSO
347

Doors: hanging and fitting

Whatever style of door you wish to fit, the procedure is similar. Two good quality 100mm (4in) butt hinges are enough for a standard door; but a third, central, hinge should be added to a fire door or a heavy hardwood one.

Fitting a door

Before attaching the hinges to a new door, make sure it fits nicely into its frame. It should have a clearance of 2mm (¹⁄₁₆in) at the top and sides, and should clear the floor by at least 6mm (¼in) – as much as 12mm (½in) may be required for a carpeted floor.

1. Saw off horns

Measure the height and width of the opening, and the depth of the rebate in the frame into which the door has to fit.

Cutting to size

New doors are often supplied with 'horns' – extensions that prevent the corners being damaged. Cut these off with a saw (1) before starting to trim the door to size.

2. Plane to size

If you need to reduce the height of the door by more than 6mm (¼in), remove the waste with a saw and finish off with a plane. Otherwise, just trim it to size with the plane (2).

Support the door on a wedge (3) and try it in the frame.

3. Wedge the door

Fitting hinges

The upper hinge is set about 175mm (7in) from the top of the door, and the lower one about 250mm (10in) from the bottom. They are cut equally into the stile and doorframe. Wedge the door and mark the positions of the hinges on both the door and frame.

Stand the door on edge. Open a hinge and, with its knuckle projecting from the edge of the door, align it with the marks and draw round the flap with a pencil (1). Set a marking gauge to the thickness of the flap and mark the depth of the recess. Chisel a series of

1. Mark round the flap with a pencil

shallow cuts across the grain (2) to the scored line. Repeat with the second hinge. Using the flaps as guides, drill pilot holes for the screws and fix both hinges into their recesses.

Wedge the door open; align the free hinge flaps with the marks on the doorframe. Make sure the knuckles of the hinges are parallel with the frame, then trace the recesses on the frame (3) and cut out as above.

2. Cut across the grain with a chisel

3. Mark the size of the flap on the frame

Adjusting and aligning

Hang the door with one screw holding each hinge, to see if it closes smoothly. If the latch stile rubs on the frame, you may have to make one or both recesses slightly deeper. If the door appears to strain against the hinges, insert thin cardboard beneath the hinge flaps to pack them out. Finally, drive in the rest of the screws. 👉

Doorframes

Because external doorframes are built into the masonry, when you replace one you inevitably have to repair damaged plaster or rendering.

In older houses, frames are recessed into the masonry, with the inside of the frame flush with the plasterwork. Modern houses may have frames close to or flush with the outer face of the masonry.

Either buy a standard frame to fit or make one yourself from standard frame sections.

Preventing wet rot damage to wooden doorframes in the first place is the best option. Check around the frame for any gaps and apply a mastic sealant where necessary.

A small outbreak of wet rot can be treated with a proprietary repair kit and a chemical preserver.

👉

SEE ALSO
335

Doors: painting

When it comes to painting a door, the end result must be even in colour, with no ugly brushmarks visible. Follow these recommended procedures for all types of door.

Preparation and technique

Remove door handles and wedge the door open so that it cannot be closed accidentally, locking you inside the room. Keep the handle in the room with you, just in case.

Paint the door and its frame separately, so there's less chance of touching wet paintwork when passing through a freshly painted doorway. Paint the door first; and then when it's dry, finish the framework.

Flush door

To paint a flush door, start at the top and work down in sections, blending each one into the other. Lay on the paint, then finish each section with light vertical strokes. Finally, paint the edges, taking extra care to avoid paint runs.

Pannelled door

The different parts of a panelled door must be painted in a logical sequence. Finish each part with strokes running parallel to the direction of the grain.

Whatever style of panelled door you are painting, start with the mouldings (1) followed by the panels (2). Paint the muntins (centre verticals) next (3), and then the cross rails (4). Finish the face by painting the stiles – the outer verticals (5). Last of all, paint the edge of the door (6).

Flush door
Apply paint in sections, working down from the top. Lay off with light vertical brushstrokes, picking up the wet edges for a good blend.

Panelled door
Follow the numbered sequence for painting the various parts of the door, finishing each part with strokes along the grain to prevent streaking.

Doors: repairing

Tongue-and-groove boards of a ledged-and-braced door tend to rot along the bottom of the door first, as the end grain absorbs moisture. They can be easily repaired.

Repairing a battened door

Nailing a board across the bottom of the door is not a satisfactory solution, because moisture will be trapped behind the board and will increase the rot.

Remove the door and cut back the damaged boards to sound material. Where a batten falls on a rail, use the tip of a tenon saw to cut through most of it, then finish off the cut with a chisel.

When replacing the end of a single batten, make the cut at right angles (1). When a group of battens is to be replaced, make 45 deg cuts across them (2) – the interlocking of the tongued and grooved edges between the old and new sections is better maintained.

When cutting new pieces of boarding to fit, leave them overlength. Apply an exterior woodworking adhesive to the butting ends of the battens, but do not get any on the tongue-and-groove joints. Tap the pieces into place and nail each to the rail with two

1. Cut the end of a single batten square

2. Cut a group of battens to 45 deg

staggered lost-head nails. Cut off the ends of the repaired battens in line with the door's bottom edge, then treat the wood with a preserver to prevent any further damage.

Sticking doors

Doors will sometimes begin to stick after years of use, normally due to hinge wear and tear or expansion of the wood in the door. The latter problem can be exacerbated by central heating or extremes of temperature; these can cause the wood either to warp, expand or contract. For a full treatment of how to deal with sticking doors, see the illustrated special project overleaf on pages 118–19.

SEE ALSO
255

Repairing and overhauling doors

A lot of people are put off repairing or overhauling doors because they think it's a difficult job. But before long the damage to the door will be beyond repair and it will require replacing altogether.

Sticking doors

With the onset of winter and damp conditions, doors may start to stick along the side and bottom and could need 'easing'. First, check that the hinges are not worn or broken. If the door rocks a bit when pushed and pulled, this is normally a sign that the hinges are worn and should be replaced.

Let's start with a side-sticking door, provided the hinges are sound. Close the door tightly and mark a pencil line down the edge against the jamb [A]. You will now see where the door needs easing back from the high points along the pencil line. You can use a hand plane to plane off the high points until the edge is the same distance from the pencil line all the way down [B].

Shut the door, and using a flat piece of wood, for

Tools

Plane
Pencil
Hammer
Chisel
Screwdriver

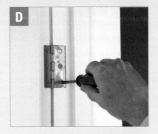

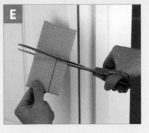

instance a piece of hardboard, scribe a line on the bottom of the door [C]. This will show any tight points on the floor. Remove the door from its hinges and plane off any points.

You may have to adjust the hinges on the door to square it to the frame for a good fit. Or you may need to pack the hinges out if they have been cut in too deep, making the door bind on the frame.

Remove the door and hinges [D] by wedging the door underneath to support it in the open position. Now cut small packers from thin card [E] and place the card packer behind the hinges [F] and screw back into position. This will adjust your door towards the jamb. You may need one or two pieces of card, depending on the amount of adjustment required.

Screw the hinge(s) back into position, just one screw per hinge while you close the door to check. Add or remove pieces of card until you have the right combination for a perfect square fit and no binding, then fix the rest of the screws.

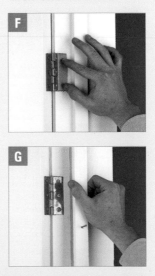

Drainage: blockages

If you find out you have a blocked drain, before resorting to professional services, hire a set of drain rods – short flexible rods made of plastic or wire, screwed end to end – to clear the blockage.

▲ Rodding points
A modern drainage system is often fitted with rodding points to provide access to the drain. They are sealed with small oval or circular covers.

Locating the blockage

Lift the cover from the inspection chamber nearest to the house. If it's stuck or the handles have rusted away, scrape the dirt from around its edges and prise it up with a garden spade.

• If the chamber contains water, check the one nearer the road or boundary. If that chamber is dry, the blockage is between the two chambers.
• If the chamber nearest the road is full, the blockage will be in the interceptor trap or in the pipe beyond, leading to the sewer.
• If both chambers are dry and yet either a yard gully or downstairs WC will not empty, check for blockages in the branch drains that run to the first inspection chamber.

Rodding the drainpipe

For a detailed, illustrated description of how to use drain rods, see the drainage clearing project on pages 122–3. For a basic summary of the technique, read on. ☞

Screw two or three rods together and fix a corkscrew fitting to the end. Insert the rods into the drain at the bottom of the inspection chamber, in the direction of the suspected blockage. If the chamber is full of water, use the end of a rod to locate the open channel running across the floor, leading to the mouth of the drain.

Pull and push the obstruction until it breaks up, allowing the water to flow away.

Extract the rods, flush the chamber with clean water from a hose, then replace the lid.

▼ Use a corkscrew fitting to clear a drain

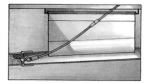

Clearing interceptor traps

Screw a rubber plunger to the end of a short length of rods and locate the channel that leads to the base of the trap. Push the plunger into the opening of the trap, then pump the rods a few times to expel the blockage.

If the water level does not drop after several attempts, try clearing the drain leading to the sewer. Access to this drain is through a cleaning eye above the trap. It will be sealed

▲ To rod an interceptor trap, fit a rubber plunger

with a stopper that is dislodged with a drain rod, unless it is attached to a chain stapled to the chamber wall. Don't let the stopper fall into the channel and block the trap.

Cesspools and septic tanks

Houses built in the country or on the outskirts of a town are not always connected to a public sewer. Instead, waste is drained into a cesspool or septic tank.

A cesspool is a collection point for sewage until it can be pumped out by the local council; a septic tank is a complete waste-disposal system, in which sewage is broken down before the water is distributed underground.

Cesspools

Building Regulations stipulate that cesspools must have a minimum capacity of 18cu m (4000 gallons), but many

cesspools are far smaller and require emptying perhaps once every two weeks.

Most cesspools are cylindrical pits lined with brick or concrete. Modern ones are sometimes prefabricated in glass-reinforced plastic.

Septic tanks

The sewage in a septic tank separates slowly: heavy sludge falls to the bottom to leave relatively clear water, with a layer of scum on the surface. A dip-pipe discharges waste below the surface, so that incoming water does not stir up the sewage. A network of drains disperses it over a wide area to filter through the soil.

SEE ALSO
122–3

Clearing blocked drains and toilets

BEGINNER

Drains are something we do not like to think about too often – unless we are forced to, when the contents of our sink or toilet refuses to leave. Here are a few easy methods for maintaining continuous flow.

To clear the kitchen sink, try a spoonful or two of caustic soda [A]; if that doesn't work, use a plunger. Place a cloth in the overflow then pump the plunger over the waste outlet [B]. Repeat until the blockage clears. If the blockage remains, undo the trap under the sink [C], placing a bucket beneath it first, and try clearing that.

If the toilet isn't flushing away properly, this would suggest a blockage has already formed. Deal with this straight away, or you could have an overflow into your bathroom.

Hire a WC auger if plunging did not shift the blockage [D].

Tools

Plunger
Auger
Wire coat
hanger
Protective
clothing
Disinfectant
and soap

This is a flexible cable, pushed as far as possible into the bend [E], with the handle cranked to unblock the toilet. When you have finished, rinse with hot water and disinfect.

Before you start any major internal operations, lift up the manhole cover in the garden

or street if possible, to check whether or not that is blocked.

Hire a set of drain rods. Screw two rods together with a plunger or corkscrew top at the head [F]; slide this into the drain run, going with the flow of the waste water. Add another rod and push the assembled line to and fro into the drain [G]. Run a hose into the manhole to help flush the blockage through.

If the manhole is not blocked, the soil stack pipe may be blocked. Undo a rodding eye on the stack using a hired auger to clear the blockage.

Blocked gullies are easily cleared. Raise the grille and remove any debris from the trap [H]. Ensure the outlet from the gully is also clear. Rinse the gully with the hose and clean with suitable cleaner.

Drainage: clearing gutters/ unblocking sinks

Don't ignore the early signs of a blockage. If water drains away slowly, use a chemical cleaner to remove a partial blockage before you are faced with a serious obstruction.

Clearing gutters

Blocked gutters and downpipes are unhygienic and can present a genuine hazard to your property. If they are left to overflow, they will eventually cause damage to the walls and roof around them, as well as the ground beneath them.

It is essential to inspect and clean out gutters regularly. They concentrate dirt and sometimes collect sand washed down from the tiles on the roof by the rain. This run-off can build up quickly if the flow of water is restricted by leaves or twigs and will collect in pools along the length of the gutter. Birds' nests can also block the guttering or downpipes. The problem becomes particularly serious if the mouth of a downpipe becomes blocked, as then the water in the gutter has nowhere to run away to. One effective way of preventing this from happening is to attach squares of chicken wire or, better still, fine nylon mesh or gauze, to the top of the drainpipe. This will prevent any build-up of debris from making its way into the pipe. Some DIY stores sell ready-made drainpipe caps specifically designed for this purpose.

Clearing the trap

The trap, situated immediately below the waste outlet of a sink or basin, gets blocked when debris collects at the lowest point of the bend.

Place a bucket under the basin to catch the water, then release the cleaning eye at the base of a standard trap; on a bottle trap, remove the large access cap by hand.

Drain the contents of the trap into the bucket, then bend a hook on the end of a length of wire and probe the section of waste pipe beyond the trap. Rinse the trap out thoroughly with detergent.

E

Electrics: basic principles

Many people imagine that working on the electrical circuits of a house is an extremely complicated business – but the circuitry is, in fact, based on very simple principles.

▲ *Double insulation*
A square within a square, either printed or moulded on an appliance, means it is double-insulated and its flex does not need an earth wire.

For any electrical appliance to work, the power must have a complete circuit – the electricity must be able to flow along a wire from its source (a battery, for instance) to the appliance (say a light bulb) and then back to the source along another wire. If the circuit is broken, the appliance will stop working – the bulb will go out.

Breaking the circuit – and restoring it – is what a switch is for. When the switch is in the 'on' position, the circuit is complete and the bulb or other appliance operates. Turning the switch off makes a gap in the circuit, so the electricity stops flowing. Although a break in either of the two wires would stop the power flow, a switch must always be wired so that it interrupts the live wire – the one that takes power to the appliance. In this way, the appliance is completely dead when the switch is off.

Although mains electricity is much more powerful than that produced by a battery, it operates in the same way, flowing through a live wire linked to every socket outlet, light and fixed electrical appliance in the home. For identification, live wires are coloured red or brown. Neutral wires, which take current back out of the house, are either black or blue.

Earthing

Any material through which electricity can flow is known as a conductor. Most metals conduct electricity – which is why metal (most often copper) is used for electrical wiring.

However, the earth itself – the ground on which we stand – is also an excellent conductor, which is why electricity always flows into the earth whenever it has an opportunity to do so,

SEE ALSO
176–7

IDENTIFYING CONDUCTORS

The insulation used to cover the conductors in electrical cable and flex is colour-coded to indicate live, neutral and earth.

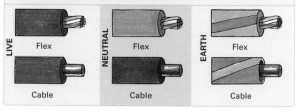

LIVE Flex / Cable

NEUTRAL Flex / Cable

EARTH Flex / Cable

taking the shortest route. If you were to touch a live conductor, the current would divert and take the route through your body to the earth – perhaps with fatal results.

A similar thing happens if a live wire comes into contact with metal components of an appliance, including its casing. To prevent this, a third wire is included in the wiring system and connected to the earth, usually via the outer casing of the electricity company's main service cable. This wire – the earth – is attached to the metal casing of some appliances or earth terminals in others, providing a direct route to the ground should a fault occur.

Double-insulated appliances – which usually means they have a nonconductive plastic casing insulating the user from metal parts that could become live – must not be earthed with a third wire.

The earth wire either has a green-and-yellow covering or is a bare copper wire sandwiched between the insulated live and neutral wires in an electrical cable.

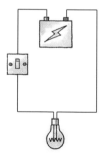

▲ **A basic circuit**
Electricity runs from the source (battery) to the appliance (bulb) and then returns to the source. A switch breaks the circuit to interrupt the flow of electricity.

Electrics: basic safety

It cannot be stressed too strongly that you must take steps to safeguard yourself and others while working on your electrical system. Faulty wiring and appliances are dangerous, and can be lethal.

Whenever you are dealing with electricity, the rule must be 'safety first'.

- Never inspect or work on any part of an electrical installation without first switching off the power.
- Always unplug a portable appliance or light.
- Double check all work before you turn the electricity on again.
- Always use the correct tools for an electrical job, and use good quality equipment and materials.
- Fuses are vital safety devices. Never fit one that's rated too highly for the circuit it is to protect – do not use any other type of wire or metal strip in place of proper fuses or fuse wire.
- Wear rubber-soled shoes when you're working on an electrical installation.

Using professionals

Always seek the advice and/or help of a professional electrician – registered with NICEIC (the National Inspection Council for Electrical Installation Contracting) – if you don't feel competent to handle a job yourself.

Testing an installation

Any significant rewiring, especially new circuits, must be tested by a competent electrician. Never attempt to make connections to the meter or to the company's earth terminal yourself.

Is the power off?

Having turned off the power, you can make doubly sure that it is safe by using an electronic mains voltage tester.

▶ **Using an electronic tester**
Touch the neutral terminal with one probe and touch the live terminal with the other probe.

Electrics: fittings

Today, standard 13amp square-pin plugs are used for most appliances and light fittings. They come with rigid plastic or unbreakable rubber casings. Some plugs have pins insulated for part of their length to prevent the user getting a shock from a plug pulled partly from the socket.

Fuses for plugs

Square-pin plugs have a small cartridge fuse to protect the appliance. Use a 3amp (red) fuse for appliances of up to 720W and a 13amp (brown) fuse for those of 720W to 3000W (3kW). There are also 2, 5 and 10amp fuses, but these are less often used in the home. ☞

Wiring a 13amp plug

Loosen the large screw between the pins and remove the cover. Position the flex on the open plug to gauge how

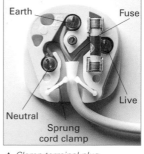

▲ *Clamp-terminal plug*

much sheathing to remove (remember that the cord clamp must grip sheathed flex, not the conductors).

Strip the sheathing and position the flex on the plug again, so that you can cut the conductors to the right length. These should take the most direct routes to their terminals and lie neatly within the channels of the plug.

Strip and prepare the ends of the wires, then secure each to its terminal. If you are using

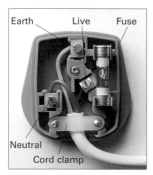

◀ *Post-terminal plug*

☞
SEE ALSO
161

Mending a fuse and fitting a plug

One of the first things to do when moving into a new home is to locate the fuse box or 'consumer unit'. When all the lights suddenly go off, you don't want to be stumbling around in the dark trying to find it then.

A very useful piece of advice is to keep a torch, spare batteries, fuses, candles and matches as back-up in an accessible location close to the fuse board.

Mending a fuse

Using your torch, check the fuse board master switch is in the OFF position. Most consumer units will contain easily replaceable cartridge fuses (see page 162), or you may find old-style rewirable fuse holders.

To locate the blown fuse, remove the fuses one at a time and inspect the thin fuse wire to make sure the wire is unbroken. On the card of fuse wire, select the appropriate amp fuse wire to match the blown fuse.

Using a small screwdriver, carefully unscrew the two screws a little way at either end of the fuse. Remove the damaged remains of the old

fuse wire and carefully thread the new wire through the centre porcelain part of the

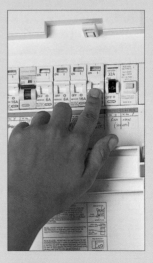

▲ *Locate the position of your consumer unit or fuse board. Ensure that the master switch is in the OFF position and then find the individual fuse or miniature circuit breaker that needs mending or replacing*

Tools

Torch
Electrical
screwdriver
Wire cutters
Ordinary
screwdriver

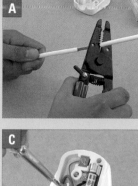

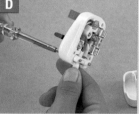

fuse. Wind the wire around the first screw then the second and tighten down the screws, snipping off any excess wire.

Replace the repaired fuse and then the consumer unit cover. Throw the master switch to the ON position.

Fitting a plug

Open up the plug case with a screwdriver and use wire strippers to remove the outer sheathing from each of the wires in the flex [A]. Use the ends of the wire cutters or a pair of pliers to position the exposed copper ends of each coloured wires in the correct terminals – brown to live, yellow and green to earth, and blue to neutral [B].

Holding the wires carefully in place in the terminals, drive the terminal screws tightly down on top of the wires using a screwdriver [C]. Ensure that no loose bits of wire protrude from the terminals.

Finally, tighten up the screws securing the cord clamp [D], replace the plug cover and switch on.

two-core flex, wire to the live and neutral terminals, and leave the earth terminal empty.

Tighten the cord clamp to grip the end of the sheathing and secure the flex (one type of plug has a sprung cord grip that tightens if the flex is pulled hard). Check that a fuse of the correct rating is fitted, then replace the plug's cover and tighten up the screw.

Round-pin plugs

Old round-pin sockets will only take round-pin plugs, which are not fused. Use 2amp plugs for lighting only; 5amp plugs for appliances of up to 1kW; and 15amp plugs for appliances between 1kW and 3kW. Have your wiring upgraded as soon as possible, so you can use modern fused square-pin plugs.

▼ *Round-pin plug*

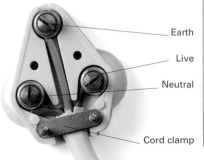

Earth

Live

Neutral

Cord clamp

Socket outlets

Whatever type of circuits exist in your home, use only standard 13amp square-pin sockets.

Before you start work on any socket, switch the power off at the consumer unit and remove the fuse or MCB for the relevant circuit – then test the socket with an appliance to make sure the socket has been switched off properly.

Types of 13amp socket

For most situations, you are likely to use either a single or double socket. Both are available switched or unswitched, and all are wired in the same way. Sockets can either be surface-mounted (screwed to the wall in a plastic box) or flush-mounted in a metal box buried in the wall.

Simple replacement

Replacing a damaged socket with a similar one is fairly simple. An unswitched socket outlet can be replaced with a switched with no change to the wiring or fixing.

Switch off the power and take out the circuit fuse, then remove the fixing screws from the faceplate and pull the socket out of the box.

▲ Types of sockets
1. Switched single
2. Unswitched single
3. Switched double
4. Switched single with
   indicator

Loosen the terminals to free the conductors. Connect the conductors to the terminals of the new socket. Fit the face-plate, using the original screws if the new ones don't match the thread in the box.

Surface to flush
You may want to replace a surface socket with a flush one.

Turn off the power, remove the old socket, then recess the new metal box into the wall.

Single sockets to doubles

A single socket on a spur can be replaced with a double, so long as it's the only socket on that spur – it needs to be connected to a single cable.

Surface to surface
Remove the old socket outlet and fix the new, double box to the wall in the same place.

Flush to surface
Fit a socket converter, which is made with two fixing holes that line up with the fixing lugs on the buried metal box (1). The faceplate of a converter is only 20mm (¾in) thick.

Flush to flush
Either centre the new box over the hole or align it with one end (2), whichever is more convenient. Trace the outline of the box on the wall and cut out the brickwork. ☞

1. Fixing a socket converter over a flush box

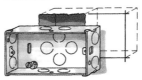

2. Cut out extra brickwork for a double box

SEE ALSO
134–5

Fitting a socket

Before you start, plan your room carefully to take into account where your furniture and appliances are going to be located. If you do this properly you can ensure that the power points are installed within easy reach.

Tools

Small electricians screwdriver
Medium screwdriver
Wire strippers
Drill
Masonry drill bit
Clubhammer
Small bolster or cold chisel
Padsaw

Single power points are not much cheaper than doubles, so you might just as well fit a double when fixing a new one.

When you remove the faceplate of the existing socket, you will see that the socket is either wired to a ring main (in which case two cables will be connected), or to a spur (which will have only one cable). In either case, the wire connections are the same: red to live; black to neutral; and green and yellow to earth.

Single to a double socket

Turn OFF the power from the mains. Unscrew the retaining screws on the socket faceplate [A]. Unscrew the wires and

remove the faceplate. Disconnect the interior of the single socket box and remove the back box by hand [B].

If the power point is mounted in a plasterboard partition wall, mark the outline of the box on to the wall with a pencil and, using a padsaw, cut out a piece of plasterboard [C]. Fix the new back box, pulling the cable through to the front of the box [D]. The wiring will be the same for a single or double socket outlets – red wire (live), black wire (neutral) and green and yellow wire (earth). Connect up the wires [E], replace the double socket cover and secure the screws [F].

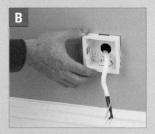

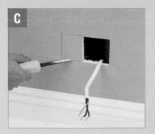

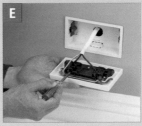

If the power point is mounted in a solid wall, position the new double back box and mark the wall with a pencil. Using a masonry bit and drill, create a series of holes following your pencil line to the depth of the new mounting box. Then cut out the brickwork with the clubhammer and small bolster or cold chisel.

Place the new double socket box in the new opening, mark two of the fixing holes. Using plugs and screws drill the holes, pull the cables through and fix the mounting box in position.

Adding a power point

To add a new power point to the existing ring main, locate and fix the new power point box as described. Wire a length of spur cable into the new socket first, as shown in the photographs on these pages.

Turn OFF the power from the mains and remove the face of the existing socket to which you wish to connect the new spur socket. Strip back the ends of the new wires and add these to the existing wires – black to black (N), red to red (L), yellow and green (E) – then fix the socket face back in place.

Light switches

The type of switch that's most commonly used for lighting is the plateswitch. This has a switch mechanism mounted behind a square faceplate with either one, two or three rockers. Although that's usually enough for domestic purposes, double faceplates with as many as four or six rockers are also available.

A one-way switch simply turns a light on and off, but two-way switches are wired in pairs so that the light can be controlled from two places – typically, at the head and foot of a staircase.

Any type of switch can be flush-mounted in a metal box buried in the wall or surface-mounted in a plastic box. Boxes 16 and 25mm (⅝ and 1in) deep are available.

Where there is not enough room for a standard switch, a narrow architrave switch can be used. There are double versions with two rockers, one above the other.

As well as turning the light on and off, a dimmer switch controls the intensity of illumination. Some types have a single knob that serves as both switch and dimmer. Others incorporate a separate knob for switching, so the light level does not have to be adjusted every time the light is switched on.

The Wiring Regulations forbid the positioning of a conventional switch within reach of a washbasin, bath or shower unit – so only ceiling-mounted double-pole switches with pull-cords must be used in bathrooms.

Methods for fixing mounting boxes are similar to fitting socket outlets (pp132–135).

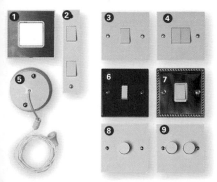

◀ Selection of light switches

1. Touch dimmer switch
2. Two-gang architrave switch
3. One-gang rocker switch
4. Two-gang rocker switch
5. Ceiling switch
6. Coloured rocker switch
7. Reproduction antique switch
8. One-gang dimmer switch
9. Two-gang dimmer switch

F

Fireplaces: fitting/reinstating

Once discarded as outdated and worthless, period fireplaces are now much sought after – both for the character they inject into a living room and for the improved resale value they bring to an older house.

Fitting an insert grate

Before proceeding with the installation, make sure the fireplace opening, hearth and chimney are all in good condition and that the proposed alterations comply with the current Building Regulations. As a precaution, check with the Building Control Officer.

To reinstate a 'missing' fireplace, either buy an original from an architectural salvage company or choose from the range of good-quality reproduction inserts and surrounds. A typical fireplace consists of a cast-iron insert grate (which includes the fire basket) and a decorative surround.

Position the insert on the back hearth, placing it

▶ *Reduce the size of the opening if necessary*

centrally in the fireplace opening. Check that it's plumb and square. If the opening is larger than the front plate of the insert, fill in the space at the sides with mortared bricks. If there's space above the insert, add a concrete lintel supported by the side brickwork. If the opening is not in the centre of the chimney breast, move the insert sideways.

Temporarily position the surround to see whether it fits snugly against the wall and grate. If necessary, pull the

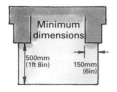

▲ Constructional hearth
Before reinstating a fireplace, check that the constructional hearth complies with current Building Regulations

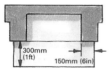

▲ Superimposed hearth
Minimum dimensions for an open fire. The width of the hearth should not be less than the width of the fire surround

insert forward to butt up against the back of the surround. Now remove the surround and pack fibreglass rope behind the rim of the insert and seal the gap with fire cement. If the insert is made with fixing lugs, use them to fix it to the wall with brass screws and heat-resistant wallplugs.

▶ *Fill the void behind the insert with concrete*

One-piece surround

The method for fitting the surround will depend on its construction. Wooden and cast-iron types are usually made in one piece and fixed with screws through lugs or fixing plates at each side.

Hold the surround against the wall and centralize it on the grate. Check that the surround is level and plumb, then mark the positions of the fixings. Remove the surround, drill and plug the wall, and screw the surround in place.

Fill the void behind the insert with a lightweight concrete mix, and form a 'throat' (the throat draws the smoke from the fire into the flue itself). Fit a superimposed hearth. **☞**

☞
SEE ALSO
144–5

Fireplaces: marble surrounds

A marble surround is constructed from separate pieces – two hollow jambs, a frieze and a mantle shelf. Ideally the frieze and jambs should overlap the edges of the insert grate. Lay the hearth before you erect the surround.

A metal loop on the inside of each jamb is wired to a screw driven into the wall. The loop, which is located near the top

▲ *The jambs and frieze overlap the insert*

▲ *Lay the mantle shelf on a thin bed of plaster*

of the jamb, can be reached through the open top when the jamb is in place.

Bond the base of each jamb in a bed of plaster of Paris laid on the hearth. Working quickly before the plaster sets, bind the metal loops back to the wall with copper wire. Make sure each jamb is plumb, then apply dabs of plaster on the inside, to stick it to the wall.

The frieze is located in notches on the inside of the jambs. Apply plaster to the notches and stick the frieze in place. Lay the mantle shelf onto a thin bed of plaster spread along the frieze, and bond it back to the wall. If need be, prop the front edge of the shelf until the plaster sets.

Use a piece of wood to scrape away any plaster that has squeezed out from the joints. Finally, repair the plasterwork around the fireplace with either a one-coat plaster or standard gypsum plaster. 🖝

Fireplaces: stripping

The availability of DIY paint removers has created a trend for stripping painted surfaces to expose the underlying material – such as cast iron, wood and marble. However, stripping a fireplace is not always appropriate, as some surrounds were intended to be painted.

Stripping a cast-iron surround may uncover much of the detail that has been obscured under layers of old paint – but repaint it afterwards to stop the metal rusting.

Restoring a marble mantlepiece may well be worth the effort – but make sure the marble is genuine. A lot of old wooden and slate fireplaces were painted to resemble marble. Marble feels cold to the touch – so allow the surround to cool down, then compare it with an adjacent wooden skirting. Similarly, it was once common practice to paint cheap softwood surrounds to imitate better-quality woods; but if you look closely, you should be able to distinguish painted graining from real wood. You can have paint finishes such as marbling or graining restored by specialist decorators.

Mouldings on Adam-style surrounds are sometimes made of plaster. These are easily damaged by solvents and stripping tools, so take extra care when removing paint.

Stripping methods

Cast-iron fireplaces can be dipped In an industrial stripping tank, but it is safer to strip most materials by hand. Use a gel or paste stripper and follow the manufacturer's instructions.

▶ *Cast-iron fireplace*
Strip thick paint to reveal fine detail in the original ironwork

SEE ALSO
268

Fireplaces: removing fireback

Some people abandon all thoughts of using an existing fireplace, just because the cast fireback is damaged and looks unsightly. However, a functioning fireplace is such an asset that it is well worth removing a damaged fireback and replacing it.

Removing an old fireback

If you plan to replace a fireback, first measure the width across its mouth and order a new one of the same size. The standard sizes are 400 and 450mm (1ft 4in and 1ft 6in), although larger firebacks are available.

Before you remove the old fireback, cover the floor with a dust sheet and protect a tiled hearth with thick cardboard. Wear a mask and goggles when removing the grate and fireback.

The grate (1) may simply rest on the back hearth; or it may be screwed down and sealed to the fireback with asbestos rope and fire cement (2). If so, dampen the area with water, then take out the screws and chip away the cement with a hammer and cold chisel. Next, break out the old fireback (3) with a hammer and chisel, starting at one corner. Open up cracks as they develop, until you can remove larger pieces.

Take care not to damage the

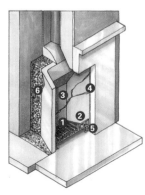

Taking out an old or damaged fireback
1. The grate may be fixed or freestanding.
2. The grate may be sealed with asbestos rope and fire cement.
3. The fireback will have to be broken out.
4. The surround is bonded to the fireback with fire cement.
5. Expansion-joint packing may need replacing.
6. You will need to clear rubble from the brick-lined opening

fire surround when you are breaking the cement seal (4) between it and the fireback. Don't touch the asbestos-rope packing (5) between the surround and fireback unless it's in poor condition and needs replacing.

You will find heat-retaining rubble in the space behind the fireback (6). Dislodge this rubble with a hammer and chisel until you have cleared the brick-lined opening completely.

To replace a fireback, it may be worthwhile seeking professional help or advice.

Fireplace ventilation

An open fire has to have oxygen to help it burn well. If the air supply is reduced, thorough draughtproofing or double glazing, then the fire smoulders and the slightest downdraught will blow smoke into the room.

There may be other reasons – such as a blocked chimney flue – but if you find the fire picks up within a few minutes of partially opening the door to the room, you can be certain that inadequate ventilation is the cause.

A simple solution is to fit a slim trickle ventilator over the door or window. Ventilators with sliding grilles are fine for a room with an open fireplace; but if you are heating a room with a fuel-burning appliance connected to a flue, the ventilator must be permanently open.

Some trickle ventilators are fitted with acoustic baffles to reduce noise penetration from outside. 🖝

Ventilating unused fireplace
If you close off an unwanted fireplace you should fit a vent, so air can flow up the chimney to dry out condensation or penetrating damp. Provided the chimney is uncapped, the moist warm air from inside the room will not condense on the cold surface of the flue.

Cut a hole in the plasterboard or leave a single-brick space in the masonry. Screw a face-mounted ventilator over the hole or use one that's designed to be plastered in.

◀ Face-mounted grille for an unused fireplace

SEE ALSO
405

Fitting a false fireplace surround

INTERMEDIATE

Even rooms without a chimney breast can have a fire surround – it can be fitted straight onto the wall, as long as it is an outside wall if you want a gas fire.

If you're lucky enough to have a chimney breast, make sure the chimney is checked and swept by a qualified chimney sweep if you are going to use it as a proper fireplace, with either an open coal or gas fire.

The surround featured in here is purely decorative and can be fixed to a straight wall or chimney breast.

Put a centre mark on the wall and hearth so they line up [A]. Turn the hearth on to its face (protect the face with a dustsheet) then apply adhesive or silicone mastic to the framework [B] and fix into position, using the alignment marks [C]. Then check its level.

Place the mantel assembly upside down; slide the legs into position and screw the block inside it [D]. To secure the legs, first check they are square to the mantel and then screw them in place with 6 x 35mm (1⅜in) screws.

To simply fix this surround to the wall, screw two mirror

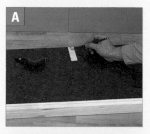

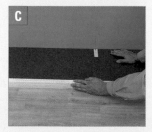

Tools

Tape measure
Spirit level
Screwdriver
Drill
Pilot bit
Mastic gun

plates with screws to the back edge of the legs about 230mm (9in) from the top [E]. Next fix the marble effect insert to the surround as shown, with screws about 380mm (15in) apart [F]. (Pre-drill pilot holes to avoid break-out damage.)

Offer up the surround and mark the hole positions on the wall through the mirror plates [G]. Remove, then drill and plug the wall, and fix the surround with screws.

Finally, place the reveal insert into position to cover the wall behind and leave a neater finish [H].

WORKING FIREPLACES

Talk to suppliers before you buy your surround to make sure it is safe to use with the working fire you intend to use.

All gas fires MUST be installed by a CORGI-registered gas installer.

Flatpacks: assembling

No matter what unit you're assembling, a few basic rules apply. Check that the contents of the kit match the checklist; read instructions thoroughly; leave yourself plenty of work space; and keep the packing, just in case.

Here are two common flatpack assemblies – a wooden upright storage system (a shelf unit) and a kitchen base unit.

1. Attach the two uprights with the screws supplied

3. Secure the unit to the wall to prevent it from falling over

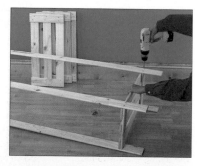

2. Turn over the shelving system and attach the remaining two uprights as above

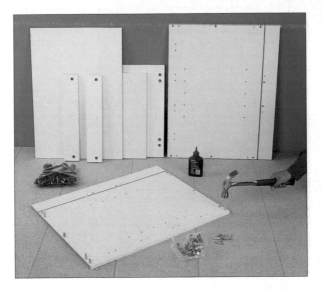

4. Apply PVA woodworking adhesive to the dowels and gently tap them in

Fitting the shelving unit

Starting with the shelf unit (to the left), which is fairly simple to assemble and a good place to start practising your DIY skills, attach two of the uprights to the top and bottom shelves, screwing through the pre-drilled pilot holes [1]. Turn the unit over and attach the remaining two uprights [2]. Insert the remaining shelves to the desired height in the same way. Turn the unit over and screw the shelves tight.

Stand the shelf unit upright and secure it to the wall to prevent it falling over [3].

Fitting kitchen flatpacks

Kitchen flatpacks are all fairly similar. This one (above) is a standard 500mm (19¾in) base unit. Assemble one unit at a time, then fit them all together. Next, fit the worktops and, finally, hang the doors.

Lay the side panel face down onto the bench or floor.

SEE ALSO
198

5. Place the locking nuts in position, with the arrow pointing to the outside edge

Apply PVA glue to the dowels and tap them home [4]. Screw in the special connecting bolts where indicated. Repeat for the second panel. 🔨

The bottom panel and top connecting rails have pre-drilled fixing positions for the connecting bolt locking nuts. There is an indicator arrow on the locking nut. Ensure the arrow points to the outer edge [5]. Apply glue to the dowels, position end panels and

6. Place the end panels and connecting rails into position and tighten the bolts

7 Turn the cabinet upside down and fix the adjustable legs

connecting rails and tighten the bolts [6]. Repeat for the second side panel.

For the back panel, run a small bead of glue the length of both slots and slide the back panel into position. Drill two pilot holes into the top rail and secure with two 15mm (⅝in) screws. Wipe off any excess glue with a damp cloth.

Up-end the cabinet and screw in the legs [7]. Turn the cabinet onto its legs. Check with a spirit level. Insert shelf supports at required height, tilt and slide in the shelf [8].

8. Finally, put in shelf supports at the desired height, then tilt and slide in the shelf

SEE ALSO
14–5

Floors: chipboard flooring

Chipboard is an excellent material for a floor that will be invisible beneath some kind of covering, such as vinyl, cork or fitted carpet. It can be laid relatively quickly and is a lot cheaper than the equivalent amount of timber flooring. It comes square-edged or tongued and grooved. Each type has its own laying technique.

Laying square-edged boards

All the edges of square-edged sheet flooring must be supported. Lay the boards with their long edges along the joists and nail 75 x 50mm (3 x 2in) softwood noggings between the joists to support the ends of the boards. The noggings against the wall are inserted in advance; those supporting joints between boards can be nailed into place as the boards are laid.

Start with a full-length board in one corner and lay a row of boards the length of the room, cutting the last one to fit, as required. Leave an

▲ *Laying square-edged boards*
The long edges rest on joists and the ends are supported by noggings

expansion gap of about 9mm (⅜in) between the outer edges of the boards and the walls. The boards' inner edges should fall on the centre line of a joist. If necessary, cut the boards to width – but remove the waste from the edges closest to the wall, preserving the machine-cut edges to make neat butt joints with the next row of boards. Nail down

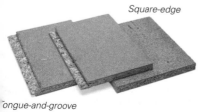

Square-edge

Tongue-and-groove

the boards, using 50mm (2in) ring-shank nails, spaced about 300mm (1ft) apart along the joists and noggings. Place the nails about 9mm (⅜in) from the board edges.

Cut and lay the rest of the boards, with the end joints staggered on alternate rows.

Laying tongue-and-groove boards

Tongue-and-groove boards are laid with their longer edges running across the joists. Noggings are required only to support the outer edges close to the walls. The ends of the boards should be supported by joists.

Working from one corner, lay the first board with its grooved edges about 9mm (⅜in) from the walls and nail in place. Apply PVA wood adhesive to the joint along the end of the first board, and then lay the next one in the row. Knock it up to the first board with a hammer for a close joint, protecting the edge with a piece of scrap wood. Nail the board down as before, then wipe surplus adhesive from the surface before it sets with a damp rag.

Continue in this way across the floor, gluing all of the

▶ **Ring-shank nails**
Nail down square-edged boards, using 50mm (2in) ring-shank nails, spaced about 300mm (1ft) apart

joints as you go. Cut boards to fit at the ends of rows or to fall on the centre of a joist, and stagger end joints on alternate rows.

Finally, fit the skirting boards, which will cover the expansion gaps around the perimeter of the floor.

If you want to keep the chipboard clean, seal the surface with two coats of clear polyurethane varnish. ◀

▲ **Laying tongue-and-groove boards**
Lay T&G boards crosswise, with their ends falling on a joist

SEE ALSO
439

Floors: levelling

Tiles, sheet vinyl or carpet should not be laid directly onto an uneven suspended timber floor; the undulations would cause the covering to lift or even crack. The solution is to panel over the floorboards with hardboard 3mm (⅛in) thick or, preferably, with 6mm (¼in) plywood. Whichever board you use, the method is the same.

Conditioning boards

Before you seal the floor with plywood or hardboard, make sure the underfloor ventilation is efficient, to prevent damp or dry rot problems.

The moisture content of the board should match the humidity of the room or the board will buckle after it has been laid. If the house is not regularly heated, wet the textured back of hardboard or both sides of plywood with warm water and leave the sheets stacked back-to-back in the room for 24 hours.

If central heating has been in use for some time, there is no need to dampen the board: just stack the sheets in the room for 48 hours. ☞

Laying the boards

Cut the boards to form 1200mm (4ft) squares. Nail loose floorboards and sink the nail heads.

Use chalked string to snap two centre lines across the room, crossing at right angles. Lay the first board on the centre so that its edges do not align with gaps between the floorboards. Lay hardboard rough side up, as a key for the adhesive. Loose-lay the boards in both directions: reposition if the margins are narrow.

Nail the first board to the floor with 20mm (¾in) hardboard pins. Start near the centre of the board and fix it every 150mm (6in) until you get within 25mm (1in) of the edge, then nail around the edge every 100mm (4in).

To cut edge strips, lay the board touching the skirting but square to the edges of the nailed boards (1). Use a block of softwood to scribe along it to fit the skirting (2). Cut the scribed line, butt it up to the skirting, then mark the position of the nailed boards on both sides of the edge strip. Join the marks, then cut along this line. Nail the board to the floor (3).

4. Scribe to skirting

5. Trace frame shape

6. Cut and nail down

1. Butt to skirting

2. Scribe to fit

3. Nail to floor

To fit into a doorway, butt a board up to the frame and measure to the doorstop. Cut a block of softwood to this size and scribe to the skirting (4). Trace the shape of the architrave (5);

cut the shape with a jigsaw. Slide the board into the doorway, mark and cut the other edge that butts up against the nailed boards, then nail the board to the floor (6).

Draughtproofing floors and skirtings

The ventilated void below a suspended wooden floor is a common source of draughts that penetrate through large gaps between floorboards and under the skirting. Fill between floorboards or cover them with hardboard panels.

Seal gaps between skirting boards and the floor with mastic applied with an applicator gun, or use

caulking strips. For a neat finish, pin a quadrant moulding to the skirting to cover the sealed gap.

▲ *Seal the gap with mastic and wooden quadrant*

SEE ALSO
402

Repairing damaged floorboards

INTERMEDIATE

If your home has had central heating fitted or been rewired, when you take up the carpets the floorboards could be in a bit of a shambles. Not a problem under a carpet, but it will be if you want the boards exposed.

Carefully remove the skirtings around the area of floorboards to be replaced. This will allow easier lifting of the boards.

Removing the first board is the trickiest. Carefully insert the nail bars on opposite sides of the board and central to the

length, and lever the board upwards [A]. Use wooden blocks for extra leverage – this can help prevent damaging the adjacent boards [B].

Repeat along the length of the wood. Starting at the middle will help spring each board away from the joists. Once the first board is up, it is easier to remove the others, using the same technique.

To replace a section easily, remove damaged sections in a square form. Carefully mark the board around the section using a square [C]. Use two wooden battens to keep the

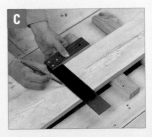

Tools

Cordless drill
2 flat-type
nail bars
Claw hammer
Pinchers
Cramps
Wood chisel
Tenon saw
Hand saw
Electric sander
PVA wood glue
Pins
Floor brads

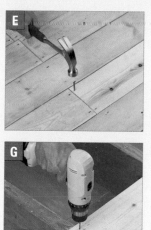

rogue board supported above the floor, allowing the damaged section to be cut out using a tenon saw [D].

Cut a matching piece from another board. Cut the replacement 2mm (⅛in) oversize to ensure a tight fit

with no gaps. Tap the new section into position with a wooden block and hammer. Nail the board in place [E]. Smooth with a sander or with sandpaper and block by hand.

To replace boards, remove all the old nails from the joists using the nail bars and claw hammer [F]. Drill fine pilot holes in your new boards to prevent splitting and locate and direct the position of the fixings [G]. Stagger the cut boards to avoid two joints abutting side by side. Secure with floor brad nails [H].

Floors: repairing and lifting floorboards

Floorboarding is produced in lengths running from wall to wall. Shorter lengths are often laid to save on materials. When lifting, start with these shorter pieces if possible.

Square edge boards

Tap the blade of a bolster into the gap between the boards, close to the cut end (1). Lever up the edge of the board, but try not to crush the one next to it. Fit the bolster into the gap at the other side of the board and repeat the procedure.

Ease the end of the board up in this way, then work the claw of a hammer under it until there is room to slip a cold chisel under the board (2). Lift the next pair of nails, and proceed in the same fashion along the board until it is free.

▲ *2. Place a cold chisel under the floorboard*

Lifting a continuous board

Floorboards are nailed in place before the skirting, so the ends of a continuous board will be trapped under it. Cut the board in half before you can lift it; prise up the floorboard centre until you can slip a cold chisel under it to keep the board bowed. Remove the nails and cut through the board over the centre of the joist. Then lift the two halves of the board.

If a board is too stiff to be bowed upwards or is tongued and grooved, it will have to be sawn in situ. This means cutting it flush with the side of the joist, instead of over its centre. 🔖

▲ *1. Lever up the board with a bolster chisel*

To locate the side of the joist, pass the blade of a padsaw vertically into the gaps on both sides of the board (the joints of tongue-and-grooved boards will have to be cut beforehand). Mark both edges of the board where the blade stops, and draw a line between these points. Make an access slot for the padsaw by drilling three or four holes.

Work the tip of the padsaw blade into the hole, and start making the cut with short strokes. Lever up the board with a bolster chisel, as above.

Laying new floorboards

Lay a few loose floorboards together as a work platform. Measure the width or length of the room – whichever is at right angles to the joists – and cut the boards 9mm (⅜in) short of the walls at each end. Lay four to six boards at a time.

Fix the first board parallel to the wall, and nail in place. Place the nails in pairs, about 25mm (1in) from each edge of the board, centred on the joists.

Lay the other cut boards in place and clamp them to the fixed one. Wedges cut from offcuts work as well as cramps. To clamp the boards with

wedges, temporarily nail another floorboard less than a board's width away. Insert pairs of wedges in the gap, resting on every fourth or fifth joist; then, using two hammers, tap the wedges together (1). After nailing the clamped boards in place, remove the wedges and repeat, continuing in this way across the room.

At the far wall, cut the last board to fit by removing its tongued edge – roughly 9mm (⅜in). If you can't slide it onto the previous board's tongue, cut away the bottom section of its grooved edge to drop into place (2).

▲ 1. Make wedges to clamp boards

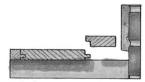

▲ 2. Cut away part of the last board's grooved edge

SEE ALSO
154–5

Sanding floors

Wooden flooring, both the solid and laminate-type, has become more popular. Sanding and lacquering old original floorboards is particularly popular. It's noisy, dusty, messy and hard work, but it can be incredibly rewarding.

The first job is to inspect the condition of the floorboards. Tap down the fixing nails with a suitable nail punch [A] and remove other nails or screws. All this will help to avoid tearing the sanding belts.

If woodworm has attacked the floor, lift the boards carefully, treat the joists and the back and front of the contaminated boards, then re-fix. Sanding over woodworm gives the floor 'character'. But if it is too severe or a board is damaged, cut it down in length or slot in a repair using wood glue and pins or a clamp. Replacements can be taken from elsewhere in the house or from a reclamation yard – new boards will look out of place.

Lay the floor drum sander on its back (unplugged); undo the retaining bar and fix the sanding belt [B]; screw it tightly to stop the belt coming loose. There are three grades of sandpaper – coarse, medium and fine. Unless the boards are very rough, medium and fine grades are usually enough.

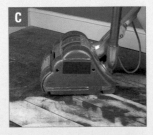

Tools

Drum floor
sander
Edging sander
Hook scraper
Corner sander
Claw hammer
Pinchers
Screwdriver
Nail punch

If the boards have cupped or curled, this can be helped by running the belt sander across the room at 45 deg [C] and again at 45 deg from the other angle. When the floor is flat, use a fine belt and sand along the board length and grain [D].

An edging sander reaches the edges where the drum sander is cannot reach. Pads are fitted by a central bolt on the underside [E]. Do not overrun this machine on the floor [F], or you may make make swirl scratches. Use the hook scraper for difficult tight areas or corners [G].

Dust the whole floor area thoroughly and wipe over with a cloth and white spirit, ready for the lacquer. You will need at least two coats of lacquer, but for a better finish apply more coats. Always apply lacquer along the grain of the wood – never across it [H].

Floors: sealing gaps

Many people ignore gaps between floorboards, but you will end up with a more attractive floor, and improved draughtproofing, if you make the effort to fill the gaps or close them up.

Closing up
Over a large area, the quickest and most satisfactory solution is to lift the boards a few at a time and re-lay them butted side by side, filling in the final gap with a new board.

Filling with papier mâché
If there are just a few gaps, make up a stiff papier mâché paste, plus a little water-based wood dye to match the sanded floor. Scrape out dirt and wax from between the boards, and press the paste into the gap with a filling knife. Press it well below the level likely to be reached by the sander and fill flush with the floor surface,

▲ *Wedge a wooden lath into a wide gap*

smoothing the exposed surface with the filling knife.

Inserting a wooden lath
Large gaps can be filled with a thin wooden lath planed to fit tightly between the boards. Apply a little PVA adhesive to the gap and tap the lath in place with a hammer until the wood is flush with the surface. If necessary, skim with a plane. Don't bother to fill several gaps this way: it is easier to close up the boards and fill one larger gap with a new floorboard.

▶ *Force papier mâché between the boards*

Fuses

In the consumer unit there is a fuseway for each circuit. A fuse carrier, essentially a bridge between the main switch and that particular circuit, is plugged into the fuseway. When the fuse carrier is removed from the consumer unit, the current cannot pass across the gap.

Identifying a fuse

Turn off the power and then pull any of the fuse carriers out of the consumer unit to see what kind of fuse it contains.

At each end of the carrier you will see a single-bladed or double-bladed contact. A rewirable carrier will have a thin wire running from one contact to the other, held by a screw terminal at each end. Fuse wire is available in various thicknesses, carefully calculated to melt at given currents when a circuit is substantially overloaded, thus breaking the 'bridge' and isolating the circuit.

Alternatively, the carrier may contain a cartridge fuse similar to those used in 13amp plugs, though circuit fuses are larger, varying in size according to their rating. The cartridge is a ceramic tube containing a fuse wire packed in fine sand. The wire is connected to metal caps at the ends of the cartridge that snap into spring clips on the contacts of the fuse carrier.

Cartridge fuses provide better protection, since they blow faster than ordinary fuse wire; it is therefore advisable to use cartridge fuse carriers wherever possible.

FUSE RATINGS

Circuit	Fuse	Colour coding
Door bell	5amp	White
Lighting	5amp	White
Immersion heater	15amp	Blue
Storage heater	15amp	Blue
Radial circuits –		
20sq m maximum floor area	20amp	Yellow
50sq m maximum floor area	30amp	Red
Ring circuits –		
100sq m maximum floor area	30amp	Red
Shower unit	45amp	Green
Cooker	30amp	Red

SEE ALSO
126–7

Fuses: checking/changing

The first thing to check when everything on a circuit stops working is the fuse. Turn off the main switch on the consumer unit and look for the blown fuse. Cartridge fuses are more likely to be used in modern houses.

▲ *Continuity tester*

Checking a cartridge fuse

The simplest way to check a suspect cartridge fuse is to replace it with a new one and see if the circuit works.

Alternatively, you can check the fuse with a metal-cased torch. Remove the bottom cap of the torch, and touch one end of the fuse to the base of the battery while resting its other end against the torch's metal casing. If the torch bulb lights up, the fuse is sound.

Using a continuity tester

You can check a suspect cartridge fuse with a continuity tester. Place one of the tester's probes on each of the fuse's metal caps, then

press the appropriate circuit-test button. If the indicator of the tester doesn't illuminate, the fuse has blown.

If the fuse blows again

If a replaced fuse blows again as soon as the power is switched on, then there is either a fault or an overload (too many appliances plugged in) on that circuit – and it must be detected and rectified before another fuse is inserted.

Unplug all appliances on the faulty circuit to make sure that it is not simply overloaded, then switch on the consumer unit again.

If the circuit is still faulty, get professional advice.

▶ **Testing a cartridge fuse**
With the torch switched on, hold the fuse against the battery and the metal casing.

Fuses: circuit breakers

Instead of fuses, miniature circuit breakers (MCBs) are sometimes used to protect circuits. There are many types of MCB on the market, but only buy ones that are made to the required standards of construction and safety.

Make sure any MCB you use is marked BSEN 60898, which is the relevant British Standard. There are also different classes of MCB (you need to look for Type B). And lastly, MCBs are classified according to the largest potential fault current they are able to clear; ask for M6 or M9, as these will clear any potential domestic current.

If for any reason these MCBs are unavailable, ask your electricity company whether they will accept alternatives.

MCB ratings

To conform to European standards, MCB ratings tend to vary slightly from circuit-fuse ratings. However, it is perfectly acceptable if you have MCBs that match

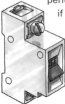

◀ Switch-operated miniature circuit breaker

▶ Button-operated miniature circuit breaker

the slightly smaller ratings shown for circuit fuses.

Resetting MCBs

Even though MCB current ratings tend to differ very slightly from fuse ratings, the main difference is that circuit breakers switch to the 'off' position automatically, so a faulty circuit is obvious as soon as you inspect the consumer unit.

Turn the consumer unit's main switch off, and then simply close the switch on the miniature circuit breaker to reset it (there is no fuse to replace). If the MCB's switch or button won't stay in the 'on' position when power is restored, then there is still a fault on the circuit – which must be detected and rectified as soon as possible.

SEE ALSO
128

Fuses: consumer units

The consumer unit is the heart of your electrical installation: every circuit in your home has to pass through it. Although there are several different types and styles, all consumer units are based on similar principles.

Every consumer unit has a large main isolating switch, which turns off the entire electrical system of the house. On some of the more expensive units, the switch is in the form of a residual current device (RCD) that can be operated manually but will also 'trip' automatically should any serious fault occur, isolating the whole system.

Having turned off the main switch, remove the cover so

that you can see how the unit is arranged. Remember, even when the unit is switched off the cable connecting the meter to the main switch is still live – so take care.

Ideally, cables should be spaced apart to prevent any overheating.

Some wires will be joined together in a single terminal. These are the two ends of a ring circuit, and that is how they should be wired.

A typical cartridge fuse unit
1. *Circuit cables*
2. *Earth block*
3. *Neutral block*
4. *Fuse carrier removed from bell circuit*
5. *Spare fuseway (unconnected)*
6. *Bell circuit*
7. *Lighting circuits*
8. *Immersion heater circuit*
9. *Ring circuits*
10. *Cooker circuit*
11. *Main switch*
12. *Earth lead*
13. *Meter leads*

G

Gates/fences

Gates are designed to offer access to cars or people through a fenced or walled boundary, while fences are one of the cheaper forms of boundary marker.

Types of gates

Where a gate is hung has the greatest influence on its design and style. When choosing a gate, consider the character of the house and its surroundings. Buy a gate that matches the style of fence or complements the wall from which it is hung. If in doubt, aim for simplicity.

Side gates

An unprotected side entrance is an open invitation for intruders to slip in unnoticed and gain access to the back of your house. Side gates are designed to deter burglars while affording easy access for tradesmen.

Side gates

Entrance gates

An entrance gate is designed as much for its appearance as its function, but it must be sturdy enough to withstand frequent use.

Entrance gates

Drive gates

Decide whether hanging a gate across your drive is a good idea. Stepping out of

Drive gates

your car to open the gate can be risky unless there's plenty of room to pull the car off the road.

Gateposts and piers

Gateposts and masonry piers need to be anchored securely to the ground to take the leverage exerted by a heavy gate. Choose hardwood posts whenever possible, and select the size according to the weight of the gate.

Types of fencing

In the short term a fence is cheaper to put up than a masonry wall and need not necessarily be made from wood.

Various forms of fencing include: chain-link fencing, trellis fencing, post-and-chain fencing, closeboard fencing, prefabricated fencing, interlap fencing, picket fencing, ranch-style fencing and even cast-concrete fencing, which provides the security and permanence of a wall built from brick or stone.

Gates/fences: erecting fences

Whichever type of fence you choose, the fence posts need to be secure and solid enough to support the fencing, so erecting the posts is also important.

Marking out fence posts

Drive a peg into the ground at each end of the fence run, and stretch a length of string between the pegs to align the row of posts.

Erecting the posts

Digging the hole

Hire post-hole augers to remove the central core of earth. Twist the tool to drive it into the ground (1) and pull it out after every 150mm (6in) to remove the soil.

Anchoring the post

Ram a layer of hardcore into the bottom of the hole to support the base of the post. Get someone to hold the post while you brace it with battens nailed to the post and to stakes driven into the ground. Check that the post is vertical (2).

Ram more hardcore around the post, leaving a hole about 300mm (1ft) deep for concrete. Top up with a fast-setting dry concrete mix, then pour in the water, or mix up general-purpose concrete (3). Build the concrete just above the level of the soil and smooth it to slope away from the post (4).

Leave the concrete to harden before removing the struts.

1. Dig the post hole

2. Brace the post

3. Fill with concrete

4. Slope the concrete

SEE ALSO
88–9

Erecting panel fences

To prevent a prefabricated panel rotting, either fit gravel boards, as on a closeboard fence, or leave a gap at the bottom by supporting a panel temporarily on two bricks while you fix it to the fence posts.

Using timber posts

Pack the first post into its hole with hardcore; get someone to hold a panel against the post while you nail through the frame into the post. If you can work from both sides, drive three nails from each side of the fence. If the wood is likely to split, blunt the nails (tap their points with a hammer).

Or use rustproofed metal angle brackets to secure the panels. Construct the entire fence by erecting panels and posts alternately.

Fit pressure-treated gravel boards; nail capping strips across the panels, if they have not already been fitted by the manufacturer. Finally, cut each post to length and cap it.

Wedge struts, made from scrap timber, against each post to keep it vertical, then top up the holes with concrete.

Using concrete posts

Grooved concrete posts will support panels without the need for additional fixings. Recessed concrete posts are supplied with metal brackets for screw-fixing the panels.

▼ **Building a panel fence**
Posts and panels are erected alternately. Dig a hole for the post (1) and hold it upright with hardcore. Support a panel on bricks (2) and get a helper to push it against the post (3) while you nail it (4). Fit gravel boards (5) and capping strips (6), then cap the posts (7). Top up the holes with concrete (8) and allow it to set

Gates/fences: hanging gates

Gateposts are set in concrete, in the same way as ordinary fence posts, but the post holes are linked by a concrete bridge that provides extra support.

Erecting gateposts

Lay the gate on the ground with a post on each side. Check that the posts are parallel and that they are the required distance apart to accommodate hinges and catch. Nail two battens from post to post and another diagonally to keep the posts in line while you erect them (1).

Dig a trench, 300mm (1ft) wide, across the entrance. Dig an adequate post hole at each

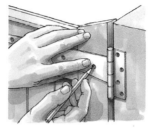

▲ *Hanging a gate*
Stand the gate between the posts, and prop it up on bricks or wooden blocks to hold it the required height off the ground. Tap in pairs of wedges on each side until it is held securely. Then mark the positions of the hinges and catch

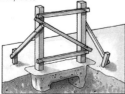

1. Nail temporary struts to the gateposts

2. Support the posts until the concrete sets

end – 450mm (1ft 6in) deep for a low entrance gate, 600mm (2ft) deep for a taller side gate.

Set the battened gateposts in the holes with hardcore and concrete, using temporary battens to hold them upright until the concrete has set (2). Fill the trench with concrete, and either level it flush with the pathway or allow for the thickness of paving slabs.

SEE ALSO
240–2

Repairing gates

Damaged or worn gates can be a problem. Latches drop, which means the gate no longer sits properly, or sometimes even the wood itself rots. It's worth remembering that adequate maintenance can prevent many problems.

General repairs

The first thing to do is to check that your gate post is absolutely aligned. Gates and posts are exposed to all-weather conditions, and so will often contract, expand and move slightly with time.

To re-align the catch, hold the gate in the optimum closed position and then simply work out where the new holes should be. Then, use a drill to create pilot holes [A] to receive the screws. Use long screws to ensure a firm fixing [B], ensuring that they are galvanized and therefore less prone to weather deterioration.

On some occasions – if the gate has 'dropped' particularly severely, for example – it may be necessary to re-align the hinges of the gate as well as its catch.

If the gate has a rotten section, remove it and lay it flat on a workbench. Remove the damaged pieces with a claw hammer [C] and/or screwdriver. Then use an existing piece of gate as a template – draw around the piece onto new timber and cut out the replacement strut. Prime and paint the new piece of timber to ensure it will be suitably weather-resistant [D].

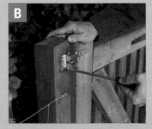

When you are satisfied that the replacement strut is dry, fix it to the existing gate, again using strong, galvanized screws for maximum security.

Re-hang the gate on its hinges, taking care to ensure that it clears the path and aligns neatly with both posts [E]. This can be a little time-consuming and fiddly, but it is important to make sure that the gate hangs comfortably – otherwise, further damage to the wood may occur.

Many wooden gates are made from relatively cheap softwood, but a wood such as cedar or oak will last much longer. Most so-called 'wrought iron' gates are made from mild-steel bar, which must be primed and painted.

If you do re-decorate your gate after repairing or re-hanging it, don't forget to paint the gateposts as well.

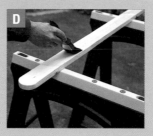

USING WOOD PRESERVATIVE

Try not to use traditional paint finishes on gates or fences. Although painted gates (as shown here) look good initially, you will generally make a better job using wood preservative, which is available in a wide array of colours. This will help to protect the wood as well, making it less prone to rotting. If you do choose paint instead of wood preservative for your gate, be warned that it will not protect the gate as thoroughly, which could mean that the life of your gate is foreshortened.

Gate and fence repairs INTERMEDIATE

A wooden fence can have a fairly short life compared to a wall as it is susceptible to insect infestation and rot. However, if treated correctly with the right preserver, your fence can last for years with the minimum repairs.

Tools

Cordless drills
Spirit level
String line
Shovel
Long bar
Hole borer
Hammer
Sledgehammer

▼ If the base of your wooden post rots underground, brace the upper section with a short concrete spur.

With wooden fences, there are various types to choose from. One choice is the gravel board variety (named after the bit of the fence which comes in contact with the soil). It generally doesn't rot and is used in conjunction with concrete posts and wooden panels. Another common type is made completely of wood – preferably pressure-treated. When the bottom gravel board panels rot, they are just replaced with a new piece by fixing a couple of screws at either end into the base of the post [A].

If you are replacing panels, before you erect them apply your own preservative

coating, either water- or spirit-based, which are available in a myriad of colours, including blue [B].

Erecting a new post is fairly straightforward once you have removed the remains of the old one. Dig a hole for the new post a minimum depth of 460mm (18in) to achieve the best support. Use a stiff concrete mix dry or with not too much water – it should have the consistency of double cream. Pack down the concrete around the post with a wooden batten [C].

Make sure that the post is level and lined up straight with the other posts by means of a string line. While the

A

B

concrete is setting, fix up some temporary braces to ensure that the post remains upright [D].

Softwood posts are not going to last as long as hardwood or concrete posts in the soil. To increase the post life, use pressure-treated posts. Alternatively, stand the posts upright in a bucket of preservative for a minimum of two days; this will help extend the lifespan of the post [E].

Instead of digging holes, you can plug the base of posts into a fence-post (metpost) spike. They can be a useful

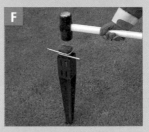

alternative to concreting. Drive the spike partially into the ground with a sledgehammer [F]. Check it is upright with a spirit level, then hammer until just the socket is visible. Once the metpost is firmly in the ground, slip the end of your post into it [G].

Gates/fences: specialized hinges and latches

There is a wide range of hardware for hanging heavy garden gates, to cope with the strain on their fixings.

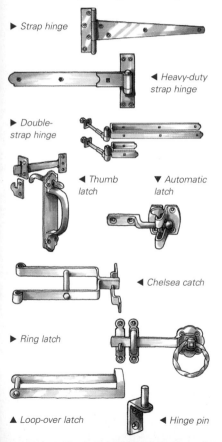

▶ Strap hinge

◀ Heavy-duty strap hinge

▶ Double-strap hinge

◀ Thumb latch

▼ Automatic latch

◀ Chelsea catch

▶ Ring latch

▲ Loop-over latch

◀ Hinge pin

Hinges

Strap hinges

Most side and entrance gates are hung on strap hinges.

Hinge pins

Collars, welded to metal gates, drop over hinge pins that are attached to gateposts.

Latches and catches

Automatic latches

Simple wooden gates are usually fitted with a latch.

Thumb latches

Operated by thumb pressure from the operator.

Ring latches

Operated by twisting the ring handle to lift the latch beam.

Chelsea catches

A Chelsea catch drops into a slot in the catch plate, which is screwed to the gatepost.

Loop-over catches

Normally used for a pair of wide gates.

H

Health and safety 176

Health & safety: bathrooms

Water and electricity are a dangerous combination. For this reason, in respect to electricity, bathrooms are potentially the most dangerous areas in your home. Where there are so many exposed metal pipes and fittings, regulations must be stringently observed if fatal accidents are to be avoided.

General safetey

- Sockets must not be fitted in a bathroom – except for special shaver sockets that conform to BS EN 60742 Chapter 2, Section 1.

- The IEE Wiring Regulations stipulate that light switches in bathrooms must be outside zones 0 to 3 (see pp22–23). The best way to comply with this is to fit only ceiling-mounted pull-cord switches.

- Any bathroom heater must comply with the IEE Wiring Regulations.

- If you have a shower in a bedroom, it must be not less than 3m (9ft 11in) from any socket outlet, which must be protected by a 30 milliamp RCD.

- Light fittings must be well out of reach and shielded – so fit a close-mounted ceiling light, properly enclosed, rather than a pendant fitting.

- Never use a portable fire or other electrical appliance, such as a hairdryer, in a bathroom – even if it is plugged into a socket outside the room.

Supplementary bonding

In any bathroom there are many nonelectrical metallic components, such as metal baths and basins, supply pipes to bath and basin taps, metal waste pipes, radiators, central-heating pipework and so on –

▼ *Single-core cable insulated with green-and-yellow PVC and earth clamps*

all of which could cause an accident during the time it would take for an electrical fault to blow a fuse or operate a miniature circuit breaker (MCB). To ensure that no dangerous voltages are created between metal parts, Wiring Regulations state that all metal components must be connected by a conductor which is itself connected to a terminal on the earthing block in the consumer unit. This is known as supplementary bonding and is required for all bathrooms – even when there is no electrical equipment installed in the room, and even though the water and gas pipes are bonded to the consumer's earth terminal near the consumer unit.

When electrical equipment such as a heater or shower is

fitted in a bathroom, that too must be supplementary bonded by connecting its metalwork – such as the casing – to the nonelectrical metal pipework.

Planning the connections

Wiring Regulations specify the minimum size of earthing conductor that can be used for supplementary bonding in different situations, so that large-scale electrical installations can be costed economically. In a domestic environment, use 6mm^2 single-core cable insulated with green-and-yellow PVC for supplementary bonding. This is large enough to be safe in any domestic situation. For a neat appearance, plan the route of the bonding cable to run from point to point behind the bath panel, or under floorboards. If necessary, run the cable through a hollow wall or under plaster.

▼ Supplementary bonding in a bathroom

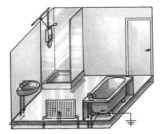

SEE ALSO
26–7

Health & safety: general

As with most rules of health and safety, commonsense generally comes out on top. Never take risks with your equipment or materials – err on the side of caution.

Ladder safety

More accidents are caused by using ladders unwisely than by faulty equipment. Erect the ladder safely before you climb it; and move it when work is out of reach. Never lean to the side, or you will overbalance. Follow these simple, commonsense rules:

Securing the ladder

If the ground is soft, place a wide board under the feet of a ladder; screw a batten across the board to hold the ladder in place. On hard ground, make sure the ladder has anti-slip end caps, and lay a sandbag (or a tough polythene bag filled with earth) at the base. Secure the stiles with rope tied to stakes driven into the

1. Staking a ladder
Secure the base of the ladder by lashing it to stakes in the ground

2 Securing the top
Anchor the ladder to a batten held inside the window frame.

ground at each side and just behind the ladder (1).

When you extend a ladder, the sections should overlap by at least a quarter of their length. Don't lean the top of the ladder against gutters, soil pipes or drainpipes, as these may give way, and especially not against glass.

Anchor the ladder near the top by tying it to a stout timber rail held across the inside of the window frame. Make sure that the rail extends about 300mm (1ft) on each side of the window, and pad the ends with cloth to protect the wall from damage (2).

It's a good idea to fix ring bolts at regular intervals into the masonry just below the fascia board: this is an excellent way to secure the top of a ladder, as you will have equally good anchor points wherever you choose to position it. Alternatively, fix large screw eyes to the masonry or a sound fascia board and attach the ladder to them.

Safety aloft

Never climb higher than four rungs from the top of the ladder, or you will not be able to balance properly and there will be no handholds within reach. Keep both your feet on a rung, and your hips centred between the uprights. Avoid slippery footholds by placing a sack or doormat at the foot of the ladder to dry your boots before you ascend.

Unless the manufacturer states otherwise, don't use a ladder to form a horizontal walkway – even with a scaffold board lying on it.

Stepladders are prone to toppling sideways. On uneven floors, clamp a strut to one of the stiles (3).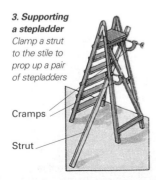

Safety when bleaching wood

Wood bleach is a dangerous substance that must be handled with care and stored in the dark, out of the reach of children.

- Wear protective gloves, goggles and an apron.
- Ensure that ventilation is adequate, or work outside.
- Have a supply of water handy, so you can rinse your skin immediately if you do accidentally splash yourself with bleach.
- If you get bleach in your eyes, rinse them thoroughly with running water and see a doctor.
- Never mix both parts of the bleach except on the wood, and always apply them with separate white-fibre or nylon brushes.
- Discard unused bleach.
- Wear a face mask when sanding bleached wood.

3. Supporting a stepladder
Clamp a strut to the stile to prop up a pair of stepladders

Cramps

Strut

SEE ALSO
81

SEE ALSO
82–5

Safety when painting

Solvents in paint (volatile organic compounds – VOCs) contribute to atmospheric pollution and can exacerbate conditions such as asthma. Where possible, use paints and varnishes with low VOC emissions. Most manufacturers label their products to indicate the level of VOCs.

Take sensible precautions when using solvent-based paints:

- Ensure good ventilation indoors while applying a finish and when it is drying. Preferably wear a respirator.
- Don't smoke while painting or in the vicinity of drying paint.
- Contain paint spillages outside with sand or earth; don't allow any paint to enter a drain.
- If you splash paint in your eyes, flush them with copious amounts of water, with your lids held open. If symptoms persist, visit a doctor.
- Always wear barrier cream or gloves if you have sensitive skin. Use a proprietary skin cleanser to remove paint from your skin, or wash it off with warm soapy water. Don't use paint thinners.
- Keep all paints out of reach of children. If a child swallows a substance, don't induce him or her to vomit – instead, seek medical help.

Safety when using lacquer

Although cold-cure lacquer is safe to use, take care when applying to a large surface such as a floor, as there will be a concentration of fumes.

If possible, open all windows and doors for ventilation – but remember the necessity for a warm atmosphere, too. Wear a respirator, to prevent breathing in the fumes. The hardener is acidic, so wash thoroughly with water if you spill any on your skin.

▼ *Wear a suitable respirator when applying cold-cure lacquer over a large area*

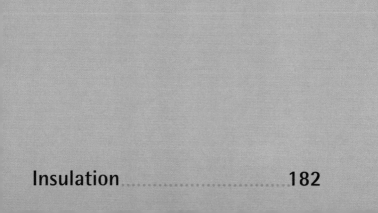

Insulation

The cost of heating a home continues to rise. Saving money is a major consideration – but equally important is the need to conserve energy to protect the environment.

Local-authority grants

Because home insulation is of benefit to the economy, the government has made discretionary grants available through local authorities to encourage people to insulate their lofts, storage tanks and pipework. You may also be eligible for a grant towards the cost of draughtproofing, double glazing and cavity-wall insulation. To qualify for a grant, you must obtain local authority approval before carrying out the work or purchasing insulation materials.

Insulating materials

There's a wide range of insulating materials available.

▼ *Blanket insulation*

Blanket insulation

Blanket insulation – which is made from glass fibre, mineral fibre or rock fibre – is widely available in the form of rolls that fit snugly between the joists. All types are non-flammable and are proofed against damp, rot and vermin.

Loose-fill insulation

Loose-fill insulation (either fibrous or granular) is poured between the joists, up to the recommended depth. Exfoliated vermiculite and mineral fibre are two common types of loose-fill insulation suitable for DIY installation.

Blown-fibre insulation

Inter-joist fibrous insulation is blown through a large hose by professional contractors. An even depth of 150 to 200mm (6 to 8in) is required.

Rigid and semi-rigid sheet insulation

Sheet insulation, such as semi-rigid batts of glass fibre or mineral fibre and slabs of foamed polystyrene or polyurethane, can be fixed between the rafters. It pays to install the thickest insulation possible.

Insulating cavity walls

When constructing a new house, builders include a layer of insulation between the two masonry leaves of exterior walls. Insulating an existing wall requires a skilled and experienced contractor to introduce an insulant through holes cut in the outer brick leaf and to fill the cavity in such a way that a substantial reduction of heat loss is achieved, while avoiding the possible side effect of damp penetrating to the inner leaf.

It is advisable to hire contractors that are registered with the British Standards

2. Introducing the insulant
A hose is then inserted into each hole and the insulant is injected or blown into the cavity under pressure, filling it from the base. Afterwards, the holes are plugged with colour-matched mortar

1. Drilling holes in the outer leaf
A professional contractor will begin by drilling large-diameter holes through the outer skin of brickwork to gain access to the cavity

Institution or belong to the National Cavity Insulation Association.

The contractor should carry out a thorough initial survey of the building to make sure that the walls are structurally fit for filling and that there is no evidence of frost damage or failed pointing.

The whole process is carried on outside the house, where holes are drilled at regular intervals in the brickwork (1). The insulant is either injected or blown through a hose (2), then the insertion holes are plugged.

SEE ALSO
346

Insulating lofts

BEGINNER

As well as taking precautions to prevent falling through to the room below, when working with insulation, make sure that you are well covered. Fibreglass tends to irritate the skin and lead to uncomfortable rashes.

Insulation comes in two forms – blanket (in rolls) or loose fill (in bags). The recommended minimum depth of insulation is 150mm (6in), but the more the merrier – don't forget that 25–30 per cent of heat loss occurs through un-insulated roofs.

Preparation is the key. Lay a couple of short scaffold boards across the joists. Hang a lead light at a high vantage point if you don't have a permanent light in your loft. Bring all the insulation into the loft space but don't open any of the rolls until you are ready to lay it.

Rolls are roughly 39–41cm (15–16in) wide x 7.5m (25ft)

long. Trim the ends to allow airflow from the eaves, then start rolling out [A]. Lift any electrical cables and roll the insulation underneath [B]. This will avoid any cables overheating. Also closely trim around any light casings or lamp fittings protruding into the loft with an extended craft knife or sharp kitchen knife [C].

To make really sure that none of the heat escapes from your home, lay a second layer of insulation at right angles to the first and cover right over the joists [D]. Follow the same procedures as for the first insulation layer, remembering not to cover up any cables.

Tools

Handsaw
Meauring tape
Short timber batten (straight edge)
Craft knife or kitchen knife
Lead light
Protective clothing
Mask
Goggles, etc.

A

B

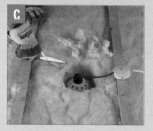

If you are using loose fill insulation, it's vital to cut strips of plywood or hardboard fixed between the joists to form a barrier and keep the eaves clear. The depth of fill is roughly 15cm (6in) – you may need to raise the height of the joists by fixing battens to allow boarding to be laid down for walking on.

To help prevent cold water pipes freezing in the winter, make a bridge out of hardboard before filling with loose fill insulation [E]. This will allow warm air from below to circulate around the cold water pipes.

Pour in the insulation fill [F], and spread with a timber or plywood off-cut. Tamp down and level the insulation so that it lies evenly between the joists [G].

Insulation: double glazing

Secondary double glazing consists of a separate pane of glass or sheet of plastic fitted over an ordinary single-glazed window and is relatively easy to install yourself.

Glazing with renewable film

Quite effective double glazing can be achieved using double-sided adhesive tape to stretch a thin flexible sheet of plastic across a window frame. The taped sheet can be removed at the end of the winter.

Clean the window frame (1) and cut the plastic roughly to size, allowing an overlap all round. Apply double-sided tape to the edges of the frame (2), then peel off the backing paper.

Attach the plastic film to the top rail (3), then tension it onto the tape on the sides and bottom of the window frame (4). Apply only light pressure until you have positioned the film, and then rub it down onto the tape all round.

Remove all creases and wrinkles in the film using a hot hairdryer (5). Starting at an upper corner, move the dryer slowly across the film, holding it about 6mm (¼in) from the surface. When the film is taut, cut off the excess plastic with a knife (6). ☞

1. Wipe woodwork to remove dust and grease

2. Apply double-sided tape to the fixed frame

3. Stretch the film across the top of the frame

4. Pull the film taut and fix to sides and bottom

5. Use a hairdryer to shrink the film

6 Trim the waste with a sharp knife

Demountable systems

A simple method of interior secondary glazing uses clear-plastic film or sheet. These lightweight materials are held in place by rigid moulded sections. Most strip fastenings use magnetism or some form of retentive tape, allowing its removal for cleaning or ventilation. This type of glazing can be left in place throughout the winter and removed for storage during the summer. ☞

Insulation: floors

The Building Regulations stipulate that new floors must be insulated. So far as existing floors are concerned, it's possible to upgrade a concrete surface by installing an insulated floating floor on top of it.

Suspended wooden floors lose heat to the crawlspace below, which must be ventilated to keep them free from rot. Reduce draughts by lining the floor with hardboard covered with carpet and underlay – but really effective insulation entails additional measures.

Methods of treatment

Working from above, by lifting the floorboards you can lay a substantial amount of insulation between the joists. Staple some plastic netting to the sides of the joists as support for blanket insulation. Alternatively, nail battens to the joists to support panels cut from sheet insulant.

If you can gain access from below, it makes the job easier. Simply push insulating material between the joists and then staple plastic netting or wire mesh to the undersides to hold it in place.

▶ **Insulating from below**
If you have a cellar or basement below the room you want to insulate, it makes sense to press batts between the joists (1) and hold them in place by stapling netting to the timbers (2). Line with plasterboard for a neat finish

◀ **Insulating from above**
Lift the floorboards and staple plastic netting (1) to the sides of the joists (2). Lay blanket insulation (3) between the joists. Alternatively, nail battens (4) to the sides of the joists to support sheet insulation (5)

SEE ALSO
346

SEE ALSO
429–31

SEE ALSO
344–5

Lagging pipes and tanks

BEGINNER

Good pipe and tank insulation keeps the water hot and saves in heating costs. On cold water pipes and tanks, it keeps the cold out and prevents burst pipes or leaks.

Lagging a cold water tank

The easiest method of lagging a cold water tank is to buy a purpose made 'insulation jacket' – or Bylaw 30 kit – which is fibreglass wadding inside a plastic covering. It is usually pretty straightforward and self-explanatory to fit.

You can make your own by cutting pieces of hardboard to match all four sides of the tank (as well as its lid). Cut some roof insulation and stick it to the hardboard by painting PVA adhesive on with a brush and placing the insulating material on top of the glue. Or you could just place a cut-down piece of insulating material in a black plastic sack and make a blanket that way [A]. Secure the panels or blankets in place around the tank with string [B].

Insulating pipework

Pipe insulation is very simple to fit. There is a felt-sock type of material on a roll that you slide over the pipe, normally when the pipes are being installed, and more often used under floors and screeds, or the foam type, which comes in long lengths and is usually pre-split along its length for easy installation. The latter is much better for

pipes which are already in position.

Cut the tubes to length with a bread knife or hacksaw. Open the tube by the split and pop on over the pipe [C]. Use insulating tape to seal the joints [D].

A right or left hand bend requires a mitre cut. Using an adjustable square, mark the 45 deg angle and cut the tube to length. Repeat the process in the other direction to complete the angle [E], press the two angled ends of the insulating material together to make the joint [F]. Tape the join with insulating tape.

To make a tee joint, cut a 90 deg angled cut to half-depth on a straight length of insulating sock, and then cut a matching shape to fit snugly against this [G]. Complete the joint by taping the pieces together with insulating tape.

Insulating the cylinder

Many people think that an unlagged cylinder has the advantage of providing a useful source of heat in an airing cupboard – but this wastes a surprising amount of energy. Even a lagged cylinder should provide ample heat in an enclosed airing cupboard.

Buying a water-cylinder jacket

Proprietary water-cylinder jackets are made from mineral-fibre insulation, 75–100mm (3–4in) thick, wrapped in plastic. Measure the height and circumference of the cylinder to choose the right size.

If need be, buy a jacket that is too large, rather than one that is too small. Make sure that it is marked with the British Standard Kite mark.

▶ Fit the jacket snugly around the cylinder and wrap foamed-plastic tubes around the pipework, especially the vent pipe directly above the cylinder

Reflecting radiator heat

As much as 25 per cent of the radiant heat from a radiator against an outside wall is lost to the wall behind it. Reclaim maybe half this wasted heat by applying a sheet of foil-faced expanded-polystyrene lining to the wall behind the radiator, to reflect the heat back into the room. Fix with adhesive pads or paste.

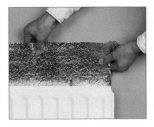

▲ *Slide lining behind radiator and press to wall*

Lagging pipe runs

Insulate hot water pipes in the house where their radiant heat is not contributing to the warmth of the rooms, and cold-water pipes in unheated areas of the building (where they could freeze). Pipework can be lagged in lagging bandages, but it is often more convenient to use foamed-plastic tubes designed for the purpose (see pages 188-9).

Joinery: woodworking joints

Craftsmen have invented countless ingenious ways of joining pieces of timber together. Some are as decorative as they are practical, but for general joinery and home maintenance requirements, here are just a few of the basic woodworking joints.

▲ *Nailed butt joints*

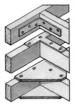

▲ *Bracket and plate fixing*

▲*Timber connectors*

▲ *Corner blocks*

Butt joints

When you cut a piece of wood square and butt it against its neighbour you need some kind of mechanical fixing to hold the joint together, as the end grain doesn't glue strongly enough for adhesive alone to be used.

Nailed butt joints

When you nail-fix a butt joint, drive the nails in at an angle, to clamp the two pieces together. 🖙

Bracket and plate fixing

A screwed-on metal right-angle bracket or T-bracket makes a strong, though not very attractive, butt joint. Similarly, you can reinforce a butt joint by nailing or screwing a plywood plate across it.

Timber connectors

The sharp pointed teeth of metal timber connectors hammered onto a butt joint grip the wood like a bed of nails.

Corner blocks

Either pin and glue or screw a square or triangular block of wood in the angle between two components.

Overlap joint

You can make a simple overlap joint by laying one square-cut board across another and fixing them with nails or screws. 🖙

▲ *Overlap joint*

Making an overlap joint

Clamp the components together accurately with a G-cramp, and drill pilot and clearance holes for the screws.

Remove the cramp, apply glue, and then screw the components together.

Halving joints

Halving joints can be adapted to join lengths of wood at a corner or T-joint, or where components cross one another.

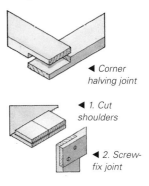

◄ *Corner halving joint*

◄ *1. Cut shoulders*

◄ *2. Screw-fix joint*

Cutting a corner halving joint
To join two pieces of wood at a corner, cut identical tongues in their ends as for a T-halving joint – but clamp the components side by side and cut their shoulders simultaneously (1).

Reinforce the glued joint with screws (2).

Cutting a T-halving joint
Lay the crossrail on the side rail (1) and mark the width of the housing on it with a marking knife, extending the lines halfway down each edge of the rail.

With a marking gauge set to exactly half the thickness of the rails, score the centre lines on both rails (2). Mark the shoulder of the tongue on the crossrail (3), allowing for a tongue slightly longer than the width of the side rail. Hold the crossrail at an angle in a vice (4) and saw down to the shoulder on one edge, keeping to the waste side of the line. Then turn the rail round and saw down to the shoulder on the opposite edge. Finally, saw down square to the shoulder line (5) and remove the waste

1. Mark the housing

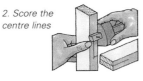

2. Score the centre lines

3. Mark the shoulder

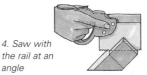

4. Saw with the rail at an angle

SEE ALSO
240–2

SEE ALSO
332–5

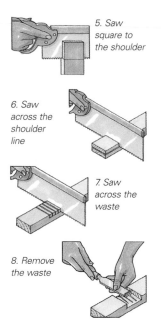

5. Saw square to the shoulder

6. Saw across the shoulder line

7. Saw across the waste

8. Remove the waste

Lap joint

This is a simple joint for joining two wide boards at a corner.

Cutting a lap joint
Cut the square-ended board first and use it to mark out the width of the rebate on the other board. Set a marking gauge to about half the timber's thickness and mark out the tongue. Cut out the rebate with a tenon saw, then glue and dovetail-nail the joint.

by sawing across the shoulder line (6).

To cut the housing in the side rail, saw down both the shoulder lines to the halfway mark, then make several sawcuts across the waste (7). Pare out the waste with a chisel down to the marked lines, working from both sides (8).

Glue and assemble the joint; and when it has set, plane the end of the tongue flush with the side rail. ☛

Bridle joint

A bridle joint is used for making strong joints for a frame.

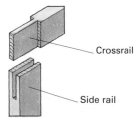

Crossrail

Side rail

Housing joints

Housing joints are often used for shelves and similar structures. A through housing can be seen from both sides of the structure, whereas a stopped housing is not visible from the front.

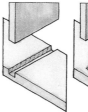

▲ Through housing   ▲ Stopped housing

Dowel joints

Dowel joints are strong and versatile. They can secure butt-jointed rails, mitred frames and long boards butted edge to edge.

Cutting a dowel joint
When joining boards edge to edge, cut dowels about 38mm (1½in) long; otherwise, saw dowels two-thirds the width of the rails. Saw a groove along each one (1) so air and surplus glue can escape.

If you are using a dowelling jig, then you won't need to mark the centres of the dowel holes. Otherwise, set a marking gauge to the centre line on both rails (2), drive panel pins into the edge of the side rail to mark dowel-hole centres, then cut them to short sharp points with pliers (3). Line up the rails, push them together for the metal points to mark the end grain of the crossrail (4), and then pull out the cut panel pins.

Bore holes to a depth just over half the length of the dowels; then glue and assemble the joint. This is easier if the drill is mounted in a vertical drill stand.

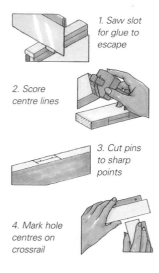

1. Saw slot for glue to escape

2. Score centre lines

3. Cut pins to sharp points

4. Mark hole centres on crossrail

SEE ALSO
15

Mortise-and-tenon joints

A mortise and tenon is a strong joint for narrow components – and essential for chair and table frames. A through tenon can be wedged for extra strength, but a stopped tenon is neater.

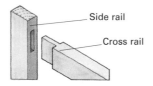

Side rail

Cross rail

▲ *Stopped mortise and tenon*

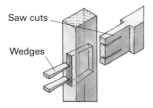

Saw cuts

Wedges

▲ *Through mortise and tenon*

Mitre joint

Mitre joints are used for joining corners of frames. They are also especially useful for decorative mouldings and skirting boards.

Cutting a mitre joint

A right-angled mitre joint is made by sawing the ends of two rails to 45 deg in a mitre

▲ *Mitre joint*

box, then butting them together. Trim the mitres with a finely set plane on a shooting board, and assemble the glued joint in a mitre cramp. If the meeting faces of the rails are fairly large, glue alone will hold them together; but you can reinforce a mitre joint by sawing two slots across the corner and gluing strips of veneer into them (1). Plane the veneers flush with the rails after the glue has set.

▲ *1. Inserting veneer strips*

Scarf joint

A scarf joint is used for joining two lengths of timber end to end.

▶ *Scarf joint*

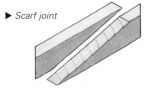

K

Kitchens

The kitchen is one of the most practical rooms in the home, so as well as the cost factor, functionality must play a big part in the design and layout.

Buying kitchens

Fitted kitchens come in many shapes, sizes – and prices. At the cheaper end are units from a DIY store, which you assemble and build yourself, according to your own particular needs. At the other end of the scale there are companies that discuss your requirements, offer a choice of fixtures and fittings, then come and refit your entire kitchen.

Whatever your budget, you still need to make the following similar decisions.

▼ *Storage should be carefully planned*

Decor for cooking and eating

Kitchens need to be functional areas capable of taking a great deal of wear and tear, so the materials you choose will primarily be dictated by practicalities. However, that does not mean you have to restrict your use of colour in any way. Kitchen sinks and appliances are made in bright colours as well as the standard stainless steel and white enamel, while tiled worktops and splashbacks, vinyl floorcoverings and melamine surfaces offer further opportunity to introduce a range of colours. ☞

Textures are an important consideration, offering a range of possibilities. Natural timber remains a popular material for kitchen cupboards and will provide a warm element that you can either echo in your choice of paint, paper or floorcovering or contrast with cool colours and textures. Some people prefer to rely entirely on plastic, ceramic and metallic surfaces, which give a clean and purposeful character.

If the kitchen incorporates a dining area, you may decide to decorate the latter in a fashion more conducive to relaxation and conversation. Softer textures, such as carpet tiles and fabric upholstery, will absorb some of the clatter that is generated by kitchen utensils. Another possibility is to decorate the walls in a different way that changes the mood, perhaps using darker tones or a patterned wallcovering to define the dining area. ☞

Planning

The quality of kitchen furniture and fittings varies enormously – but every well-designed kitchen should incorporate the following features.

A labour-saving layout
Preparing meals is a chore unless the facilities for food preparation, cooking and washing up are grouped in a layout that avoids unnecessary movement.

To use design terminology, the kitchen needs to form an efficient work triangle (*see above right*). Ideally, the sides of the triangle combined should not exceed 6 to 7m (20 to 22ft) in length.

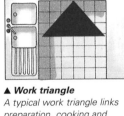

▲ *Work triangle*
A typical work triangle links preparation, cooking and washing-up areas

Storage and appliances

If the work triangle is to be effective, a kitchen must incorporate enough storage space in each area. The fridge and foodstuffs should be close to where the meals are prepared (continued on page 204)

SEE ALSO
383–96

SEE ALSO
244–9

Fitting new kitchen cupboard doors

A quick and relatively inexpensive way to achieve a brand new kitchen without buying brand new units is to change the fronts and so change the appearance.

Tools

Screwdriver
Tape measure
Square
Drill
Wood bits
Cramp
Circular
hinge-cutter
Bradawl

Firstly, the old doors need to come off. Unscrew the door hinges but leave the hinge plates attached to the unit [A]. Replacement doors usually have hinge holes pre-cut, but if not, they can be put in easily using a circular hinge-cutter, which fits into the end of your drill.

You can easily buy replacement hinges from DIY stores and hardware shops. Transfer the hinges from the old door. Use a bradawl to start the screw holes and fit them to the new door with the two fixing screws [B].

Hold up the new door to the unit, and screw the hinge in

place on the hinge plate with the large central screw [C]. The second screw is to align the door to the unit. Repeat this process for the bottom hinge.

Replace the door handles by marking the position and drilling through to attach the handle. To avoid any damage when you drill through the

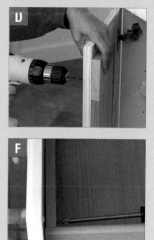

the door to allow the bolt to protrude a little further.

Swapping over kitchen drawer fronts is also simple. Firstly, remove the old drawer front by undoing the two retaining screws inside the drawer [F]. Attach the new drawer handle, by drilling a hole through the centres of the drawer front [G]. Countersink the hole on the back of the drawer front to prevent the bolt head protruding out of the edge of the drawer.

Attach the new drawer front by screwing through the two fixing points [H].

door, temporarily attach a block of wood to the door behind the drilling point with a cramp [D].

Hold the handle and screw in the threaded bolt [E]. If the bolt is a bit short, countersink the hole a bit on the inside of

Repairing kitchen cupboard doors and sticking drawers

INTERMEDIATE

Hinges and runners in older kitchen units are bound to become sticky or wobbly over time. Lubricating with oil and tightening everything up every year or so will help.

There are three areas of door adjustment on a cabinet hinge. The first is the large central screw that attaches the door to the cabinet. This screw tightens over a slot to allow adjustment

away from the cabinet if the door is rubbing [A].

The second is made by tightening or loosening the smaller fixed screw, next to this central screw. This adjusts the door to the left or right of the cabinet (as you look at it) when closed, allowing you to centralize and equally space the doors apart [B].

The third is on the hinge plate attached to the cabinet. This plate has a vertical slot to allow the door to be raised or lowered and align with the cabinet and other doors [C]. All you need to make these

SOLID WOOD UNITS

Drawer units that work on wooden battens as runners need an occasional rubbing over with candle wax along the runner and drawer base to ensure smooth and effortless operation.

A solution of vinegar removes greasy finger marks and grime from wooden doors and drawer fronts.

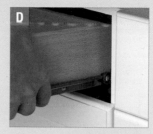

adjustments is a cross-head
screwdriver.

To adjust a drawer (not just
the drawer front), take out the
drawer from the unit. Extend
the drawer right out, then lift
the front of the drawer to free
it from the runners [D].

Unscrew the runners and
reposition [E]. Use a cramp to
hold the runner in position
while new pilot holes are
drilled [F] before securing with
screws. Only drill to half the
screw's length with these pilot
holes, using a drill bit that is
slightly narrower than the
indended screw.

If the drawer runs perfectly
but its front rubs on a door or
worktop as it closes, you may
be able to solve this just by
unscrewing the front from the
drawer, repositioning the
drawer front and screwing it
back together again [G].

Tools

Cross-head
screwdriver
Sandpaper
Drill
Drill bits
Cramp
Candle wax
(optional)

and adequate work surfaces need to be provided. You may be able to find a place for a freezer elsewhere, but it needs to be somewhere conveniently close to the kitchen.

The hob and oven should be grouped together, with heat-proof surfaces nearby to receive hot dishes. Cooking equipment should be within easy reach.

Appliances that require plumbing are best grouped together, with the sink, on an outside wall. In a small house the kitchen area may contain a dishwasher, washing machine and tumble dryer, although a separate laundry room is really the ideal solution.

Kitchen safety

Check the layout of the kitchen with a view to safety. A cramped kitchen can lead to accidents, so make sure that more than one person at a time can circulate in safety.

When building storage into a kitchen, make sure every item is within easy reach and that there is room to open drawers and doors without backing into a wall or injuring other people.

- If possible, avoid an arrangement that encourages people to use the working part of the kitchen as a through passage to other parts of the house or the garden.
- Make sure children cannot reach the hob, and construct a barrier that will keep small children outside the work triangle.
- Placing a hob or cooker in a corner or at the end of a run of cupboards isn't advisable – try to plan for a clear worktop on each side. Don't place it under a window, either – a draught could extinguish a gas pilot light, and someone will eventually get burned trying to open the window.

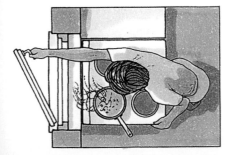

◄ *A dangerously placed cooker Don't position cookers under windows*

L

Lighting: bulbs and fittings

Properly planned lighting can create an atmosphere of warmth and wellbeing, highlight objects of beauty and transform the entire character of your home.

Light bulbs

Choosing the right light bulb is the key in any lighting plan. Nowadays this means trawling through a vast array of designs, effects and strengths. Do you want subdued, atmospheric lighting in one part of the room but more functional –

ENERGY-SAVING LAMPS

Compact fluorescent lamps can be used in place of conventional bulbs. They last up to eight times longer and use up to 80 per cent less electricity. The tube is folded to make a very small unit. The lamps either have built-in control circuits or are supplied with plug-in holders containing these controls.

▶ *Changing a bulb can dramatically change the lighting effect in a room.*
1. screw-thread reflector bulb;
2. daylight bulb;
3. screw-thread pearl bulbs;
4. fluorescent strip lamp;
5. candle bulbs;
6. bayonet reflector bulb;
7. bayonet bulb

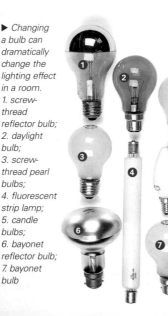

for example, for reading purposes – in another area of the same room? Would installing a dimmer switch help? Or do you want concealed downlighters for a kitchen, in which case low voltage halogen bulbs are the answer.

Whatever your lighting requirements, there is a bulb for you. Depending on the lighting effect, this may entail changing the actual light fitting to accommodate, so make sure you are certain of the type of illumination you wish to achieve.

Light fittings

There is a vast range of light fittings for the home – but, although they may differ greatly in their appearance, they can be grouped roughly into six basic categories according to their functions.

Pendant lights

The pendant light is probably the most common fitting. At its most basic, it consists of a lampholder, with a bulb and usually with some kind of shade, and is suspended from a ceiling rose by a length of flex.

Many decorative pendant lights are designed to take more than one bulb, and they may be much heavier than the simpler ones. Heavy pendant lights should never be attached to a standard plastic ceiling rose. However, they can be connected to a detachable ceiling rose .

▲ Close-mounted lights

Close-mounted ceiling lights

A close-mounted fitting is screwed directly to the ceiling, without a ceiling rose, most often by means of a backplate that houses the lampholder or holders. The fitting is usually enclosed by some kind of rigid light-diffuser, also attached to the backplate.

Recessed ceiling lights

The lamp housing itself is recessed into the ceiling void, and the diffuser either lies flush with the ceiling or projects only slightly below it. These discreet light fittings are ideal for rooms with low ceilings; they are often referred to as downlighters. ▬

▲ Pendant light

▲ Decorative pendant

▲ Recessed fitting

SEE ALSO
136

Changing a light bulb holder

Before starting this task, turn the power off at the mains. It's fine to change a light bulb just by turning the light switch off, but you'll be in contact with wires on this job.

Removing the old holder

First unscrew the top section of the bulb holder [A] to expose the connecting wires. Undo the two screws [B] to release the wires and remove the damaged bulb holder. The top part of the bulb holder will then be free to slide down over the wires and off.

The ends of the wires often become brittle over a period of time, so cut off the last 25mm (1in) of flex. Then strip back the sheathing a further 12mm (½in) [C] before you fit the new bulb holder.

Fitting the new holder

Unscrew the top section of the new bulb holder and slide this over the wires. Use a strip of tape [D] to stop it from sliding down and getting in the way.

Undo the grub screws of the new bulb holder, put in the wires and tighten the screws one at a time [E]. It doesn't matter which side you put the wires in. Loop them over the

Tools

Stepladders
A small neon electric screwdriver
A pair of wire strippers
Sticky tape

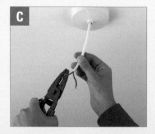

supporting lugs to prevent the weight from being carried to the terminals.

Remove the tape and carefully screw the top section onto the main body. Unscrew the plastic retaining ring which holds the lampshade in place, and insert the shade [F].

Carefully screw the retaining ring back on to the bulb holder [G]. Finally, insert your new bulb, and turn the power back on.

If there are problems, either the bulb has blown or wiring is not properly secured. Check both until you get a result.

CHANGING A BULB

There are basically two types of bulb or light fittings – a (threaded) screw-in type and the more common double pronged, push and twist (bayonet) type.

Make sure that the light switch is in the OFF position before you start. However, if the bulb holder is faulty, then you must TURN OFF the power from the mains fuseboard before you do anything.

Put your steps under the light (don't use a chair) and put the replacement bulb holder and tools on the platform. Undo the threaded plastic ring to release the lampshade and put it aside.

Track lights

Several individual light fittings can be attached to a metal track, which is screwed to the ceiling or wall. Because a contact runs the length of the track, lights can be fitted anywhere along it.

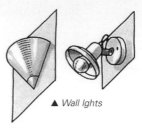
▲ Wall lghts

Wall lights

Light fittings designed for screwing to a wall can be supplied either from the lighting circuit in the ceiling void or from a fused spur off a ring circuit. Various kinds of close-mounted fittings and adjustable spotlights are the most popular wall lights.

Fluorescent light fittings

A fluorescent light uses a glass tube of mercury vapour. The voltage makes electrons flow between electrodes at the ends of the tube and bombard an internal coating which produces bright light.

Different types of coating make the light appear warmer or cooler. For the home, choose warm white or daylight.

The light fitting, which includes a starter mechanism, is usually mounted directly on the ceiling – though, as they produce very little heat, they are also frequently fitted to the underside of cupboards above kitchen work surfaces.

Striplights

These slim lights are often mounted above mirrors and inside display cabinets. They can be controlled by separate microswitches to come on each time the door is opened. They take 30W or 60W tubular tungsten filament bulbs with a metal cap at each end.

Some under-cupboard strip lights are designed to be linked with short lengths of cable so that they can all be powered from a single 13amp plug.

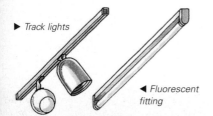
▶ Track lights

◀ Fluorescent fitting

Lighting: planning

Lighting must allow you to work, read or study without straining your eyes. Yet the decorative possibilities of lighting, though no less versatile, are often ignored.

Illuminating living rooms

With lighting for a living room, the accent should be on versatility – creating areas of light where they are needed most, both for function and dramatic effect. Seating areas are best served by lighting placed at a low level (so that naked bulbs are not directed straight into the eyes) and in such a position that a book or newspaper is illuminated from beside the reader.

Sleeping areas

Bedside lamps are a basic requirement in any bedroom – but better still, fit concealed lighting above the bedhead. If you decide to do so, position the fitting low enough to prevent light falling on your face as you lie in bed.

Dining areas and kitchens

Because its height can be adjusted exactly, a rise-and-fall unit is the ideal light fitting to illuminate a dining table. If you eat in the kitchen, have separate controls for the table lighting and work areas, so you can create a cosy dining area without having to illuminate the rest of the room.

Bathrooms

Safety must be your first priority when choosing light fittings for a bathroom. They have to be designed to protect electrical connections from moisture and steam, and must be controlled either from outside the room or by a ceiling-mounted switch.

▼ *Atmospheric lighting works well in a living room*

SEE ALSO
128

Fitting a spotlight track

INTERMEDIATE

A track system offers you the flexibility of positioning individual lights along the track to highlight specific areas or throw more light onto a work surface.

The connecting blocks of track systems are usually situated at one end of the track, so bear this in mind, as it will affect where you are able to locate the spotlights. You can get tracks with the connection block situated in the middle of the track, which may save you having to make alterations to the lighting circuit.

Turn off the power and unscrew the cover of the existing ceiling rose by hand [A]. Disconnect the wires from the terminals [B]. Next, unscrew the base of the rose from the ceiling [C]. Go to the floor above and lift the floorboard directly above the ceiling rose; replace the existing rose for a junction box between the floorboards and the ceiling. If possible, try and fix the track to some of the floor joists.

Mark drilling points with a pencil [D], drill holes and press in rawlplugs to receive the screws to hold up the base

Tools

Measuring tape
Electrical screwdriver
Hammer
Insulating tape
Nail bar
Ordinary screwdriver
Drill and pilot bit
Wire strippers

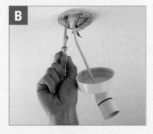

of the track [E]. Or you could fix battens in the ceiling void to take the track fittings. Screw the base of the track to the joists or battens [F], then pull any excess flex into the ceiling void. Follow the instructions supplied with the track (ceiling

fixings and instructions normally come with all spotlight track systems).

Wire one end of the flex into the junction box and the other end into the track connections [G]. Attach the cover of the spotlight track [H] and switch the power back on.

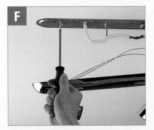

Lofts: installing a loft hatch

Many houses have a hatch in the ceiling that provides access to the roof space. If your house has a large roof space without any openings, installing a hatch will provide you with extra room for storage.

▲ Housing joints
A housing joint will give better support to the trimmer joist than using nails alone

▼ Alternative ways to install hatch covers
1. Drop-in recessed
2. Drop-in flush
3. Hinged up
4. Hinged down

In older houses cutting away part of the roof structure is usually not a problem, as the timbers are relatively substantial. In modern houses, however, lightweight timber is used to make strong triangulated trussed-roof structures. Since these are designed to carry the weight of the roof, any alteration may weaken the structure.

Before you start work, check with your Building Control Officer that it is safe to proceed.

If you have a choice, site the hatch over a landing (although not too close to the stairs), rather than in one of the bedrooms, which is generally less convenient. Also, take into consideration the pitch of the roof, as you will need headroom above the hatch.

Making the opening

If you are planning to fit a special folding loft ladder, the size of the new opening will be specified by the ladder's

manufacturer. In general, aim to sever no more than one ceiling joist: these are usually spaced 350mm (1ft 2in) apart.

Locate three joists by drilling pilot holes in the ceiling. Mark out a square for the opening between the two outer joists. Cut an inspection hole inside the marked area to check that there are no obstacles in the way of the cutting line. Saw through the ceiling plasterwork and strip it away.

Pass a light up into the roof space, and climb up into it between the joists. Lay a board across the joists to support yourself. Saw through the middle joist, cutting it back 50mm (2in) from each edge of the opening. Cut two new lengths of joist timber, called trimmers, to fit between the joists; allow for a square housing joint 12mm (½in) deep to be cut at each end. Nail the housed joints, and the butt joints between the trimmers and joists. Use two 100mm (4in) round wire nails to secure each joint.

Nail the ceiling laths or plasterboard to the underside of the trimmers. Cut timber linings to cover the joists and the edges of the plaster. Make good the damaged edges of the plaster with filler. When it is set, nail mitred architrave moulding around the opening. Make a drop-in or hinged panel of 18mm (¾in) plywood or blockboard. If the loft is for storage, fix chipboard floor panels over the joists.

Loft-access traps

Any openings made in the ceiling will encourage the flow of water vapour into the loft space. This can increase the risk of condensation, particularly if the loft is not well ventilated.

Ready-made loft-access traps are made with seals to overcome this problem. Each trap has a moulded

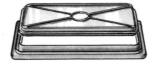

▲ *Frame and insulated trap form an airtight seal*

frame that, when fixed in the trimmed ceiling opening, forms a seal with the ceiling all round. It also neatly covers the cut edges of the hole. The insulated trap door incorporates a flexible vapour seal between it and the hatch frame.

There are hinged trap doors and lift-out ones. Some of them are fire-resistant. Hinged types can be used in conjunction with an aluminium loft ladder that is available as an accessory. 🔺

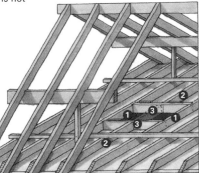

▶ **Hatch opening**
1. Ceiling joists
2. Trimmed joist
3. Trimmers

SEE ALSO
184–5

Installing a loft ladder

BEGINNER

Loft ladders are an efficient way of making use of normally inaccessible and unused space in the roof, enabling access safely and neat storage for the ladders.

Loft ladders usually operate on a slide and fold basis, or are the concertina type.

The trapdoor in the loft must be hinged to open downwards, so the hinges provided must be fixed to the same side as the loft ladder [A]. The trapdoor should be made from 19mm (¾in)

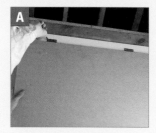

plywood, MDF or blockboard and be flush with the ceiling.

Lower the ladder to the floor and fit the loft ladder guide assembly to the frame with the screws provided [B] and [C]. Slide down the two plastic stops to the top of the guide assembly and tighten all four screws [D]. This ensures that

Tools

Screwdriver
Drill
Pilot bit
Tape measure
Handsaw

the ladder is always in the correct position for climbing into the loft.

Secure the pivot arm to the loft floor [E]. Close all the sections and push the ladder up fully into the loft. Slide the two plastic stops up to the underside of the guide assembly and tighten the four screws [F], ensuring the ladder clears the trapdoor when closed. Fix the handrails to either side of the middle or top section [G].

To fix the automatic latch, put the latch in the centre of the frame surround, opposite

the trapdoor hinges [H]. Engage the pointed marker into the latch and close the trap door. Where the point marks the trapdoor is where the striking plate is fixed. Test the position by opening and closing the trapdoor [I].

Lofts: planning your loft conversion

Although planning permission is generally not required for loft conversions, most building alterations are subject to minimum standards of construction under the Building Regulations.

If you are planning to convert your loft into a lived-in space, you should always check with your local authority's Building Control Officer for any changes to requirements.

Planning controls exist to regulate the use of buildings and other structures. Building Regulations focus on matters such as a building's structural integrity and the suitability of the materials used for its construction.

No planning permission is needed if the volume of your house is unchanged, and the highest part of the roof is not raised.

However, if you intend to install front-elevation dormer windows, or rear and side ones over a particular size, then you will need to apply for planning permission. Permission is also required if your home is a listed building or situated in a conservation area.

It may save you time and money in the long term if you arrange to meet the Building Control Officer well before you carry out any work. The officer will discuss your plans thoroughly with you, detailing any obvious building contraventions and advising you on whether you need to approach any other authorities for approval as well.

▶ *Make an outline application before preparing detailed plans*

Masonry: cleaning

You can often spruce up old masonry by washing off surface grime with water. Strong solvents, however, will harm certain types of stone – so seek the advice of an experienced local builder before applying anything other than water.

Wearing goggles, start at the top of the wall and gently hose the masonry while you scrub it with a stiff-bristle brush (1). Scrub heavy deposits with half a cup of ammonia added to a bucketful of water, then rinse again. Avoid soaking brick or stone when a frost is forecast.

▲ *2. Stipple paint stripper onto spilled paint*

Removing unsightly stains

Soften tar, grease and oil stains by applying a poultice made from fuller's earth soaked in white spirit or in a proprietary grease solvent (following any instructions).

Wearing protective gloves, dampen the stain with solvent then spread on a layer of poultice 12mm (½in) thick.

Tape a sheet of plastic over the poultice, and leave to dry. Scrape off the dry poultice with a wooden or plastic spatula, then scrub with water.

Stripping spilled paint

To remove a patch of spilled paint, use a proprietary paint stripper. Follow any instructions, and wear old clothes, gloves and goggles.

Stipple the stripper onto the stain (2). Leave for about 10 minutes, then remove the softened paint with a scraper. Gently scrub the residue out of deeper crevices with a stiff-bristle brush and water. Then rinse the wall with clean water.

▶ *1. Remove dirt and dust by washing*

Masonry: painting

There are various grades of paint suitable for decorating and protecting exterior masonry. The choice depends on economy, standard of finish, durability and coverage.

Cement paint

This comes as a dry powder to which water is added. It is based on white cement, but pigments are added to produce a range of colours. It is one of the cheaper paints suitable for exterior use. Spray new or porous surfaces with water, then apply two coats.

Mixing cement paint

Shake the container to loosen the powder, then add two volumes of powder to one of water in a clean bucket. Stir it to a smooth paste, then add a little more water until you achieve a full-bodied creamy consistency. Mix no more than you can use in one hour.

Adding an aggregate

When painting a dense wall, or one treated with a stabilizing solution so its porosity is reduced, it is advisable to add clean sand to the mix to give it body. This also provides added protection for an exposed wall and helps to cover dark colours. If the sand changes the colour of the paint, add it to the first coat only. Use one part sand to four parts powder, stirring it in when the paint is still in its paste-like consistency.

Masonry paint

When buying weather-resistant exterior masonry paints, you have a choice between a smooth matt finish or a fine granular texture. 🖝

Water-based masonry paint

Most masonry paints are water-based, being in effect exterior-grade emulsions with

▼ *Do not paint on wall that still shows signs of efflorescence*

SEE ALSO
250–1

additives that prevent mould growth. Although they are supplied ready for use, on porous walls it pays to thin the first coat with 20 per cent water – then follow up with one or two full-strength coats, depending on the colour.

Water-based masonry paints must be applied during fairly good weather. Damp or humid conditions and low temperatures may prevent the paint drying properly.

Solvent-based masonry paints

Some masonry paints are thinned with white spirit or a special solvent – but unlike most oil paints they are moisture-vapour permeable, so the wall is able to breathe. It is advisable to thin the first coat with 15 per cent white spirit, but check manufacturer's recommendations.

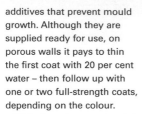

▼ *When painting heavy textures, use a roller that has a deep pile*

Solvent-based paints can be applied in most weather conditions, provided it is not actually raining.

Reinforced masonry paint

Masonry paint with powdered mica added or a similar fine aggregate dries with a textured finish that is extremely weatherproof. Reinforced masonry paints are especially suitable in coastal districts. Although large cracks and holes must be filled before painting, reinforced masonry paint will cover hairline cracks.

Textured coating

A thick textured coating can be put to exterior walls to form a thoroughly weatherproof coating, which can be overpainted to match other colours. The usual preparation is necessary; brickwork needs to be pointed flush. Large cracks should be filled, although a textured coating will cover fine cracks. The paste is then brushed or rolled onto the wall, and left to harden to give an even texture. However, you can produce a texture of your choice, using a variety of simple tools. It's a relatively easy process – but practise on a small section first. 🖌

Masonry: preparation

Before redecorating the outside of your house, check the condition of the masonry and carry out any necessary repairs. Organic growth or mould should be scraped off and any efflorescence removed.

New brickwork or stonework should be left for about three months to completely dry out before further treatment or painting is considered.

Cleaning off mould

Although colourful lichens growing on garden walls can be attractive, the spread of mould and lichens depends on damp conditions – usually not a good sign when they occur naturally on the walls of your house.

Try to identify the source of the problem before treating the growth. It could just be overhanging shrubs or trees, blocking the light, which need to be cut back.

Scrape heavy organic growth from the bricks with a non-metallic spatula, then brush the masonry vigorously with a stiff-bristle brush.

Use a nylon brush to paint on a proprietary fungicidal solution; leave to dry for 24 hours, then rinse thoroughly with clean water.

Removing efflorescence

Soluble salts within building materials gradually migrate to the surface, along with the moisture, as a wall dries out. The result is a white crystalline deposit known as efflorescence.

Old masonry can also show signs of this if a wall has been subjected to more than average moisture.

Brush the deposit from the wall regularly using a dry stiff-bristle brush or a piece of coarse sacking until the crystals stop forming. Don't attempt to wash off the crystals as they will just dissolve in the water and soak back into the wall.

Masonry paints and clear sealants that let the wall breathe are not affected by the alkali content of the masonry, so can be used without applying a primer.

If you plan to use solvent-based (oil) paint on masonry, coat the wall first with an alkali-resistant primer.

SEE ALSO
70–1

Masonry: repairing

Cracked masonry may just be the result of cement-rich mortar being unable to absorb slight movements within the building. However, it could also be a sign of a more serious problem – subsiding foundations, for example. Don't ignore the symptoms, but investigate immediately and put the necessary repairs in hand.

Filling cracked masonry

If a brick or stone wall is found to have substantial cracks, consult a builder or your local Building Control Officer to ascertain the cause. If a crack proves to be stable, you can carry out some minor repairs yourself.

Cracked mortar can be removed and repointed in the normal way, but a crack that splits the bricks cannot be repaired neatly, and the damaged masonry should be replaced by a builder.

Cracks across a painted wall can be filled with mortar that has been

▲ Cracks allow moisture to penetrate

mixed with a little PVA bonding agent to help it stick. Before you effect the repair, wet the damaged masonry with a hose to encourage the mortar to flow deeply into the crack.

Repairing render

Brickwork is sometimes clad with a smooth or roughcast cement-based render, both for improved weatherproofing and to provide a decorative finish. Render is susceptible to the effects of damp and frost, which can cause cracking, bulging and staining. Before you redecorate a rendered wall, make good any damage and clean off surface dirt, mould growth and flaky material, in order to achieve a long-lasting finish.

Repairing defects

Before you repair cracked render, have a builder check the wall for any structural faults.

You can ignore fine hairline cracks if you intend to paint the wall with a reinforced masonry paint, but rake out larger cracks with a cold chisel. Dampen them with water and fill flush with a cement-based exterior filler. Fill any major cracks with a render made of 1 part cement, 2 parts lime and 9 parts builder's sand, plus a little PVA bonding agent to help it stick to the wall.

Bulges in render normally indicate that the cladding has parted from the masonry. Tap the wall gently with a wooden mallet to find the extent of these hollow areas, then hack off the material to sound edges. Use a bolster chisel to undercut the perimeter of each hole except for the bottom edge – which should be left square, so that is does not collect water.

Brush out the debris, then apply a coat of PVA bonding agent. When it becomes tacky, trowel on a layer of 1:1:6 render, 12mm (½in) thick, using plasterer's sand. Leave the render to set firm, then scratch it to form a key.

Next day, fill flush with a weaker mix (1:1:9) and smooth the surface with a wooden float, using circular strokes.

Priming and waterproofing brickwork and masonry

You only need to prime brickwork if it shows signs of efflorescence or spalling.

If you need to waterproof masony, prepare the surface well before applying the fluid, making good any cracks in bricks or pointing.

▼ Restore painted masonry first before waterproofing

SEE ALSO
365

SEE ALSO
295

Masonry: repointing

A combination of frost action and erosion tends to break down the mortar pointing of brickwork and stonework. Cracked joints may also be caused by using a hard, inflexible mortar. Replacing defective pointing is a straightforward but time-consuming task.

Applying the mortar

Rake out the old pointing with a thin wooden lath to a depth of about 12mm (½in). Use a cold chisel, or a special plugging chisel, and a club hammer to dislodge sections that are firmly embedded, then brush out the joints with a stiff-bristle brush.

Spray the wall with water, to make sure the bricks or stones will not absorb too much moisture from the fresh mortar. Mix up some mortar in a bucket and transfer it to a hawk (plasterer's square board). If you are mixing your own mortar, use the proportions 1 part cement to 1 part lime to 6 parts builders' sand.

Pick up a small sausage of mortar on the back of a pointing trowel and push it firmly into the upright joints. This is tricky to do without the mortar falling off, so hold the hawk under each joint to catch it. Try not to smear the face of the bricks with mortar, as it will

stain. Use the same method for the horizontal joints. The actual shape of the pointing is not vital at this stage.

Once the mortar is firm enough to retain a thumbprint, it is ready for shaping. As it is important you shape the joints at exactly the right moment, you may have to point the work in stages to complete the wall. Shape the joints to match existing brickwork or choose a profile suitable for the prevailing weather conditions in your area.

Once you have shaped the joints, wait until the pointing has almost hardened, then brush the wall to remove traces of surplus mortar from the surface of the masonry.

Shaping the mortar joints

The joints shown here are commonly used for brickwork. Flush or rubbed joints are best for most stonework. Leave the pointing of dressed-stone ashlar blocks to an expert.

Flush joint

Rubbed joint

Raked joint

Weatherstruck joint

Flush joints

This is the easiest profile to produce. Scrape the mortar flush, using the edge of your trowel, then stipple the joints with a stiff-bristle brush to expose the sand aggregate.

Rubbed (concave) joints

This joint is ideal for an old wall with bricks that are not of the quality to take a crisp joint. Bricklayers make a rubbed joint using a jointer, a tool shaped like a sled runner with a handle – the semicircular blade is run along the joints. Improvise by bending a length of metal tube or rod (use the curved section only, or you will gouge the mortar). Flush the mortar first, then drag the tool along the joints. Finish the vertical joints, then shape the horizontal ones. Having shaped the joints, stipple them with a brush so that they look like weathered pointing.

Raked joints

A raked joint is used to emphasize the bonding pattern of a brick wall. It is not suitable for an exposed site where the wall takes a lot of weathering.

Rake out the new joints to a depth of about 6mm (¼in), and then compress the mortar by smoothing it lightly with a lath or piece of rounded dowel rod.

Weatherstruck joints

The sloping profile helps shed rainwater from the wall. Shape the mortar with the edge of a pointing trowel. Start with the vertical joints, sloping them either to the right or to the left (but be consistent). Then shape the horizontal joints, allowing the mortar to spill out at the base of each joint.

Finish by cutting off excess mortar with a Frenchman, a tool with a narrow blade with the tip bent at 90 deg. Use a wooden batten to guide the Frenchman along the joints. Nail scraps of wood at each end of the batten to hold it off the wall. Align the batten with the bottom of the horizontal joints, then draw the tool along it to trim off the excess mortar.

▼ Use a Frenchman to trim weatherstruck joints

SEE ALSO
56

SEE ALSO
71

Mouldings: centrepieces

Most Victorian and Edwardian houses of any quality had moulded cornices and centrepieces in the main rooms. In comparatively recent times, when they became unfashionable, many of these ceilings were destroyed. Today, thanks to renewed appreciation of period-style plasterwork, damaged mouldings are frequently restored or replaced with reproductions.

Original centrepieces

Unless you live in a very modern building, the chances are your home will have some decorative moulding, be it picture rails, plaster covings or panelled doors. If you are particularly fortunate, your house might feature the entire range of Victorian decorations, including plasterwork ceiling roses and decorative cornices. These are now very much in demand and what estate agents call original features. If you've got them, show them off!

Before the mid-18th century, decorative plaster and timber mouldings were unknown except in very important houses. Georgian craftsmen developed the art of plasterwork and examples of their elegant, classically inspired work still survive in houses of the period. At that time, the wet plaster was applied straight to the walls and ceiling, and the decoration was formed in-situ by skilled plasterers, who moulded the designs themselves.

The Victorians changed all that. In the early 1850s they developed a new material, known as fibrous plaster, which could be mass-produced in very ornate designs and installed by any builder. It was also much cheaper to produce and brought decorative plasterwork within the reach of ordinary homeowners.

▶ Fine detail can be obscured by paint

The use of plaster decoration continued until the First World War, after which it declined as the European fashion for a sparser, more modern look gathered ground.

Although they are primarily decorative, mouldings do serve a practical purpose. Decorative centrepieces often help disguise joins in ceilings. Cornices neaten joins between walls and ceilings, while skirtings do the same job at ground level.

Restoring original centrepieces

A ceiling 'rose', or centrepiece, is a decorative plaster moulding placed at the centre of a ceiling, usually with a pendant light fitting hanging from it. Original mouldings of

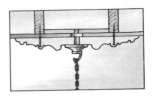

▲ Reinforce larger mouldings with screws for support

▲ Cover the screwheads in the moulding, using a filling knife

this kind are often caked with distemper, which tends to mask the fine detail (see opposite page). Restore them, whenever possible, by cleaning away the layers of old distemper with water and repairing any cracks and chipped details with filler. 🖾

◀ Reproduction fibrous-plaster centrepiece

SEE ALSO
12

Fitting a decorative ceiling rose

BEGINNER

Plaster ceiling roses or centrepieces, along with plastic and polystyrene ones, are widely available from DIY stores and good decorating shops. If you want something a bit special, you will have to visit a fibrous plaster specialist. Fixing a small or medium-sized ceiling rose on your own is straightforward, but for really large centrepeices, it is probably best to leave it to the experts.

If you have a plain ceiling with no central light, the first thing to do is find the centre of the ceiling. You can easily do this by using two lines of string each stretched diagonally from corner to corner of the ceiling [A]. The point where the strings cross each other will be the centre [B].

Where there is already a light fitting in place, remember to turn the power supply off and remove the fitting first. Make sure you have set up a safe and secure platform on which to stand and work from.

Lift up the new ceiling rose and draw around the edge onto the ceiling [C].

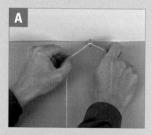

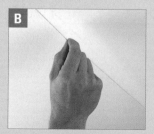

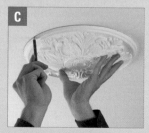

For a lightweight rose such as the one pictured here, apply a coat of PVA adhesive and water to both the ceiling and the back of the rose to seal the surfaces [D] – remember to remove any ceiling paper first. Apply

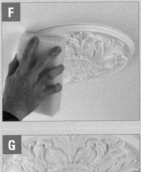

plaster or tile adhesive to the back of the rose and press into place [E]. Gently wipe off any excess plaster or adhesive [F].

Get someone to hold the rose in place while you pull the lighting flex through the centre of the rose. Cut back the cable using wire strippers and strip the wires ready for installing into the light fitting [G]. Use filler over any screwheads and leave to dry. Paint to finish.

If you are attaching a heavy rose, use a joist detector to locate the joists within close range of the rose. Take the straight edge and pencil, and draw two centre lines on the ceiling and transfer corresponding lines onto the rose. Carefully drill two pilot holes, then a light countersink and have two long brass screws ready for fixing.

Tools

New ceiling rose
Tacks
String
Pencil
Straight edge
Joist detector
Drill
PVA adhesive
Brass screws
Screwdriver
Filler

Installing cornice and coving

Victorian properties – and particularly their ceilings – deserve to be restored sympathetically. A lot of the time, not only are the centrepieces no longer intact, but the coving or cornice has been damaged or removed.

Offer up an off-cut of your coving or cornice and mark the walls and ceilings in every corner [A]. Pin one end of a chalk line onto a mark and stretch a line to another mark. Do this around the whole room. To give the adhesive something to grip, scratch the finish plaster within the lines. Apply a solution of PVA adhesive and water to the prepared surface. This stops the plaster from absorbing the water from the adhesive, helping it stick better.

There is usually a paper template with the coving to help you cut the internal and external mitre joints. An easier way is with a mitre block [B]. Four different mitres are needed – left and right internal, and left and right external.

Fixing adhesive comes in bags of dry powder, which you add to water and mix. To make mixing quicker and easier, buy

Tools

Mitre block
Saw
Pointing trowel
Scraper
String line
Tape measure
Hammer
Screwdriver

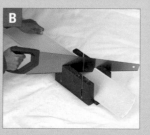

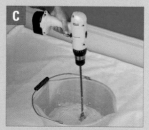

a mixing tool to fit into your electric drill [C]. The mixture should be thick but light and applied either with a pointing trowel or filling knife [D].

The joints can be filled and shaped with some of the excess adhesive if the mitre is not perfect. On a cornice, however, the joints would have to be over-filled with casting plaster when set, and the pattern cut out with a 'trowel end small tool' – a long steel drawer handle with a spoon shape at one end (for applying plaster) and a blade shape at the other end (for carving).

When pressing coving (or cornice) into position, follow the chalk line on the wall, as that is the line the eye will see [E]. Often ceilings are out of alignment, but you can pack any gaps with adhesive or filler and when painted, it will never notice. So keep it straight and fill in any gaps.

Scrape off excess adhesive with a filling knife or trowel then rub over with a damp sponge [F]. Nails temporarily hammered in underneath the cove or cornice will hold the coving or cornice in place while the adhesive dries [G].

Mouldings: interior rails

Interior wooden mouldings – referred to as architectural mouldings – are a legacy of the classically proportioned panelled walls found in grand houses. They include moulded skirting boards, dado rails, picture rails and decorative cornice mouldings. You may want to reinstate such decorative features if they have been stripped out of an older house or to add them after installing a new partition wall. Mouldings are usually made from selected softwood, certain hardwoods or MDF.

Dado rails

The dado rail, also known as a chair rail, is a reference to the waist-high dado panelling of earlier times. It provides a rubbing strip to protect the wall finish from chair backs and forms a border for textured wallcoverings – a feature which is typically found in Victorian and Edwardian houses.

Picture rails

Like the dado moulding, the picture rail is an echo from the earlier panelled walls. It is usually set about 300 to 500mm (1ft to 1ft 8in) below the ceiling cornice to form a frieze. Picture-rail mouldings have a groove in the top edge to hold metal hooks for hanging pictures.

Making corner joints

Where moulded profiles meet at a corner, it is necessary to mitre the ends where they meet. Or, for an internal corner only, you can scribe one end to fit over the moulded profile of the other. Some mouldings are pre-scribed. Cut mitres using a tenon saw and mitre box, or a mitre saw. To scribe the end of a moulding, first mitre it; and then, with a coping saw, cut

▼ *Mouldings come in many shapes and designs*

1. Make a perpendicular cut

away the waste, following the line formed by the face and the mitred end (1).

For larger mouldings, mark the profile on the back face, using an offcut as a template. Saw off the waste with the teeth of the coping saw facing backward to prevent damaging the face of the moulding.

Fixing architectural mouldings

The best method for fixing a moulding will depend on the structure of the wall. On a masonry wall, you can use nails, nailable plugs or woodscrews driven into wallplugs. If it is a cavity wall, drive nails or screws into the wooden studs, but use cavity fixings elsewhere. Alternatively, you can use gun-applied panel adhesive in all cases.

Some mouldings have a groove machined along the back for fitting onto plastic clips screwed to the wall. This offers an invisible fixing that does not require filling prior to finishing. Simply set the clips on a levelled marked line.

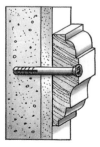

Nailable-plug fixing

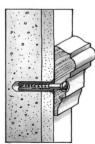

Plug and screw fixing

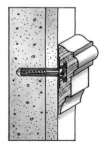

Plastic-clip fixing

SEE ALSO
192–6

SEE ALSO
240–2

SEE ALSO
330–3

Fitting picture and dado rails

Fitting a picture rail or dado rail in a room allows for more creative decorating. Just using one moulding, or even both used together, can create interest in a room.

Although the height you choose a dado rail to be is up to you, it may look odd if it is much higher than 1m (3ft 3in) from the floor. Using a spirit level, rotating it as you go, draw a line around the room [A]. The height of a picture rail is usually about 300–500mm (1ft–1ft 8in) below the ceiling

cornice. You will need a mitre block and tenon saw, or a mitre saw [B], to cut a dado or picture rail to length. Mitre the ends to make a perfect 90 deg angle for joining at corners.

There are special adhesives for fixing timber features such as picture and dado rails. Apply with a sealant gun [C], and press the rail into place [D]. Use 50–65mm (2–2½in) lost head nails through the rail fixed into vertical studwork timbers, for modern walls constructed from timber studwork (framework) and plasterboard. Knock the nails below the surface using a punch [E]. Then fill the nail

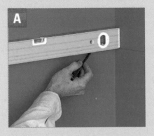

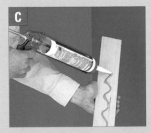

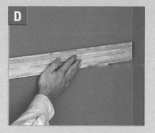

holes afterwards with proprietary filler.

If you are lucky, the corners of your room might be square. You could then cut an internal mitre to fit the corners perfectly. Another way is to cut one piece square ended and fix it; then scribe the second piece over the first. A scribe is obtained by first cutting an internal mitre. Using a coping saw, cut off the mitre leaving just the profile. This should then fit over the first piece [F].

Two pieces of rail can be joined together by mitring on

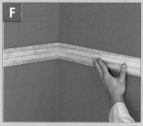

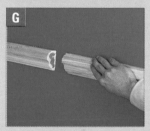

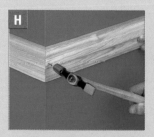

a 45 deg angle and fixing the first piece. Mitre the second piece to fit perfectly over the first, using a touch of PVA [G].

You can add an extra bit of strength to an external corner by knocking in a pin or two, joining the two pieces [H].

Tools

Measuring tape
Mitre block
Mitre saw
Nail punch
Spirit level
Hammer
Cordless drill
Tenon saw
Filling knife
Sealant gun

Mouldings: skirting boards

Skirtings are protective 'kick boards', usually moulded to form a decorative border between the floor and walls. Modern skirting boards are relatively small and simply formed, with a rounded or bevelled top edge. Skirting repairs or replacements are an inevitable consequence of major repairs to a floor.

Removing the skirting

Remove a skirting board by levering it away from the wall, using a crowbar and bolster chisel. A continuous length of skirting, with ends that are mitred into internal corners, may have to be cut before it can be removed.

Cutting a long skirting

Lever it away at its centre and insert blocks of wood, one on each side of the proposed cut, to hold the board about 25mm (1in) from the wall. Make a vertical cut with a panel saw using short strokes.

Fitting a new skirting

Whenever possible, restore a damaged skirting, particularly if it is an unusual moulding for which there is no modern replacement.

Measure the length of each wall. Mark the length of the wall on the bottom edge of the new skirting; mark a 45 deg angle for the mitre. Saw down the line at that angle.

Fix skirtings in place with cut clasp nails or masonry nails when nailing to brick or stone, but use lost head nails when attaching skirting boards to wooden grounds.

▼ *Selection of skirting mouldings*
1. Bolection mould skirting
2. Torus skirting
3. Ovolo skirting
4. Torus/ovolo reverse skirting
5. Bevelled/ rounded reverse skirting
6. Bevelled hardwood skirting

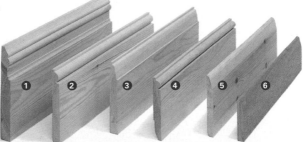

N

Nails

Nails are a cheap and simple method of fixing for a variety of timber structures, as well as holding glued joints together. There are many types of nail for general use and also for specific purposes.

▲ Round plain-head wire nail

Round plain-head wire nail
Rough general carpentry. 20 to 150mm (¾ to 6in).

Round lost-head wire nail
Can be concealed. 40 to 75mm (1½ to 3in).

Lath nail
Fixing laths and thin battens. 25 to 40mm (1 to 1½in).

Ring-shank nail
Extra-secure fixings. 20 to 100mm (¾ to 4in).

Square twisted plain-head nail
Twisted shank gives extra grip. 20 to 100mm (¾ to 4in).

Cut clasp nail
Carpentry and fixing wood to masonry. 25 to 200mm (1 to 8in).

Cut floor nail
Nailing floorboards to joists. 40 to 75mm (1½ to 3in).

▲ Ring-shank nail

Oval wire nail
Can be concealed. Less likely to split wood than round wire nails. 25 to 150mm (1 to 6in).

Oval lost-head nail
Oval nail with small head; neat finish. 25 to 150mm (1 to 6in).

Plasterboard nail
Fixing plasterboard to battens. 30 to 40mm (1¼ to 1½in).

Panel pin
Cabinet-making and fine joinery (with glue). 15 to 50mm (⅝ to 2in).

Veneer pin (moulding pin)
Applying veneers and small mouldings. 15 to 50mm (⅝ to 2in).

Hardboard panel pin
Fixing hardboard and light plywood. 20 to 40mm (¾ to 1½in).

Corrugated fastener
For making rough butted or mitre framing joints.

▶ Oval wire nail

► *Masonry nail*

Clout (slate) nail
Fixing slates and roofing materials. 20 to 100mm (¾ to 4in).

Felt/large-head clout nail
Attaching roofing felt, webbing. 12 to 50mm (½ to 2in).

Roofing nail or drive screw
Fixing corrugated sheet to timber. 65 to 115mm (2½ to 4½in).

Twisted-shank spring-head nail
Fixing sheet materials and man-made boards. 65mm (2½in).

Masonry nail
For fixing wood to masonry. 23 to 85mm (⅞ to 3⅜in).

Escutcheon pin
For fixing keyhole plates etc. 15 or 20mm (⅝ or ¾in).

Terrier nail
Extra-strong wood-to-wood fixings: countersunk head, 25 to 65mm (1 to 2½in); and with flat head, 30 to 80mm (1⅛ to 3⅛in).

Sprig
For glazing, picture-framing, and fixing linoleum. 12 to 20mm (½ to ¾in).

Timber connector
Making rough butted or mitre wood joints.

Staple
Rough carpentry; fixing fencing wire. 10 to 40mm (⅜ to 1½in).

Upholstery nail
Domed decorative head. 3 to 12mm (⅛ to ½in).

Tack
Carpeting; attaching fabric to wood. 6 to 30mm (¼ to 1¼in).

Insulated masonry nail
Securing electric cable and micro-bore pipe to masonry. Various shapes and sizes.

Screw nail
Fixing hardboard, plywood and sheet materials. 12 to 50mm (½ to 2in).

Poly-head nail
Ringed shank and shatter-proof plastic head. Fixing plastic cladding. 30 to 65mm (1¼ to 2½in). ☞

► *Clout (slate) nail*

SEE ALSO
330–3

NAILING TIPS

Hammering a nail into a wall or a piece of wood might seem like a straightforward enough task, but there is actually much more skill involved in nailing than you might think. Here is a selection of useful nailing tips, to be used in conjunction with the advice given on different types of nails in the preceding pages. Following these tips will reduce damage to walls, etc., and will save you time and energy.

Preventing split wood	To avoid splitting, if that seems likely, blunt the point of the nail with a light hammer blow. A blunt nail punches its way through timber instead of forcing the fibres apart.
Removing a dent from wood	If you dent wood with a misplaced hammer blow, put a few drops of hot water on the wood and let the wood swell. When it is dry, smooth the wood with abrasive paper.
Using a nail set	A nail set is a punch with a hollow-ground tip used for sinking nails below the surface of the wood. Nail sets are made in several sizes, for use with large and small nails. Having driven the nail almost flush, hold the set upright between thumb and fingertips and place its tip on the protruding nailhead, then tap the tool with your hammer. With a heavy hammer, very little force is needed to sink the nail.
Blind nailing	To hide a nail fixing, lift a flap of wood with a gouge, sink the nail with a nail set, then glue the flap and cramp it flat.
Hammering small nails	If the nail is very small, either set it with the hammer peen or push it through a piece of thin card to steady it. Just before you tap the nail flush with the wood, tear the card away.
Removing a bent nail	If you bend a nail while driving it in with a claw hammer, lever it out by sliding the claw under the nailhead and pulling back on the end of the shaft. The hammer's curved head will roll on the wood without doing too much damage, but you can protect the work by placing a piece of thick card or hardboard under the hammer head. A thick packing of this kind will also give you extra leverage for removing a long nail.

P

Painting

The secret with painting, as indeed with all decorating jobs, is to prepare well and, of equal importance, to take your time. Although painting may seem easy compared to some DIY tasks, a rushed job looks just that – rushed.

There seems to be an infinite range of paints and finishes available nowadays. Yet, provided you know the effect you want and the base of the paint you're using, it's not as complicated as it first appears. Water-based paints are generally faster drying and easier to clear up, but they may not be as hard-wearing as their oil-based equivalent.

TYPES OF PAINT

Type of paint	Useage	Notes	Cleaning
Oil-based			
Primer	Wood/metal	Use this to seal bare wood	White spirit
Undercoat	Wood/metal/plaster	Apply this as a base for the top coat	White spirit
Gloss	Wood/metal/plastic	Hardwearing and durable	White spirit
Eggshell	Woodwork	Hardwearing and durable	White spirit
Water-based			
Primer	Wood	Only use on interior woodwork	Water and soap
Undercoat	Wood/metal/plaster	Apply before water-based top coat	Water and soap
Satin Finish	Wood/metal/plaster	Quick and relatively durable	Water and soap
Eggshell	Wood/metal/plaster	Top coat for interior work	Water and soap
Vinyl Matt Emulsion	Plaster	General purpose coverage	Water and soap
Vinyl Silk Emulsion	Plaster	General purpose coverage	Water and soap
Others			
Varnish	Woodwork	Available as water or oil-based in a variety of finishes	Check label
Wood stain	Woodwork	See above	Check label
Knotting fluid	Woodwork	Used to seal knots in wood prior to painting, varnishing or staining	White spirit
Paints for Metals	There are a number of paints available, but by far the best paint to use is a Hammerite-type paint especially designed for finishing metal.		White spirit

So consider how much wear-and-tear the surface is likely to receive when you're choosing which type to use. ☞

Choosing colours

It's never easy getting exactly the right shade. With so many ready-made and made-to-order colours available, the decision can be a daunting one. Many paint manufacturers now sell small tester pots which you can take home and try out before making the decision to buy a larger quantity.

Bear in mind that colours can have different effects on a room – warm colours will make the room feel cosy but smaller; pale colours can increase the feeling of

▲ *Paint can be made up to match any hue exactly*

spaciousness but may not be as comforting on a cold winter night. Of course, clever use of lighting can also affect this, so try and think about the room in its entirety, complete with furniture, natural light and artificial light, when choosing your paint.

Different types of paint will have differing coverage, depending on whether they are oil-or water-based. Calculate how much you need by measuring the required area and work out the square meterage (length x width). When selecting your paints, check the coverage rate on the can to see how much you need. Always allow at least 10 per cent extra paint because you do not want to run short.

▼ *Get your choice of colours right at the start*

SEE ALSO
398–9

Painting: applying paint

Unless you are using one of the specially formulated one-coat finishes, it is necessary to apply successive layers of paint to build up a paint system.

▼ *A paint system for woodwork*
Different types of paint are required to build a protective system for woodwork

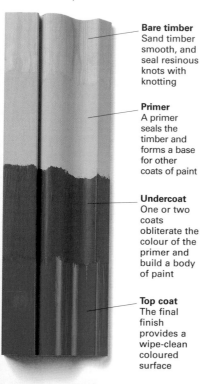

Bare timber
Sand timber smooth, and seal resinous knots with knotting

Primer
A primer seals the timber and forms a base for other coats of paint

Undercoat
One or two coats obliterate the colour of the primer and build a body of paint

Top coat
The final finish provides a wipe-clean coloured surface

Painting walls requires a simple system, comprising two or three coats of the same paint.

Painting woodwork and metalwork usually involves a more complex system, using paints with different qualities. A typical paint system for woodwork is illustrated on the left.

After preparing the surface on which you are painting, the first type of paint you require is a primer. There are many types of primer, depending on the surface, including: wood primer, acrylic wood primer, aluminium wood primer, metal primer and multi-purpose primer (suitable for wood, metal and plaster). ☞

An undercoat covers the colour of the primer and builds up a body of paint, ready to accept the top coat of paint. This top coat provides the final finish in the paint system, giving a wipe-clean, hard-wearing colour surface.

Painting: ceilings and walls

Whatever method you prefer to use to paint, it pays to use good quality tools, especially when it comes to brushes – cheaper brushes tend to shed bristles.

Paints for walls and ceilings

Emulsion paint, in its many forms, is the most practical finish for interior walls and ceilings – but use an acrylic or solvent-based paint on wall-fixed joinery such as skirtings, architraves and picture rails.

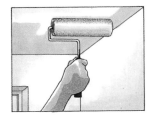

▲ *Blend in the wet edges*

Painting the ceiling

Starting in a corner near the window, carefully paint along the edges of the ceiling with a small paintbrush.

Working from the wet edges, paint in bands 600mm (2ft) wide, working away from the light. Whether you are using a brush, pad or roller, apply each fresh load of paint

▼ *Paint around the edges first*

just clear of the previous application, then blend in the junctions for even coverage.

Painting the walls

Starting at a top corner of the room, use a small brush to paint the edges, working right to left if you are right-handed and vice-versa. Moving on to a larger brush or roller, paint an area of about 600mm (2ft) square at a time. If you are using emulsion, paint in horizontal bands; gloss paints, however, are best applied in vertical strips.

Always finish a complete wall before you take a break as a change of tone may show between separate painted sections.

SEE ALSO
293–4

Painting interior surfaces

BEGINNER

Before starting your painting, ensure that the surfaces are prepared as well as they can be – filling any holes or cracks with filler, rubbing well down and washing down not only the walls but also the ceiling.

When painting ceilings, although the choice of brush, pad or roller is often down to the individual, the preferred method is to use a good quality roller [A]. To make painting easier, fit an extension pole to help you reach the ceiling comfortably from the floor. If not, set up a safe, sturdy work platform.

Cover the floor with dustsheets and use the roller slowly across the ceiling to avoid splashing. The roller will only take the paint close to the walls; paint the edges with a brush [B]. This brushwork is known as 'cutting in'. If this overlaps onto the walls a bit, it doesn't matter, as the wall colour will cover the overlap when it is applied. If you have a coving or a cornice, this should be incorporated into the ceiling colour – unless you wish to make it stand out in its own colour.

When painting walls, again the choice is down to the individual. A roller is often seen as the quickest method. However, don't be too vigorous with it or the paint will splash onto any woodwork and the newly painted ceiling.

Cover the walls with the

Tools

Dust sheets
Roller
Roller tray
Brushes
Stepladder
Platform
Radiator roller
Cling film

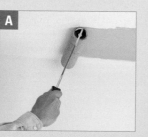

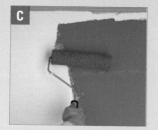

paint – in this instant, using a roller [C]. Paint the bits the roller can't reach with a brush. Any splashes on woodwork or walls should be removed while still wet with a damp sponge or cloth.

You need a steady hand to cut in at ceiling level with a brush [D].

If you need to stop in between coats, you can wrap the roller and brushes in cling film to prevent them from going hard before you've finished using them [E].

You will always come across an awkward space behind the radiator that needs doing. If you don't want the hassle of taking off the actual radiator, then just use a 'rad roller' to reach as far down or up as you will need to go [F].

From a health and safety point of view, it's important that any ladders or platforms are safely constructed and positioned. Tailor-made platforms for stairwells are available to hire or you can build your own with an interlocking network of scaffold boards, stepladders and boxes. Lash everything to secure supports for safety.

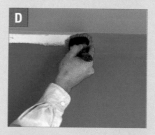

Painting: exterior masonry

The outside walls of houses are painted for two main reasons: to give a bright, clean appearance, and to protect the surface from the weather. What you use as a finish and how you apply it depends on what the walls are made from, their condition and the degree of protection they need.

Working to a plan

Before you embark upon painting the outside walls of your house, plan your time carefully. It's not necessary to tackle the whole job at once – although it is preferable, since the weather may change to the detriment of your timetable. You can split the work into separate stages with days (or even weeks) in between, provided you divide the walls into manageable sections. Use window frames and doorframes, bays, downpipes and corners of walls to form break lines that will disguise joins.

There are various grades of paint suitable for decorating and protecting exterior masonry, which take into account economy, standard of finish, durability and coverage. Use the chart (left) for quick reference and think carefully when choosing. 🔝

	①	②	③	④	⑤	⑥
Suitable to cover						
Brick	•	•		•	•	•
Stone	•	•		•	•	•
Concrete	•	•	•	•	•	•
Cement rendering	•	•	•	•	•	•
Pebbledash	•	•	•	•		
Emulsion paint		•	•	•	•	
Emulsion paint		•	•	•	•	
Solvent-based paint		•	•	•	•	
Cement paint	•	•	•	•		
Drying time: hours						
Touch-dry	1-2	1-2	2-3	4-6	6	2-3
Recoatable	24	4-6	24	16	24-48	3-16
Thinners: solvents						
Water	•	•	•			
White spirit				•	•	
Number of coats						
Normal conditions	2	2	1-2	2	1	1-2
Coverage: Depending on wall texture						
Sq metres per litre		4-10	3-6.5	6-16	2	5-10
Sq metres per kg	1-6				1-2	
Method of application						
Brush	•	•	•	•		•
Roller	•	•	•	•		•
Spray gun	•	•	•	•		

KEY 1. Cement paint **2.** Water-based masonry paint **3.** Reinforced masonry paint **4.** Solvent-based masonry paint **5.** Textured coating **6.** Floor paint

◀ *Black dot denotes compatibility. All surfaces must be clean, sound, dry and free from organic growth*

Using paintbrushes

Choose a brush 100 to 150mm (4 to 6in) wide for painting walls; larger ones are heavy and tiring to use. A good-quality brush with coarse bristles will last longer on rough walls. For effective coverage, apply the paint with vertical strokes, crisscrossed with horizontal ones. You will find it necessary to stipple paint into textured surfaces.

▲ When painting heavy textures, use a roller that has a deep pile. Switch to a medium pile for light textures and smooth surfaces.

Using a paint roller

A roller will apply paint three times faster than a brush. When painting with a roller, vary the stroke angle to ensure even coverage; use a brush to cut into angles and obstructions.

▲ Cut in with a gentle scrubbing motion

Using a spray gun

Spraying is the quickest way to apply paint to a large expanse of wall. Hold the gun about 225mm (9in) away from the wall and keep it moving with even passes.

▲ Protect downpipes with newspaper

▶ Hire a good-quality spray gun and a small portable compressor.

SEE ALSO
221

Painting: paintbrushes, pads and rollers

Brushes, rollers or pads – all have their place when painting. The choice often comes down to surface type, speed of applying or individual preference.

Paintbrushes

Some paintbrushes are made from natural animal hair. Hog bristle is the best, but it is often mixed with inferior horsehair or oxhair to reduce cost.

Synthetic-bristle brushes are generally the least expensive, and are quite adequate for the home decorator.

Bristle types

Bristle is ideal, since each hair tapers naturally and splits at the tip into even finer filaments that hold paint. Bristle is also tough and resilient.

Synthetic 'bristle' (usually made of nylon) is designed to resemble the characteristics of real bristle. A good quality nylon brush will serve most painters just as well as a bristle one.

Choosing a brush

The bristles of a good brush are densely packed. When you fan them with your fingers they should spring back into shape immediately. Flex the tip of the brush against your hand to see if any bristles work loose. Even a good brush will shed a few bristles at first, but never clumps. The ferrule (metal band) should be fixed firmly to the handle.

Flat paintbrushes

The filling is set in rubber, pitch or resin, and is bound to the wooden or plastic handle with a pressed-metal ferrule.

▼ *Paintbrushes come in a variety of sizes*

▲ *Standard paint pad*

Paint pads
Paint pads help inexperienced decorators to apply paints and wood dyes quickly and evenly. Although they aren't universally popular, they are useful for painting large flat areas.

Standard pads
Rectangular paint pads are used for decorating walls, ceilings and flat woodwork. They have short mohair pile and are generally made with D-shape handles.

Corner pad
A mohair-covered pad wrapped around a triangular applicator spreads paint onto both sides of an internal corner.

Sash pad
This has a small mohair sole for painting glazing bars of sash windows. Most have plastic guides to stop them straying onto the glass.

Paint rollers
A paint roller is ideal for painting a large area of wall or ceiling quickly. The cylindrical sleeves that apply the paint are interchangeable, and slide onto a revolving sprung-wire cage fitted to the cranked handle of the roller.

Sizes of roller sleeves
Sleeves for standard paint rollers are 175mm (7in) or 225mm (9in) long, but you can buy 300mm (1ft) rollers.

Types of roller sleeves
You can buy roller sleeves of various materials to suit different surface textures and kinds of paint. Most sleeves are made of sheepskin or synthetic fibres, cropped to different lengths. A sheepskin sleeve can hold more paint than a synthetic fibre one, but costs about 25 per cent more.

◀ *Rollers apply paint quickly*

SEE ALSO
251

Painting: preparing metal

Ferrous metals that are rusty will shed practically any paint film rapidly – so the most important aspect of finishing metalwork is thorough preparation and priming, to prevent the corrosion returning.

Methods of application

With the exception of black lead, you can use a paintbrush to apply metal finishes. In general, the techniques are identical to those used for painting woodwork – but don't attempt to brush out bitumen-based paints in the conventional manner.

Remove metal door and window fittings for painting, suspending them on wire hooks to dry. Make sure that sharp edges are coated properly, as the finish can wear thin relatively quickly.

Some paints can be sprayed, but there are few

▲ *Use card behind a downpipe when painting behind it*

situations where this is advantageous, except perhaps in the case of intricately moulded ironwork such as garden furniture, which you can paint outside. Indoors, good ventilation is essential when spraying.

A roller is suitable for large flat surfaces. Pipe-work requires the use of a special V-section roller, designed to coat curved surfaces.

Apply the same principles if you have to paint metal gutters and downpipes, metal casement windows, or lacquering metalwork.

◀ *A long slim-handled radiator brush or roller enables you to paint the back of a radiator without having to remove it from the wall. These same tools can be used for painting between the leaves of a double radiator*

Painting: wood/renovating

Wood is a fibrous material with different rates of absorption; some woods contain knots that may ooze resin. All this has a bearing on the type of paint you use

It is essential to prepare and prime all new woodwork thoroughly before applying the finishing coats. 🖙

With solvent-based paint, apply one or two undercoats. As each coat hardens, rub down with fine wet-and-dry paper to remove blemishes, and then wipe the surface with a cloth dampened with white spirit.

Apply the paint with vertical brush-strokes, then spread it sideways to even out the coverage. Finish with light strokes ('laying off') in the direction of the grain. Blend the edges of the next application while the paint is still wet. Don't go back over a painted surface that has started to dry, or you will leave brushmarks in the paintwork.

Use a different technique for spreading one-coat or acrylic paints. Simply lay on the paint liberally with almost parallel strokes, then lay off lightly. Blend wet edges quickly.

▼ Painting a straight edge
Use a small brush; place it very close the edge. As you flex the bristles, they will spread to the required width, laying on an even coat of paint

Renovating bath enamel
You can buy two-part paints prepared specifically for restoring the enamel surface of an old bath, sink or basin.

To achieve a first-class result, the bath must be scrupulously clean and dry. Paint the bath from the bottom upwards, in a circular direction. This type of paint is self-levelling, so don't brush it out too much. Pick up runs immediately, and work quickly to keep wet edges fresh.

🖙
SEE ALSO
293

Paving

If your only experience of paving slabs is the rather bland variety used for public footpaths, then cast-concrete paving may not seem a very attractive proposition for a garden. However, nowadays manufacturers offer a wide range of shapes, colours and finishes that can brighten up any patio area whether laid in a uniform shape or in mixed designs.

Colours and textures

Paving slabs are manufactured by hydraulic pressing or casting in moulds to create the desired surface finish. Pigments and selected aggregates added to the concrete mix are used to create the illusion of a range of muted colours or natural stone. Combining two or more colours or textures within the same area of paving can be very striking and look more interesting.

Shapes and sizes

Although some manufacturers offer a wider choice than others, there's a fairly standard range of shapes and modular sizes. It is possible to carry the largest slabs without help, but it's a good idea to enlist the help of another person to manoeuvre them carefully into place.

Square and rectangular
A single size and shape can

Regular or informal paving
Constructing a simple grid from square slabs is relatively easy. Though more difficult to lay, mixed paving is richer in texture, colour and shape

Hexagonal slab

Honeycomb pattern

be employed to make grid-like patterns or, when staggered, to create a bonded brickwork effect. Use rectangular slabs to form a basket-weave or herringbone pattern.

Alternatively, combine different size slabs to create the impression of random paving, or else mix slabs with a different type of paving to create a colourful contrast.

Hexagonal

Hexagonal slabs form honeycomb patterns. Use half slabs, running across flats or from point to point, to edge areas that are paved in straight lines. 👉

Tapered slabs

Use tapered slabs to edge ponds and for encircling trees or making curved steps. Progressively larger slabs can be used for laying circular areas of paving.

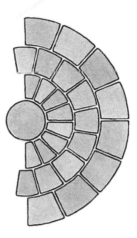

Tapered slabs

Circular slabs

Circular slabs make perfect individual stepping stones across a lawn or flower bed, but for a wide area fill the spaces between with cobbles or gravel.

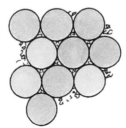

Butted circular slabs

SEE ALSO
261

Paving: paths and drives

Paths and drives are laid and compacted in the same way as rectangular pads, using similar formwork to contain the concrete. However, the proportions of most paths and drives make the inclusion of control joints essential, to allow for expansion and contraction.

Preparing the site

Excavate the site, allowing for the thickness of the subbase and concrete. Level the bottom of the excavation as accurately as you can, using a board to scrape the surface flat.

Drive accurately levelled pegs into the ground along the site, to act as datum

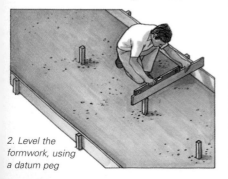

1. A water level made from a garden hose

2. Level the formwork, using a datum peg

points for the formwork. Space them about 2m (6ft 6in) apart along the centre of the pathway. Drive in the first peg until its top corresponds exactly to the proposed surface of the concrete. Use either a long straightedge and spirit level or a water level to position every other peg.

To make a water level, push a short length of transparent plastic tubing into each end of an ordinary garden hose. Holding both ends together, fill the hose with water until it appears in the tube at both ends. Then mark the level on both tubes. As long as the ends remain open, the water level at each end is constant – enabling you to establish a level over any distance, even around obstacles or corners. When you move the hose, cork each end to retain the water.

Tie one end of the hose to the first datum peg, ensuring that the marked level aligns

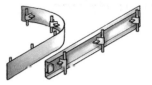

3. Curved and straight road forms

with the top of the peg. Use the other end to establish the level of every other peg along the pathway (1).

To set a fall with a water level, make a mark on one tube below the surface of the water and use that as a gauge for the top of the peg.

Erecting framework

Construct formwork from planks 25mm (1in) thick, as for a concrete pad. To check for level, rest a straightedge on the nearest datum peg (2).

If the drive or path is very long, timber formwork can be expensive and it may be

cheaper to hire metal 'road forms' (3). Straight-sided formwork is made from rigid units, but flexible sections are available to form curves.

If you want to bend wooden formwork, make a series of closely spaced, parallel sawcuts across the width of the plank in the area of the curve (4). The timber is less likely to snap if you place the sawcuts on the inside of the bend.

Installing control joints

Install a permanent expansion joint every 2m (6ft 6in) for a footpath, and every 4m (13ft) along a drive.

Cut strips of either rot-proofed hardboard or

4. Curved formwork made with wooden planks

Cuts on outside for a gentle curve

Wide cuts on inside for a tight bend

SEE ALSO
94–5

5. Support board with concrete and nails

softwood 12mm (½in) thick to fit exactly between the form-work and to match the depth of the concrete. Before pouring, hold the control joints in place with mounds of concrete and nails driven into the formwork on each side of the board (5).

As you fill the formwork, pack more concrete on both sides of each joint and tamp towards each joint from both sides, so that it is not dislodged.

On a narrow path, to prevent the concrete cracking between joints, cut grooves 18mm (¾in) deep across the compacted concrete to form dummy joints alternating with the physical ones.

The simplest method is to cut a length of T-section metal to fit between the formwork boards. Place the strip on the surface of the wet concrete and tap it down with a mallet (6). Carefully lift the strip out of the concrete to leave a neat impression. If the concrete should move, a crack will develop unnoticed at the bottom of the groove.

Place strips of thick bituminous felt between concrete and an adjoining wall to absorb expansion. Hold the felt in place with moulds of concrete before pouring the full amount of concrete.

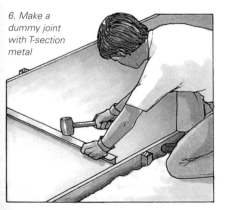

6. Make a dummy joint with T-section metal

Paving: patios

In terms of technique, laying paving slabs for a patio is no more complicated than tiling a wall, as long as you set out the area and prepare the base properly.

Lay blobs of mortar

Level the slabs

Paving slabs must be laid on a level base of sharp sand roughly 35mm (1⅜in) deep. If butting up to a lawn ensure the slabs will sit below the level of surrounding turf.

Lay the slabs on the sand, working in both directions from a corner. When satisfied, lift the slabs one at a time, so you can set them on a bed of firm mortar (1 part cement to 4 parts sand). Lay a blob under each corner,

and one more to support the centre of the slab (1).

Lay three slabs at a time, with wooden spacers between. Level each slab by tapping with a heavy hammer (2).

Gauge the slope across the paving with datum pegs along the high side. Drive into the ground so the tops correspond to the finished surface of the paving; use a straightedge with a packing piece under one end to check the fall (3). 🔨

Filling the joints

Don't walk on the paving for two to three days. If you do have to cross the area, lay planks across the slabs to spread the load.

To fill the gaps between slabs, brush a dry mortar mix of 1 part cement to 3 parts sand into the open joints (4). Remove any surplus from the surface, then sprinkle with a fine spray of water to consolidate the mortar.

3. Check the fall with a spirit level

4. Fill the joints

SEE ALSO
260

Pipes

Modern materials and technology have made it possible for anyone who is prepared to master a few techniques to upgrade pipework without having to hire a professional.

Metric and imperial pipes

Copper and stainless-steel pipes are now made in metric sizes, whereas pipework already installed in older house will have been made to imperial measurements. If you compare the equivalent dimensions (15mm – ⅝in, 22mm – ¾in, 28mm – 1in), the difference seems obvious, but metric pipe is measured externally while imperial pipe is measured internally. In fact, the difference is very small – but enough to cause problems when joining one type of pipe to another.

Metal supply pipes

Over the years, most home plumbing systems will have undergone some form of alteration. As a result, you may find any of a number of metals used, perhaps in combination, depending on the availability of materials at the time of installation or the preference of an individual plumber.

▼ *Copper pipes. The economic choice for modern, plumbing systems*

Copper

Half-hard-tempered copper tubing is by far the most widely used material for pipework. This is because it's lightweight, solders well, and can be bent easily (even by hand, with the aid of a bending spring). It is used for both hot-water and cold-water pipes, as well as for central-heating systems. ☞

Stainless steel

Stainless-steel tubing is not as common as copper. It's harder than copper, so doesn't bend easily, and is difficult to solder. It pays to use compression joints to connect stainless-steel pipes, but tighten them slightly more than you would when joining copper.

Lead

Lead is no longer used for new plumbing but there are many homes that still have a lead rising main connected to a modernized system.

Lead plumbing that is still in use must be nearing the end

of its life, so replace it as soon as possible. If you have a lead pipe supplying your drinking water, always run off a little water before you use any.

Galvanized steel (iron)
Galvanized steel was once commonly used for supply pipes, having taken over from lead. It was then superseded by copper. However, it rusts from the inside and resists water flow as it deteriorates.

Plastic supply pipes
Plastic supply pipes are made to the same standard sizes as metal pipework, but there may be a slight variation in wall thickness from one manufacturer's stock to another.

Chlorinated polyvinyl chloride (cPVC)
Versatile, suitable for hot and cold supply. It can withstand temperatures required for central-heating systems.

Polybutylene (PB)
A tough, flexible plastic pipe used for hot and cold supply, and central heating. PB resists bursting when frozen.

Cross–linked polyethylene (PEX)
PEX is used for pipes that supply hot and cold water and for underfloor heating systems. A PEX pipe resists bursting when subjected to frost.

Medium–density polyethylene (MDPE)
Widely used for underground domestic supply pipes. The pipes are resistant to pressure and corrosion.

Polybutylene (PB)

Cross-linked polyethylene (PEX)

Chlorinated polyvinyl chloride (cPVC)

Medium-density polyethylene (MDPE)

SEE ALSO
280–5

Pipes: bending

You can change the direction of a pipe run by using an elbow joint, but there are occasions when bending the pipe itself will produce a neater or more accurate result.

Using a bending spring

A bending spring is the cheapest and easiest tool for making bends in small pipe runs. It is a hardened-steel coil spring that supports the walls of copper tube to stop it kinking. Most bending springs are made to fit inside the pipe, but some slide over it.

Slide the spring into the tube, so it supports the area you want to bend. Hold the tube against your padded knee and bend it to the required angle. The bent tube will grip the spring, but slipping a screwdriver into the ring at one end and turning it anticlockwise will reduce the diameter of the spring so that you can pull it out.

If you make a bend some distance from the end of a tube, you won't be able to withdraw the bending spring in the normal way. Either use an external spring or tie a length of twine to the ring and lightly grease the spring with petroleum jelly before you insert it. Slightly overbend the

▲ *Plumbers' bending springs*

tube and open it out to the correct angle to release the spring, then pull it out with the twine.

Using a pipe bender

Although you can hire bending springs to fit the larger pipes, it isn't easy to bend a 22 or 28mm (¾ or 1in) tube over your knee – so it is well worth hiring a pipe bender to do the job.

Hold the pipe against the radiused former and insert the straight former to support it. Pull the levers towards each other to make the bend, and then open up the bender to remove the pipe.

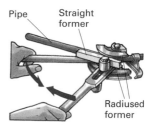

Pipe　Straight former

Radiused former

▲ *Use a pipe bender for larger tubing*

Pipes: joints

Joints are made to connect pipes at different angles and in various combinations. There are adaptors for joining metric and imperial pipes, and for connecting one kind of material to another. Consult manufacturers' catalogues to see every variation.

It would be impossible to make strong, watertight joints by simply soldering two lengths of copper pipe end to end. Instead, plumbers use capillary or compression joints.

▲ *Straight connector*
Compression joint to join two pipes of equal diameter, end to end, in a straight line

Capillary joints

Capillary joints are made to fit snugly over the ends of a pipe. The small space between the pipe and joint sleeve is filled with molten solder. When it solidifies on cooling, the solder holds the joint together and makes it water-tight. Capillary joints are neat and inexpensive – but because you need to heat the metal with a gas torch, there is a slight risk of fire when working in confined spaces under floors.

◄ *Elbow joint*
A 90 deg elbow compression joint connects two pipes at an angle

Compression joints

Compression joints are easy to use, but more expensive than capillary joints. They are also more obtrusive – it is also impossible to manoeuvre a wrench in a restricted space. Each pipe end is cut square before the joint is assembled. When the cap-nut is tightened it compresses a ring of soft metal (an olive) to fill the joint between fitting and pipe.

◄ *End-feed capillary joint (left) and integral-ring fitting (far left)*

SEE ALSO
281

Pipes: repairing

It pays to master a few techniques for coping with emergency repairs – to avoid damage to your home, as well as the high cost of calling out a plumber. All you need is a simple tool kit and a few spare parts.

Thawing frozen pipes

If water won't flow from a tap during cold weather, or a tank refuses to fill, a plug of ice may have formed in one of the supply pipes. The plug cannot be in a pipe supplying taps or float valves that are working normally, so you should be able to trace the blockage quickly. Freezing usually occurs first in the roof space.

As copper pipework transmits heat quickly, use a hairdryer to gently warm the suspect pipe, starting as close as possible to the affected tap. Leave the tap open, so water can flow normally as soon as the ice thaws.

▼ Thawing a frozen pipe
Move a hairdryer gently along a frozen pipe, working away from the blocked tap or valve

Preventative measures

Insulate pipework and fittings to stop them freezing, particularly those in the loft or under the floor. If you're going to leave the house unheated for a long time during the winter, drain the system.

A punctured pipe

Unless you know where your pipes run, it is easy to nail through one of them when fixing a loose floorboard. You may hear a hissing sound, but more likely you won't notice until you see a wet patch on the ceiling below. While the nail is in place, water will leak quite slowly, so don't pull it out until you have drained the pipe and can repair the leak. ☞

If you plan to lay fitted carpet, you can paint pipe runs on the floorboards to avoid such accidents in future.

Patching a leak

During freezing conditions, water within a pipe turns to ice, which expands until it

**◀ Binding
a split pipe**
*Bind a length of
hosepipe around a damaged
pipe, using hose clips or wire, or
use an amalgamating tape*

eventually splits the pipe or
forces a joint apart. Copper
pipework is more likely to
split than lead, which can
stretch to accommodate the
expansion. Temporarily patch
copper or lead pipes (see
above) but close up a split in
lead beforehand by tapping
the pipe gently with a
hammer. Arrange to replace
the old lead with copper as
soon as you have contained
the leak.

The only other reason for
leaking plumbing is
mechanical failure – either
through deterioration of the
materials or because a joint
has failed and is no longer
completely waterproof.

If possible, make a
permanent repair, by inserting
a new section of pipe or
replacing a leaking joint. (If it
is a compression joint that has
failed, try tightening it first.)

Binding a leaking pipe
For a temporary repair, cut a
length of garden hose to cover
the leak and slit it lengthwise,
to slip over the pipe. Bind the
hose with two or three hose
clips; or, using pliers, twist
wire loops around the hose.

Patching with epoxy putty
Epoxy putty adheres to most
metals and hard plastic and
will produce a fairly long-term
repair, although it is better to
insert a new length of pipe.

First clean a 25 to 50mm (1
to 2in) length of pipe on each
side of the leak, using wire
wool. Mix the putty and press
into the hole or around a joint,
building to a thickness of
3 to 6mm (⅛ to ¼in). It will cure
to full strength within 24
hours, but you can run low-
pressure water immediately if
you bind the putty with self-
adhesive tape.

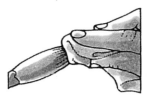

▲ Smoothing epoxy putty
*When patching a hole with epoxy
putty, smooth it with a damp
soapy cloth to give a neat finish*

SEE ALSO
382

Plaster

Plastering is carried out with modern gypsum plasters or mixes based on cement, lime and sand. Plasters are basically produced in two grades: one for 'floating' coats (basecoats) and the other for finishing coats.

Gypsum plasters

Most plaster is produced from ground gypsum by a process that removes most of the moisture from the rock. This results in a powder that sets when mixed with water. Setting times are controlled by the use of retarding additives.

Gypsum plasters are intended for interior work only; they should not be used on permanently damp walls.

Plaster of Paris

This quick-setting non-retarded gypsum plaster gives off heat as it sets. It is unsuitable for general plastering, but good for casting, and for repairs to decorative mouldings.

Carlite plaster

Carlite refers to a range of retarded gypsum plasters that are premixed with a lightweight aggregate and ready for use once water is added. The undercoat bonds well to most backgrounds. This, coupled with their light weight, makes Carlite plasters fairly easy to use.

The three types of Carlite undercoat plasters are: 'browning', 'tough coat' and 'bonding', each formulated to suit a background of a particular surface texture and suction. Browning is generally used for solid backgrounds (such as brickwork), while the more impact-resistant tough coat is for a wider range, including expanded metal lath.

Bonding undercoat is generally used for low-suction surfaces like plasterboard, dense brick or concrete blocks, or where the surface is treated with a bonding agent.

Thistle plasters

Thistle is the brand name of a range of building plasters used for a variety of conditions and backgrounds.

Two types of Thistle finishing plaster are available. Multi-finish plaster is used over sanded and hardwall undercoats, while board-finish plaster is for finishing plasterboard surfaces.

There are also special 'renovating' plasters, for use on walls with residual dampness. The undercoat is a premixed gypsum plaster with special additives; and the finish plaster, which contains a fungicide, is specially formulated for use with the undercoat.

Sanded plasters

Before modern gypsums, lime and sand for undercoats and neat lime for finishes were used in traditional wet plastering, often with animal hair added to the undercoat mix to act as a binder. Lime plasters are generally less strong than gypsum and cement-based plasters.

Single-coat plasters

A universal one-coat plaster can be used in one application on a variety of backgrounds and then trowelled to a normal finish. Ready-mixed one-coat is ideal for small repairs – but when plastering larger areas, it's more economical to buy bigger bags.

Skim-coat plaster

A brush-on skim-coat plaster is applied up to 3mm (⅛in) thick, using a wide brush, and then smoothed with a trowel or spreader. When firm, it is polished with a damp sponge.

Fillers

Fillers are fine plaster powders used for repairs. Some, reinforced with cellulose resin, are sold in small packs and are ideal for filling cracks in plaster and wood. ☛

SEE ALSO
365

Plaster: buying and storing

Plaster powder is normally sold in 25kg (55lb) paper sacks. Smaller sizes, including 2.5kg (5½lb) bags, are available from DIY stores for repairing damaged plasterwork. It is generally more economical to buy the larger sacks, but this depends on the scale of the work.

Try to buy only as much plaster as you think you need – although it's best to overestimate slightly, to allow for wastage and to avoid running out of plaster at an inconvenient moment.

Storage

Store plaster in dry conditions. If it is going to be kept in an outbuilding for some time, cover it with plastic sheeting to protect it from moisture. Keep the paper bags off a concrete floor by placing them on boards or plastic sheeting.

Once opened, bags are more likely to absorb moisture, which can shorten the setting time and weaken the plaster, so keep an opened bag in a plastic sack sealed with self-adhesive tape. Discard plaster that contains lumps.

Pre-mixed plaster

Ready-to-use plaster is available in plastic tubs. It can be more expensive to buy, but it is easier for amateurs to use and will keep for a long time, provided the airtight lid is sealed well.

This type of plaster will also stay workable for up to an hour, and some types can be built up to a thickness of 50mm (2in).

If you are attempting to cover a large area, though, it might be more economical to buy a larger bag and keep it well stored.

◄ Storing plaster
Keep an opened bag of plaster in a plastic sack sealed with adhesive tape

Plaster: mixing

Mixing plaster can be a messy job, so spread plastic dust sheets or old newspapers across the floor where you are working, and remember to wipe your feet when leaving the room.

Plaster mixed to the correct consistency will be easier to apply. Use a plastic bucket to measure the materials accurately. For large quantities, multiply the number of bucket measures; for small quantities, use half-bucket measures.

Old gypsum plaster stuck to your tools or equipment can shorten the setting time and reduce the strength of newly mixed plaster. Discard plaster that has begun to set and make a fresh batch: don't try to rework it by adding more water.

Using bonding agents

Bonding agents are used to modify the suction of the background or improve plaster adhesion. When using a bonding agent, don't apply a basecoat plaster any thicker than 10mm (⅜in) at a time.

Bonding agents can be mixed with plaster or sand and cement to fill cracks. Brush away loose particles, then use a brush to apply a priming coat of 1 part agent to 3–5 parts

▲ *Clean up as you go*
Wash tools and brushes thoroughly in clean water. On a large job, it may be necessary to rinse out your brushes as the work progresses

water. Mix to a stiff consistency, using 1 part bonding agent to 1 part water. Apply the filler with a trowel, pressing it well into the cracks.

Carrying plaster filler

It's easier to work with plaster on lightweight boards. You can use 6mm (¼in) exterior-grade plywood for mixing and carrying filler. Cut out a 300mm (1ft) square with a projecting handle, or make a thumb hole as in an artist's palette. Seal the surface with varnish, or apply a plastic laminate for a smooth finish.

SEE ALSO
276

Plaster: plasterboard

Plasterboard provides a quick and simple method of cladding walls or ceilings with a smooth surface for decorating. It offers good sound insulation as well as fire protection. It is quite easy to cut and to fix, either by bonding or by nailing it into place.

Plasterboard is fragile, having little structural strength. But despite its fragility, the sheets are quite heavy. Always carry it vertically on edge: there is a serious risk of breaking it if you carry a board face up.

Plasterboard manufacturers and suppliers store the boards flat in stacks, but this is usually inconvenient at home. Store them on edge instead, leaning them at a slight angle against a wall, with their ivory-coloured faces together to protect them.

Cutting plasterboard
You can cut plasterboard with a saw or with a stiff-blade craft knife. Support a sheet face side up on lengths of wood laid across trestles. Mark the cutting line on it with a straightedge. When sawing plasterboard, hold the saw at a shallow angle to the surface of the board. If the offcut is large, support it as you near the end of the cut to prevent the board breaking.

When slicing plasterboard with a knife, cut fairly deeply into the material, then snap the board along the cutting line over a length of wood. Cut through the paper facing on the other side to separate the two pieces.

Use a keyhole saw, power jigsaw or stiff-blade craft knife to cut openings in plasterboard for switches and other electrical fittings. ☛

▼ *Cutting plasterboard*
Cut plasterboard to size with a panel saw or craft knife. Use a keyhole saw, power jigsaw or knife to cut openings in the board

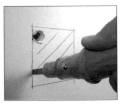

Plaster: textured coatings

Textured coatings come as a dry powder for mixing with warm water or in a ready-mixed form for direct application from the tub. You can produce a variety of textures using rollers, scrapers or improvised tools.

Applying textured coatings

You can apply the coating using a roller or broad wall brush, but finer textures are possible with the brush.

With a well-loaded roller, apply a generous coat in a band 600mm (2ft) wide across the ceiling or a wall. Don't press too hard and vary the angle of the stroke. If using a brush, don't spread it like paint. Lay it on with one stroke and spread it back again with one or two strokes only.

Texture the first band, then apply a second band and blend them together before texturing the latter.

Painting around fittings

Use a small paintbrush to fill in around electrical fittings and along edges, trying to copy the texture used on the surrounding wall or ceiling.

Creating a texture

You can experiment with a variety of tools to make any number of textures. 🐟

Creating patterns

You can make geometric patterns with a roller; achieve a stippled finish with a damp sponge, then twist a damp sponge on the surface and make a swirling design; use a toothed spatula to create combed patterns; produce a bark texture with a spiral-grooved roller, then use the rounded corner of a spatula in short straight strokes.

▲ *Painting around fittings*

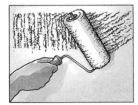

▲ *Creating a texture*

🐟
SEE ALSO
274–5

🐟
SEE ALSO
251

Plasterwork: plasterboarding

Plasterboard can be nailed to the timber studs of a partition wall, or screwed to metal ones. It can also be nailed to battens fixed to a masonry wall or bonded onto solid walls with plaster or adhesive. Generally boards are fitted vertically. Plasterboard the ceiling in a room first.

Methods for fixing

Fixing to a stud partition
Partition walls may be plain room-dividers or could include doorways. If plasterboarding a plain wall, fit the boards from one corner; if the wall includes a doorway, work away from the doorway towards the corners of the room.

Starting from a corner
Using a footlifter (see opposite), hold the first board in position. If necessary, mark and scribe the edge that meets

the adjacent wall. Then fix the board into position, securing it to all of the frame members.

Fix the rest of the boards in place, working across the partition. Butt the edges of tapered-edge boards, but leave a gap of 3mm (⅛in) between square-edge boards that are to be coated with a board-finishing plaster.

Cut a skirting board, mitring

▼ *Procedure for plasterboarding*
On a plain wall, work away from a corner. Otherwise, work away from a doorway

the joints at the corners or scribing the ends of the new board to the original. Fit the skirting board.

Starting from a doorway
Using the footlifter, hold the first board flush with the door stud and mark the position of the underside of the door head on the edge of the board. Between this mark and the board's top edge, cut out a 25mm (1in) wide strip. Reposition the board and fix it in place, securing it to all the frame members.

Fix the rest of the boards in place, working towards the corner. Butt the edges of tapered-edge boards, but leave a 3mm (⅛in) gap between boards that you intend to coat afterwards with a board-finishing plaster.

Scribe the last board to fit any irregularities in the corner before fixing it in place.

Cover the rest of the wall, on the other side of the doorway, in a similar way, starting by cutting a 25mm (1in) wide strip from the first board between its top edge and a mark indicating the lower side of the door head. 🖎

Cut a plasterboard panel to go above the doorway, fitting

▲ ***Using a footlifter***
A footlifter is a simple tool that holds the board against the ceiling, leaving both hands free for nailing. You can make one from a block of wood 75mm (3in) wide

it into the cutouts you made in the boards on each side of the door. Sand away any ragged paper at the edges before fitting the panel.

Clad the other side of the partition with plasterboard in the same way.

When all of the plasterboard is in place, fill and finish the joints. Cut and fit solid wood door linings, and cover the edges with an architrave moulding.

Cut and fit skirting boards, nailing or screwing through the plasterboard into alternate studs behind.

🖎
SEE ALSO
272

Plasterwork: preparation

As you are bound to drop some plaster at first, it pays to cover the floor with a dust sheet. Don't try to reuse dropped plaster as it can become contaminated.

Setting up

In addition to specialized plasterer's tools, you need a spirit level and some lengths of planed softwood battening 10mm (⅜in) thick. The battens, known as screeds, are nailed to the wall to act as guides when it comes to levelling the plaster. Professional plasterers form 'plaster screeds' by applying bands of undercoat plaster to the required thickness. These can be laid vertically or horizontally.

After preparing the background, fix wooden screeds vertically to the wall with masonry nails. Drive most of the nails fully home to make it easier for you to work with the trowel; leave one or two nails protruding slightly so that you can remove the screeds afterwards. The screeds should be spaced no more than 600mm (2ft) apart. Use the spirit level to get them truly plumb, packing them out with strips of hardboard as need be (see opposite).

Mix the undercoat plaster to a thick, creamy consistency and, to begin with, measure out two bucketfuls. You can increase this to larger amounts when you become more proficient.

Undercoat plastering

Use the face of a plasterer's trowel to scrape a couple of trowel-loads of plaster onto the hawk, and start the undercoat-plastering at the top of the wall. Holding the trowel at an angle to the face of the wall, apply the plaster with vertical strokes. Work from right to left if you are right-handed; if you're left-handed, work from left to right.

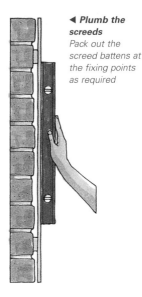

◄ Plumb the screeds
Pack out the screed battens at the fixing points as required

Using firm pressure to ensure good adhesion, apply a thin layer first, then follow it with more plaster, building up to the required thickness. If the final thickness of the plaster needs to be greater than 10mm (⅜in), key the surface with a scratcher and let it set, then apply a second or 'floating' coat.

Fill the area between two screed battens, but there's no need to pack the plaster tightly up against them. Level the surface with a rule laid across the battens, sliding the rule from side to side as you work upwards from the bottom of the wall. Fill in any hollows, and then level the plaster again. Scratch the surface lightly, to provide a key for the finishing coat, and let the plaster set.

Work along the entire wall in this way, and then remove the battens. Fill the gaps, levelling the plaster with the rule or trowel. ☞

Preparation for textured coatings
If you are planning to create a textured surface, then new surfaces will need virtually no preparation. However, joints between plasterboard must be reinforced with tape.

For older walls and ceilings, strip any wallcoverings and key gloss paint with glasspaper. Old walls and ceilings must be scrupulously clean, dry, sound and free from organic growth. Treat friable surfaces with stabilizing solution.

Although large cracks and holes in surfaces have to be filled, a textured coating will cover over most minor defects in walls and ceilings by filling small cracks and bridging shallow bumps and hollows. ☞

SEE ALSO
278–9

SEE ALSO
368–9

Plasterwork: techniques

Plastering has only two basic requirements: that the plaster should stick well to its background and that it should be brought to a smooth, flat finish. Thorough preparation and careful choice of plaster and tools should ensure good adhesion, but the ability to achieve a smooth, flat surface will come only after some practice.

1. Load the hawk

Picking up plaster

Hold the edge of your hawk below the mortar board and use your trowel to scrape a manageable amount of plaster onto its surface (1). Take no more than a trowelful to start with.

Tip the hawk towards you and, in one movement, cut away about half of the plaster with the trowel, scraping and lifting it off the hawk and onto the face of the trowel (2).

2. Lift the plaster

Applying the plaster

Hold the loaded trowel horizontally, tilted at an angle to the face of the wall (3). Apply the plaster with a vertical upward stroke, pressing firmly so that plaster is 'fed' onto the wall. Flatten the angle of the trowel as you go (4) – but never let its whole face come into contact with the plaster, or it may induce suction and pull it off the wall.

Levelling up

Build a slight extra thickness of plaster onto the wall with the trowel, applying it as evenly as possible. Use a straightedged rule to level the

3. Tilt the trowel

4. Apply the plaster

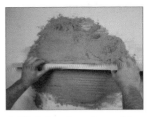

▲ *Work the rule up the wall to level the surface*

surface. Hold the rule firmly against the original plaster or against wooden screeds nailed in place at either side. Work the rule upwards while moving it from side to side, then lift it carefully away, taking the surplus plaster with it. Fill in any hollows, with more plaster from the trowel, then level the surface again. Allow one-coat plaster to stiffen before you smooth it finally with a trowel. For two-coat work, scrape back the edges slightly ready for the finish coat.

Finishing the plaster

Apply the finish coat of plaster over a gypsum-plaster undercoat as soon as it has set. 🐟

A cement-based sanded plaster must be allowed to dry thoroughly, but dampen its surface in order to adjust suction before applying finish plaster. The papered face of plasterboard can be finished immediately, without the need for wetting.

Use a plasterer's trowel to apply the finish plaster, spreading it evenly to a thickness of 2mm (½2in) – and not more than 3mm (⅛in) – judging this by eye.

As the plaster stiffens, brush it or lightly spray it with water, then trowel the surface so as to consolidate it and produce a smooth matt finish. Avoid pressing too hard or overworking the surface, as the plaster can be easily disturbed at this stage, before it has properly 'gone off'. Sponge off any surplus water, again taking care not to interfere with the smooth finish of the plaster.

▼ *Spray plaster occasionally as you smooth it*

🐟
SEE ALSO
268–9

Plumbing: dishwashers and washing machines

Nowadays dishwashers and washing machines are to be found in most kitchens or utility rooms. Made to standard sizes to conform with kitchen fitments, they fit neatly under a work surface and are attached by flexible hoses to a dedicated waste pipe or to the waste from the kitchen or utility-room sink.

Water pressure

The instructions accompanying the machine should indicate what water pressure is required. If the machine is installed upstairs, make sure the drop from the storage tank to the machine is big enough to provide the required pressure. In a downstairs kitchen or utility room there is rarely any problem with pressure, especially if you can take the cold water from the mains supply at the sink. However, check with your water supplier if you want to connect more than one machine.

Running the supply

Washing machines and dishwashers are supplied with PVC hoses to link the water inlets at the back of the appliance to special miniature valves connected to the household plumbing. Using these valves, you can turn off the water when you need to service a machine, without

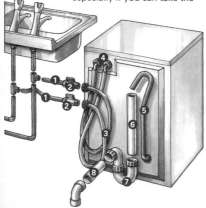

Plumbing a washing machine
1. Supply pipe – 15mm (⅝in)
2. Appliance valve
3. PVC inlet hoses
4. Machine inlets
5. Outlet hose
6. Standpipe
7. Trap
8. Waste pipe – 40mm (1½in) – to gully

Appliance valves

▶ *In-line valve*

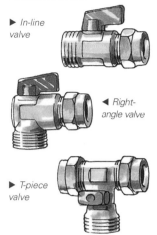

◀ *Right-angle valve*

▶ *T-piece valve*

having to disrupt the supply to the rest of the house. There are a number of valves to choose from. Select the type that provides the most practical method of connecting to the plumbing, depending on the location of the machine in relation to existing pipework.

Self-bore valves

When 15mm (⅝in) cold and hot pipes run conveniently behind or alongside the machine, use a valve that will bore a hole in the pipe without your having to turn off the water and drain the system. Each valve is colour-coded for hot or cold, and has a threaded outlet for the standard machine hose. The only problem with self-bore valves is that occasionally the cut disc of metal can restrict the water supply.

To fit a valve, screw the backplate to the wall behind the pipe. Place the saddle with its rubber seal over the pipe. Before screwing the saddle to the backplate (1), ensure that the seal in the saddle is positioned correctly.

Make sure that the valve is turned off, then screw it into the saddle (2). The integral cutter will bore a hole in the pipe. With the valve in the vertical position, tighten the adjusting nut with a spanner (3); then connect the hose to the valve outlet (4).

1. Fit the saddle

2. Insert the valve

3. Tighten the nut

4. Attach the hose

SEE ALSO
262–5

Connecting a washing machine

There is no great mystery to connecting up a washing machine or even running a water supply for one, providing you follow a few simple rules.

First of all, thoroughly read the manufacturer's instructions that come with the washing machine. Check that wherever you are going to install the machine, the water pressure level will be high enough to run it satisfactorily.

The most common location for a washing machine is in the kitchen near the sink. There are two good reasons for this: firstly, the mains water feed normally begins in the kitchen, so the water pressure here will be more than sufficient to run the machine; and secondly, the dirty water from the machine can be connected to the waste system very simply.

When you purchase a new washing machine, it will come with two inlet hoses – a blue one for the cold water supply and a red one for the hot water. These hoses are connected to the outlets on the back of the machine [A] via washing machine valves

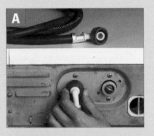

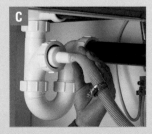

Tools

Screwdriver
Spirit level
PTFE tape

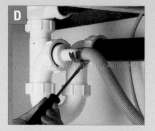

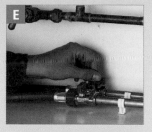

attached to the water supply [B]. These are colour coded.

Some machines have only a cold supply with just one hose, in which case the fitting procedure is exactly the same as for a machine with a dual water supply. However, it is generally much slower to run this type of appliance, because the water has to be heated in the machine.

The hook-shaped waste hose is fitted into a 40mm (1⅝in) vertical plastic waste pipe attached to a deep seal trap and away to a gully. The hose is loosely fitted into the standpipe to avoid dirty water being siphoned back into the machine. Ensure that the pipe is a minimum of 610mm (24in) in height from the floor [C].

Some sink waste traps have a spigot end to attach a washing machine. Make sure you fit an in-line anti-siphon valve, to avoid dirty water

returning into the machine. The valve fits in the machine outlet hose simply with a hose connector at each end [D].

Don't forget to turn on the power and the valves before you slide the machine into place [E]. If you spot a slight leak on the valve connection, wrap some PTFE tape around the thread [F] and reconnect the fittings.

Plumbing in a dishwasher involves exactly the same process as that used for the washing machine, except that a dishwasher normally only has a single cold water supply.

Running branch pipes

If you have to extend the plumbing to reach your machine, take branch pipes from the hot and cold pipes supplying the kitchen taps. Terminate the branch pipes at a convenient position close to the machine, and fit a small appliance valve that has a standard compression joint for connecting to the pipework and a threaded outlet for the machine hose.

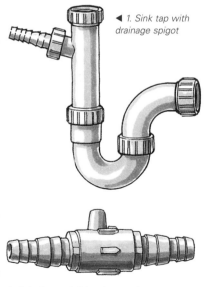

◄ 1. Sink tap with drainage spigot

▲ 2. In-line anti-siphon hose valve

Supplying drainage

The outlet hose from a dishwasher or washing machine must be connected to a waste system that will discharge the dirty water into either a yard gully or a single waste stack.

Standpipe and trap

The standard method, approved by all water suppliers, employs a vertical 40mm (1⅝in) plastic standpipe attached to a deep-seal trap.

The standpipe, trap and wall fixings come as a kit. The machine hose fits loosely into the open-ended pipe, so that dirty water won't be siphoned back into the machine. Cut a hole through the wall and run the waste pipe to a gully; or use a pipe boss to connect the waste to a drainage stack.

Draining to a sink trap

You can drain a washing machine to a sink trap that has a built-in spigot (1), but you should insert an in-line anti-siphon return valve in the machine's outlet hose. This is a small plastic device with a hose connector at each end (2). In order to drain a washing machine and dishwasher together, you will need a dual-spigot trap.

Plumbing: water softeners

Hard water scale will discolour baths and basins, fur-up kettles and eventually block pipework. Most people resign themselves to living with these effects, but they can be reduced or even eliminated by installing a water softener.

Domestic water softeners
Water softeners work on the principle of ion exchange. The incoming water flows through a compartment containing a synthetic resin that absorbs scale-forming calcium and magnesium ions and releases sodium ions in their place.

The unit must be connected to the rising main at the point where the water supply enters the house. For this reason, water softeners are usually designed to fit under a kitchen worktop.

Installing a water softener
Be sure to include the fittings that are necessary to comply with the Water Regulations – a bypass assembly allowing for the unit to be isolated for servicing, as well as a branch pipe, in order to supply unsoftened drinking water to the kitchen sink. 🔺

Install a non-return valve in the system, to prevent the reverse flow of salty water. A pressure-reducing valve may also be required. You will need a draincock, in order to empty the rising main. You will have to provide drainage in the form of a standpipe and trap, as for a washing machine.

Get an electrician to wire the water softener to a switched fused connection unit that contains a 3amp fuse.

◄ **Plumbing a water softener**

Drain rising main and insert the following installation. Use 15mm (⅝in) pipes and joints

1. Main stopcock
2. Drinking-water pipe
3. Supply to garden tap
4. Non-return valve
5. Draincock
6. Softener inlet valve
7. Bypass valve (open this valve and close the others to service the softener)
8. Softener return valve
9. Rising main

SEE ALSO
380

Ponds: choosing a pond liner

It is not by chance that the number of garden ponds has greatly increased in recent years. Their popularity is largely due to the fact that easily installed rigid and flexible pond liners are now readily available, which make it possible to create a water garden by putting in just a few days' work.

In the past it was necessary to line a pond with concrete. While concrete is a very versatile material, there is always the possibility of a leak developing through cracks caused by ground movement or the force of expanding ice.

There are no such worries with flexible liners or those made from rigid plastic. Building formers for a concrete pond involves both labour and expense, and when the pond is finished it has to be left to season for about a month – during which time it needs to be emptied and refilled a number of times to ensure the water will be safe for fish and plant life. In contrast, you can introduce plants into a pool lined with plastic or rubber as soon as the water has matured, which takes no more than a few days.

Ordering a flexible liner

Use a simple formula to calculate the size of liner you will need. Disregard any complicated shapes, planting shelves, and so on; simply take the overall length and width of the pond and add twice the maximum depth to each dimension to arrive at the size of the liner. If possible, adapt your design to fall within the nearest stock liner size.

POND DIMENSIONS	
Length – 3m	9ft 9in
Width – 2m	6ft 6in
Depth – 450mm	1ft 6in
SIZE OF LINER	
3m + 0.900m = 3.9m	9ft 9in + 3ft = 12ft 9in
2m + 0.900m =2.9m	6ft 6in + 3ft = 9ft 6in

Choosing a pond liner

The advantages of proprietary pond liners over concrete are fairly obvious, but there are a number of options to choose from – depending on the size and shape of the pond you

▲ *Rigid liners are moulded from plastic*

wish to create and how much you are planning to spend.

Rigid plastic liners

Regular visitors to garden centres will be familiar with the range of preformed plastic pond liners. A rigid liner is in effect a ready-made one-piece pond – including planting shelves and, in some cases, recessed troughs to accommodate marsh or bog gardens.

The best pond liners are those made from rigid glass-reinforced plastic (fibreglass), which is very strong and is also resistant to the effects of frost or ice. Almost as good, and more economical, are liners made from vacuum-formed plastic. Provided they are handled with a reasonable degree of care and installed correctly, rigid plastic pond liners are practically leak-proof. A very acceptable water garden can be created with a

carefully selected series of pond liners linked together by watercourses.

Flexible liners

For complete freedom of design, choose a flexible-sheet liner that will hug the contours of a pond of virtually any shape and size. Flexible plastic pond liners range from inexpensive polyvinyl acetate (PVC) and polythene sheet to better-quality low-density polythene and nylon-reinforced PVC. Plastic liners, especially those reinforced with nylon, are guaranteed for many years of normal use – but if you want your pond to last for 50 years or more, choose a thicker membrane made from synthetic butyl rubber. Black and stone-coloured butyl liners are made in a wide range of stock sizes, up to 6.5 x 10.75m (22 x 35ft); and larger liners can be supplied to order.

▼ *The best-quality flexible pond liners are made from butyl*

SEE ALSO
86–9

Ponds: constructing a pond

A pond must be sited correctly if it is to have any chance of maturing into an attractive, clear stretch of water. Don't place a pond under deciduous trees: falling leaves will pollute the water as they decay, causing fish to become ill or die. Laburnum trees are especially poisonous.

The need for sunlight
Although sunlight promotes the growth of algae, which cause ponds to turn a pea-green colour, it is also necessary to encourage the growth of other water plants. An abundance of oxygenating plants will compete with the algae for mineral salts and, aided by the shade that is cast by floating and marginal plants, will help to keep the pond clear.

Volume of water
The pond's dimensions are important in creating harmony between plants and fish. It is difficult to maintain the right conditions for clear water in a pond that is less than 3.75sq m (40sq ft) in surface area – but the volume of water is even more vital. A pond up to about 9sq m (100sq ft) in area needs to be 450mm (1ft 6in) deep. As the area increases you will have to dig deeper, to about 600mm (2ft) or more,

although it's hardly ever necessary to dig deeper than 750mm (2ft 6in).

Designing the shape of your pond
Although there's a huge variety of rigid-plastic liners available, you are limited to the shapes selected by the manufacturers. There are no such limitations if you use a flexible pond liner, although curved shapes take up the slack better than straight-sided pools do.

The profile of the pond must be designed to fulfil certain requirements. To grow marginal plants, you will need a shelf 225mm (9in) wide around the edge of the pond, 225mm (9in) below the surface of the water. This will take a standard 150mm (6in) planting crate, with ample water above, and you can always raise the crate on bricks or pieces of paving. The sides of the pond should

▼ *Important dimensions for a garden pond*

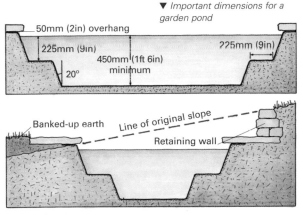

50mm (2in) overhang

225mm (9in)

225mm (9in)

450mm (1ft 6in) minimum

20°

Banked-up earth

Line of original slope

Retaining wall

▲ *A sloping site*

slope at about 20 deg, to prevent the collapse of soil during construction and to allow the liner to stretch without promoting too many creases. It will also allow a sheet of ice to float upwards without damaging the liner. Judge the angle by measuring 75mm (3in) inwards for every 225mm (9in) of depth. If the soil is very sandy, increase the angle of slope slightly for extra stability.

Installing a rigid liner

Stand a rigid pond liner in position and prop it up with cardboard boxes, both to check its orientation and to mark its perimeter on the ground.

Use a spirit level to plot key points on the ground (1), and mark them with small pegs. You will need to dig outside this line, so absolute accuracy is not required.

As you remove the topsoil, either take it away in a

1. Mark the perimeter of the liner

SEE ALSO
258

2. Measure the depth of the excavation

same time, pour sifted soil or sand behind the liner (4). There's no need to hurry as you do this, as it will take some time to fill the pond, but try to keep pace with the level of the water. Reach into the excavation and pack soil under the marginal shelves with your hands in order to firm them up.

When the liner is firmly bedded in the soil, either finish the edge with stones as for a flexible liner (see opposite) or re-lay turf to cover the rim of the liner.

wheelbarrow or pile it close by, ready to incorporate into a rockery. Lay a straightedge across the top and measure the depth of the excavation (2), including marginal shelves. Keep the excavation as close as possible to the shape of the liner, but extend it by 150mm (6in) on all sides. Compact the base and cover it with a layer of sharp sand 25mm (1in) deep. Lower the liner and bed it down firmly into the sand. Check that the pool stands level (3) and wedge it temporarily with wooden battens until the backfill of soil or sand can hold it.

Start to fill the liner with water from a hose and, at the

3. Make sure the liner stands level

4 Infill with sifted soil or sand

Installing a flexible liner

Mark out the shape of the pond on the ground – a garden hose is useful for trying out curves. Before you start excavating the soil, look down from an upstairs window at the shape you have plotted, to make sure that you are happy with the proportions of your pond.

1. Dig the excavation as accurately as possible

Excavating the pond

Excavate the pond to the level of the planting shelf, then mark and dig out the deeper sections (1). Remove sharp stones and roots from the sides and bottom of the excavation.

2. Level the edge using datum pegs

The slabs surrounding the pond need to be 18mm (¾in) below the turf. Cut back the turf to allow for the stones and then, every metre (3ft) or so, drive wooden datum pegs into the exposed surround. Level the tops of all the pegs, and use a straightedge (2) to check the level across the pond as well. Remove or pack earth around the pegs to bring the surrounding soil to a consistent level.

When the pond's surround is level, remove the pegs and, to cushion the liner, spread a 12 to 25mm (½ to 1in) layer of

3. Line the excavation with damp sand

slightly damp sand over the base and sides of the excavation (3). Alternatively, cover the excavation with a proprietary pond-liner underlay.

SEE ALSO
258

Installing the liner

Drape the liner across the excavation with an even overlap all round. Hold it in place with bricks while you introduce water from a hose (4). Filling a large pond will take several hours, but check the liner regularly, moving the bricks as it stretches. A few creases are inevitable, but you can lose most of them if you keep the liner fairly taut and ease it into shape as the water rises.

When the level reaches 50mm (2in) below the edge, turn off the water. Cut off surplus liner with scissors, leaving a 150mm (6in) overlap all round (5). Push long nails through the overlap into the soil, so the liner can't slip.

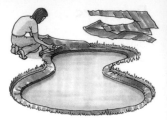

5. Cut the flexible liner to fit

6. Lay edging stones to complete the pond

Laying the surround

Select flat stones that follow the shape of the pond, with a reasonably close fit between them. Let the stones project over the water by about 50mm (2in).

Wearing goggles, use a bolster to cut stones to fit the gaps behind the larger edging stones. Lift the stones one or two at a time and bed them on two or three strategically placed mounds of mortar (1 part cement : 3 parts soft sand) (6).

Tap the stones level with a mallet and fill the joints with a trowel. Use an old paintbrush to smooth the joints flush.

4. Stretch the liner by filling the pond

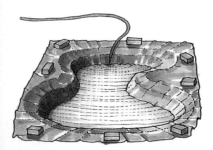

Primers

Thorough preparation of all surfaces is a vital first step in redecorating. This means removing dirt and flaking finishes, as well as repairing serious deterioration. However, it is not only old surfaces that need attention: new timber and surfaces should also be thoroughly sealed and primed.

Types of primer and sealer

There are numerous primers and sealers to suit a variety of materials. 👉

Stabilizing primer
Used to bind powdery or flaky materials. A clear or white liquid.

Wood primer
Standard solvent-based pink or white primer prevents other coats of paint soaking in.

Acrylic wood primer
Fast-drying water-based primer. Some types can be used for undercoating.

Aluminium wood primer
Used to seal oily hardwoods and resinous softwoods. It will also cover creosote.

General-purpose primer
Seals porous building materials and covers patchy walls and ceilings. Some multi-purpose primers are suitable for wood, metal and plaster.

Metal primers
Essential to prevent corrosion in metals and to provide a key for paint. Special rust-inhibitive primers treat rust and prevent its recurrence.

PVA bonding agent
A general-purpose liquid adhesive for many building materials. An excellent primer and sealer when diluted, even for bituminous paints.

Water repellent
A liquid used for sealing masonry against water penetration. It dries colourless.

Alkali-resistant primer
Used to prevent the alkali content of some materials attacking oil paints.

Aluminium spirit-based sealer
Formulated to obliterate materials likely to 'bleed' through subsequent coatings. Effective over bituminous

SEE ALSO
348–9

paints, creosote and metallic paints.

Stain sealer
Permanently seals problem stains such as nicotine, water, soot, crayon, lipstick and ballpoint pen.

Panel-system primer
Provides better adhesion for masonry paints. Can also be used to reinforce repaired cracks in exterior render.

▼ Primers and sealers
Suitability, drying time and coverage. Black dot denotes that primer and surface are compatible

	1	2	3	4	5	6	7	8	9	10	11	12	13	14
Suitable for														
Brick	•				•				•	•	•			
Stone	•				•				•	•	•			
Cement rendering	•				•				•	•	•			•
Concrete	•				•				•	•	•			
Plaster	•				•				•		•		•	
Plasterboard	•				•						•		•	
Distemper	•													
Limewash	•													
Cement paint	•													
Bitumen-based paints									•			•		
Asbestos cement	•				•				•		•			
Softwoods/hardwoods		•	•	•	•									
Oily hardwoods				•										
Chipboard		•	•	•	•									•
Hardboard		•	•	•	•									•
Plywood		•	•	•	•									•
Creosoted timber				•								•		
Absorbent fibre boards	•										•			
Ferrous metals (inside)						•		•						
Ferrous metals (outside)						•	•							
Galvanized metal						•	•							
Aluminium						•	•							
Drying time: Hours														
Touch-dry	3	4-6	0.5	4-6	4-6	4	0.5	2	3	1	4	0.25	2-3	-
Recoatable	16	16	2	16	16	16	6	6	16	16	16	1	6-8	24
Coverage (sq m per litre)														
Smooth surface	6	12	12	13	12	13	8	8	9	3-6	10	4	18	6
Rough/absorbent surface	7	10	10	11	9	10	-	6	7	2-3	7	3	-	3

KEY
1. Stabilizing primer 2. Wood primer 3. Acrylic wood primer 4. Aluminium wood primer
5. General-purpose primer 6. Zinc-phosphate primer 7. Fast-drying metal primer 8. Rust-inhibitive primer
9. PVA bonding agent 10. Water repellent 11. Alkali-resistant primer 12. Aluminium spirit-based sealer
13. Stain sealer 14. Panel system primer

Priming brickwork for painting

Brickwork will only need to be primed if it is showing signs of efflorescence or spalling. An alkali-resistant primer will guard against the former. A stabilizing solution will bind crumbling masonry and also help to seal it.

When you are painting a wall for the first time with masonry paint, you may find that the first coat is difficult to apply due to the suction of the dry, porous brick. Thin the first coat slightly with water or solvent.

▲ *Spalled bricks should be painted with a clear water-repellent*

Waterproofing masonry

Colourless water-repellent fluids are intended to make masonry impervious to water without colouring it or stopping it from breathing – which is important in order to allow moisture within the walls to dry out.

Prepare the surface before applying the fluid: make good any cracks in bricks or pointing and remove organic growth, then allow the wall to dry out thoroughly. Cover adjacent plants.

The fumes from water-repellent fluid can be dangerous if inhaled, so be sure to wear a proper respirator as recommended by the manufacturer. Also, wear eye protectors.

Apply the fluid generously with a large paintbrush, from the bottom up, and stipple it into the joints. Apply a second coat as soon as the first has been absorbed, to ensure that there are no bare patches where water could seep in. So that you can be sure you are covering the wall properly, use a sealant containing a fugitive dye, which disappears after a specified period of time.

Carefully paint up to surrounding woodwork. If you accidentally splash sealant onto it, wash it down immediately with a cloth dampened with white spirit.

SEE ALSO
225

If you need to treat a whole house, it may be worth hiring a company that can spray the sealant. Make sure the workmen rig up plastic-sheet screens to prevent overspray drifting across to your neighbours' property.

Priming cork wall tiles

Dense prefinished cork wall tiles can be painted directly, provided that they are clean and firmly attached to the wall. Prime very absorbent cork with a general-purpose primer first or, when using emulsion or water-based acrylic paint, thin the first coat in order to reduce absorption.

Unless the tiles are textured or pierced, they can be papered over – but size the surface with commercial size or heavy-duty wallpaper paste, and then apply lining paper to prevent joins showing through.

Treating bare metal

Remove light deposits of rust by rubbing with wire wool or wet-and-dry abrasive paper, dipping them in white spirit. If the rust is heavy and the surface of the metal pitted, use a wire brush or, for extensive corrosion, a wire wheel or cup brush in a power drill. Wear goggles while you are wire-brushing, to protect your eyes from flying particles.

Use a zinc-phosphate primer to protect metal inside the house. You can use the same primer outdoors, too – but if you are painting previously rusted metal, especially if it is in a very exposed location, you will need to use a high-performance rust-inhibitive primer.

Work primers into crevices and fixings, and make sure sharp edges and corners are coated generously.

Preparing previously painted metal

If the paint is perfectly sound, wash it with sugar soap or with a detergent solution, then rinse and dry it. Rub down gloss paint with fine wet-and-dry abrasive paper, to provide a key.

If the paint film is blistered or is flaking (where water has penetrated and corrosion has set in), remove all loose paint and rust with a wire brush or with a wire wheel or cup brush in a power drill. Apply rust-inhibitive primer to any bare patches, working it well into joints, bolt heads and other fixings. Prime bare metal immediately, as rust can re-form very rapidly.

When you are preparing cast-iron guttering, brush out dead leaves and other debris, then wash it clean. Coat the inside with a bitumen paint. If you want to paint over old bitumen paint, use an aluminium primer first, to prevent it bleeding to the surface.

Priming plasterboard

Before plasterboard can be decorated, it must be sealed by the application of a primer. One coat of general-purpose primer evens out the absorption of the board and joint fillers, and provides a sound surface for most decorative treatments. It also protects the board when steam-stripping wallpaper.

An alternative is to use a proprietary sealer coat, applied with a brush or roller. It is suitable for most decorative treatments. Two coats will serve as a vapour barrier and provide a more durable finish.

▶ Apply a primer to even out absorption

SEE ALSO
274–7

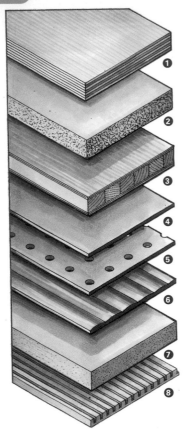

Man-made boards
1. Plywood 2. Chipboard
3. Blockboard 4. Standard hardboard
5. Perforated hardboard 6. Textured
hardboard 7. Medium-density
fibreboard (MDF) 8. Flexible MDF

Preparing man-made boards for decoration

Wallboards such as plywood, MDF, chipboard, blockboard, hardboard and softboard are all made from wood, but they must be prepared differently from natural timber. Their finish varies according to the quality of the board: some are compact and smooth, and may even be presealed ready for painting; others must be filled and sanded before you can get a really smooth finish.

As a rough guide, no primer will be required when using acrylic paints, other than a sealing coat of the paint itself, slightly thinned with water. However, any nail or screw heads must be driven below the surface and coated with zinc-phosphate primer to prevent rust stains.

Apply one coat of panel-system primer before painting building boards with masonry paint. If you are using solvent-based paint, prime the boards first with a general-purpose primer or, for porous softboard, a stabilizing primer. Where possible, you should prime both sides of the board. If the boards are presealed, you can apply undercoat directly to the surface.

Q

Quantity estimation

Estimating quantities is an intrinsic part of any DIY job which involves acquiring materials. Buying too much is wasteful, but equally there is nothing more annoying than running out of materials halfway through a job.

Estimating quantities of concrete

To estimate the amount of materials that will be required, you need to calculate the volume of concrete in the finished pad, path or drive. Measure the surface area of the site, and multiply that figure by the thickness of the concrete. Different jobs require very different thicknesses of concrete, so be sure to calculate the correct depth for the job in hand.

Use the gridded diagram to estimate the volume of concrete you will need, by reading off the area of the site in square metres (square yards) and tracing it across horizontally to meet the angled line indicating the thickness of the concrete. Trace the line up to find the volume in cubic metres (cubic yards).

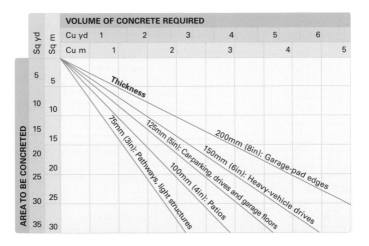

	1.00	1.50	2.00	2.50	3.00	3.50	4.00	4.50	5.00
General purpose mix	Cubic metres of concrete								
Cement (50kg bags)	7.00	10.50	14.40	17.50	21.00	24.50	28.00	31.50	35.00
plus Sand (cubic metres)	0.50	0.75	1.00	1.25	1.50	1.75	2.00	2.25	2.50
or Aggregate (cubic metres)	0.75	1.15	1.50	1.90	2.25	2.65	3.00	3.40	3.75
or Ballast (cubic metres)	0.90	1.35	1.80	2.25	2.70	3.15	3.60	4.05	4.50
Foundation mix									
Cement (50kg bags)	6.00	9.00	12.00	15.00	18.00	21.00	24.00	27.00	30.00
plus Sand (cubic metres)	0.55	0.80	1.10	1.40	1.65	1.95	2.20	2.50	2.75
or Aggregate (cubic metres)	0.75	1.15	1.50	1.90	2.25	2.65	3.00	3.40	3.75
or Ballast (cubic metres)	1.00	1.50	2.00	2.50	3.00	3.50	4.00	4.50	5.00
Paving mix									
Cement (50kg bags)	9.00	13.50	18.00	22.50	27.00	31.50	36.00	40.50	45.00
plus Sand (cubic metres)	0.45	0.70	0.90	1.15	1.35	1.60	1.80	2.00	2.25
or Aggregate (cubic metres)	0.75	1.15	1.50	1.90	2.25	2.65	3.00	3.40	3.75
or Ballast (cubic metres)	1.00	1.50	2.00	2.50	3.00	3.50	4.00	4.50	5.00

Estimating quantities of ingredients

Use the bar charts above to estimate the quantities of cement, sand and aggregate you will require to mix up the volume of concrete arrived at by using the chart on the opposite page.

The figures are based on the quantity of ingredients required to mix one cubic metre of concrete for a particular type of mix, plus about 10 per cent in order to allow for wastage.

Estimating quantity of mortar

The quantity of materials you will require when mixing mortar will vary according to the 'stiffness' of the mix required and the prevailing conditions at the building site. Use a general-purpose mortar for moderate conditions where the wall is reasonably sheltered. A stronger mix is required for severe conditions where the wall will be exposed to wind and driving rain, or if the site is elevated or near the coast.

As a rough guide to estimating how much mortar you will need when building a single-skin wall, allow approximately 1cu m (1⅓ cu yd) of sand (other ingredients in proportion) to lay either 3364 bricks, 1946 average concrete blocks, or 1639 decorative screen blocks.

SEE ALSO
88–9

SEE ALSO
72–3

Calculating areas

Buying materials to cover outdoor ground surfaces can be an expensive business, particularly if you are intending to lay real stone or paving slabs. For this reason it is essential to calculate as accurately as possible the dimensions of the area that you wish to cover.

Squares and rectangles

Calculate the area of rectangular paving by multiplying width by length.

Example:
2m x 3m = 6sq m
78in x 117in = 9,126sq in or 7sq yd

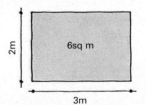

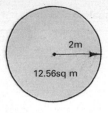

Circles

Use the formula πr^2 to calculate the area of a circle ($\pi = 3.14$, r = radius of circle).

Example:
3.14×2sq m = 3.14×4 = 12.56sq m
3.14×78sq in = $3.14 \times 6,084$ = 19,104sq in or 14.75sq yd

Irregular shapes

Draw an irregular area of paving onto a piece of squared paper, applying a scale that corresponds to the size of each square. To find the dimensions of the area that you wish to cover, count the whole squares and average out the portions. It is safer to over-estimate the total count of the portions in your plan, so that you do not have to fill gaps with odd bits of paving.

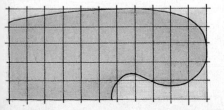

◀ Square-up an irregular shape to calculate area.

Estimating sheet and vinyl carpet

Measure the floor area and draw a freehand plan, including the position of doors, window bay, alcoves and so on, plus the full width of the doorframe. Make a note of the dimensions on the plan and take it to the flooring supplier, who will advise you on the most economical way to cover the floor.

The ideal solution is to achieve a seamless wall-to-wall covering; but this is often impossible, either because a particular width is unobtainable or because the room is such an irregular shape that there would be too much wastage if it were cut from one piece. Carpet or

▼ Vinyl floorcoverings can easily be cut to fit, whatever their type.

sheet-vinyl widths have to be butted together in these circumstances – but try to avoid seams in the main walkways. You also have to consider matching the pattern and the direction of carpet pile: it must run in the same direction, or each piece of carpet will look different. Remember to order 75mm (3in) extra all round for fitting.

Standard widths

Most manufacturers produce carpet or vinyl to standard widths. Some can be cut to fit any shape of room, but the average wastage factor is reflected in the price. Not all carpets are available in the full range of widths and you may have difficulty in matching a colour exactly from one width to another, so ask the supplier to check.

Carpet widths of 2.74m (9ft) and over are known as broadlooms; narrower widths are called body or strip carpets.

Carpet squares

Carpet squares – not to be confused with tiles – are large, rectangular loose-laid rugs. Simply order whichever size suits the proportions of your room. ☞

SEE ALSO
408–9

Wallcoverings: estimating quantities

Calculating the number of rolls of wallcovering you need will depend mainly on the size of the roll – both the length and width. However, you also need to take into consideration the pattern repeat and slight colour differences between rolls of wallcovering, as well as making an allowance for cutting around obstructions such as windows and doors.

The width of a standard roll of wallcovering is

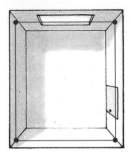

▲ *Measuring walls for standard rolls*

A standard roll of wallcovering is 520mm (1ft 9in) wide and 10.05 metres (33ft) long. To be on the safe side, you may want to include windows and doors in your estimate.

520mm (1ft 9in), the length 10.05 metres (33ft). Use the chart on this page to estimate how many rolls you are likely to need for walls and ceilings. If in doubt, it is always advisable to over-estimate slightly.

Non-standard rolls

If the wallcovering you have chosen is not cut to a standard size, calculate the amount of material that you need by applying the following methods:

Measurement in metres around walls, including doors and windows

Walls	▲ Height of room in metres from skirting								Number of rolls required for walls
	2-2.5m	2-2.5m	2-2.5m	2-2.5m	2-2.5m	2-2.5m	2-2.5m	2-2.5m	
10m	5	5	6	6	7	7	8	8	
11m	5	6	7	7	8	8	9	9	
12m	6	6	7	8	8	9	9	10	
13m	6	7	8	8	9	10	10	10	
14m	7	7	8	9	10	10	11	11	
15m	7	8	9	9	10	11	12	12	
16m	8	8	9	10	11	11	12	13	
17m	8	9	10	10	11	12	13	14	
18m	9	9	10	11	12	13	14	15	
19m	9	10	11	12	13	14	15	16	
20m	9	10	11	12	13	14	15	16	
21m	10	11	12	13	14	15	16	17	
22m	10	11	13	14	15	16	17	18	
23m	11	12	13	14	15	17	18	19	
24m	11	12	14	15	16	17	18	20	
25m	12	13	14	15	17	18	19	20	
26m	12	13	15	16	17	19	20	21	
27m	13	14	15	17	18	19	21	22	
28m	13	14	16	17	19	20	21	23	
29m	13	15	16	18	19	21	22	24	
30m	14	15	17	18	20	21	23	24	

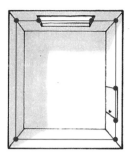

▲ Measuring walls for non-standard rolls

Do not include doors and windows when estimating for expensive materials. Allow for short lengths afterwards.

Walls

Measure the height of the walls from skirting to ceiling. Divide the length of the roll by this figure to find the number of wall lengths you can cut from a roll.

Measure around the room, leaving out windows and doors, to determine how many widths fit into the total length of the walls. To estimate how many rolls you will need, divide this number by the number of wall lengths you can get from one roll.

Make an allowance for short lengths above doors and under windows.

Ceilings

Measure the length of the room to determine one strip of paper. Work out how many roll widths fit across the room. To estimate how many rolls you need, multiply the two figures and divide the answer by the length of a roll. Check for waste and allow for it in your calculations.

Checking for shading

If rolls of wallcovering are printed in one batch, there should be no problem with colour-matching one roll to another. When you buy, look for the batch number printed on the wrapping; if the number is the same on all the rolls you buy, you should not experience any difficulties.

Make a careful visual check before hanging the covering, especially for hand-printed papers or fabrics. Unroll a short length of each roll and lay them side by side on your pasting table. You may obtain a better colour match by changing the rolls around – but if the colour difference is too obvious, go back to the shop and ask for replacement rolls. If you hang rolls that do not match, you will regret your decision for evermore! ☞

SEE ALSO
414–5

Quotations

If you are planning to appoint a builder to undertake a job for you, it is advisable to request an estimate or preferably a detailed quotation before he begins work. Ideally, get more than one builder to quote, so that you can compare prices.

Choosing a builder

Personal recommendation is the only safe way to find a builder. If someone whose opinion you respect has found a professional who is skilful, reliable and easy to communicate with, then the chances are you will enjoy the same experience. Even so, ideally you should inspect the builder's work yourself before you make up your mind. If a personal recommendation is hard to come by, choose a builder who is a member of a reputable association such as the Federation of Master Builders. To be represented by the Federation, a builder must have a good reputation and supply bank and insurance references.

A good builder will be booked up for weeks ahead, so allow plenty of time to find someone who will be free when you need him or her to start work. If a builder is very highly recommended, you may feel you do not want to look elsewhere – but, unless you get two or three firms to estimate for the same job, you will not know whether the price is fair. A builder who is in demand may quote a high price because he doesn't need the work; on the other hand, an inexperienced builder may submit a price that seems tempting, but then cut corners or ask for more money later because he or she has failed to anticipate all the problems that might arise before the job is completed.

◀ *Royal·Institution of Chartered Surveyors*
12 Great George Street, London SW1P 3AD
Telephone: 020 7222 7000

▲ *Association of Building Engineers*
Lutyens House, Billing Brook Road, Weston Favell, Northampton NN3 8NW
Telephone: 01604 404121

Subcontractors

Unless a builder is a 'jack of all trades', he may have to employ independent electricians, plumbers and plasterers. The builder is responsible for the quality of subcontracted work unless you agree beforehand that you will appoint the specialists yourself. Discuss anything relating to the subcontracted work with the builder himself. It is essential that a subcontractor receives clear instructions from one person only, or there is bound to be confusion.

Using professionals

There are certain jobs it is worth paying to have done quickly and efficiently – ones that are holding up a series of other projects, for example, or that call for techniques with which you do not feel sufficiently confident. You may prefer to ask an electrician to do major wiring or a plumber to install a new bathroom, although you plan to carry out all the peripheral labouring and finishing yourself.

Then there are certain skills that require time and practice before you can become really proficient at them.

Professional advice

In most cases, you will need to seek professional advice in order to obtain planning permission and Building Regulations approval; and if you apply for a mortgage, the bank or building society will insist on the building being professionally surveyed. If the surveyor's report highlights a serious defect, the mortgage company will want the fault rectified by a specialist firm.

▲ *Royal Institute of British Architects*
66 Portland Place, London W1N 4AD
Telephone: 020 7580 5533

SEE ALSO
218

Getting an estimate

When you ask several builders to tender for work, what they give you is only an estimate of the costs. These will be based on current prices and the amount of information you have supplied at the time. If you take a long time to make up your mind, or alter the specification, the prices are likely to change.

▲ Federation of Master Builders
14 Great James Street, London WC1N 3DP Telephone: 020 7242 7583

Before you officially engage a builder, always obtain a firm quotation with a detailed breakdown of costs. Part of the quotation may still be estimated. If you still have not decided on certain items, then you can both agree on a provisional sum to cover them – but make it clear that you are to be consulted before that money is spent. Also, a builder may have to employ a specialist for some of the work, and that fee might be estimated. If so, try to get the builder to firm up on the price before you employ him – and certainly before the work begins.

Agree how payment is to be made. Many builders are willing to complete the work before any money changes hands; others ask for stage payments to cover the cost of materials. If you agree to stage payments, it should be on the understanding that you will only pay for work completed, or that at least the materials will have been delivered to the site. Never agree to an advance payment. Provided you make it clear to the builder before he accepts the contract, you can retain a figure for an agreed period after the work is completed to cover the cost of faulty workmanship. Between 5 and 10 per cent of the overall cost is a reasonable sum to retain.

Neither you nor the builder can anticipate all the problems that might arise. If something unexpected occurs that affects the price for the job, ask the builder for an estimate of costs before you decide what course of action to take. Similarly, if you change your mind or ask for work that is extra to the specification, you must expect to pay for any resulting increase in costs – but make sure you agree the amount at the time, rather than trying to negotiate it at the end of the job.

ESTIMATES AND QUOTATIONS

A builder's initial estimate is usually an approximate price only. Before you engage him or her, make sure you obtain a firm written quotation that reflects current prices.

R

Radiators: bleeding and hanging

Trapped air prevents radiators heating up fully. If a radiator feels cooler at the top than at the bottom, it's likely that a pocket of air has formed inside it. Getting the air out of a radiator – 'bleeding' it – is a simple procedure.

First switch off the circulation pump. Each radiator has a bleed valve at one of its top corners, identifiable by a square-section shank in the centre of the round blanking plug. Buy a key for bleeding radiators at any DIY shop or ironmonger's.

Use the key to turn the valve's shank anticlockwise about a quarter of a turn. Have a small container and some rags handy to catch spurting water, in case you open the valve too far.

You will hear a hissing sound as the air escapes. Keep the key on the shank of the valve; then when the hissing stops and the first dribble of water appears, close the valve tightly.

Blocked bleed valve

If no water or air comes out when you attempt to bleed a radiator, check whether the feed-and-expansion tank in the loft is empty. If the tank is full of water, then the bleed valve is probably blocked with paint.

Close the inlet and outlet valve at each end of the radiator, then remove the screw from the centre of the bleed valve. Clear the hole with a piece of wire, and reopen one of the radiator valves slightly to eject some water from the hole. Close the radiator valve again and refit the screw in the bleed valve. Open both radiator valves and test the bleed valve again.

▶ Dispersing an air pocket in a radiator.

Installing a different-pattern radiator

Drain your central-heating system, then take the old brackets off the wall. Slide one of the new radiator's brackets onto the hangers welded to the back of the radiator. Measure the position of the brackets and transfer these measurements to the wall (1). Line up the new radiator brackets with the pencil marks on the wall, and mark the fixing-screw holes for them. Drill and plug the holes, then screw the brackets in place (2).

Take up the floorboards below the radiator and sever the vertical portions of the feed and return pipes. Connect the valves to the

▲ **1. Transferring the measurements**
Measure the positions of the radiator brackets and transfer these dimensions to the wall.

bottom of the radiator and hang it on its brackets.

Slip a new vertical pipe into each of the valves and connect these pipes to the original pipework running under the floor (3). Tighten the nuts connecting the new pipes to the valves. ☞

▼ **2. Securing the brackets**
Screw the mounting brackets to the wall.

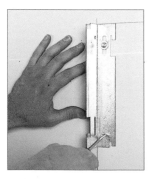

▲ **3. Connecting the new pipework.**
Make sure the vertical section of pipe aligns with the radiator valve.

SEE ALSO
318

Radiators: cabinets

Whereas a standard panel radiator may suit a modern interior, it can look out of place in a period-style room. One solution is to enclose the radiator in a cabinet that's more in keeping with the character of the interior.

Making your own cabinet

A radiator cabinet can be designed to stand on the floor or to be hung on the wall at skirting height. A floor-standing version is described here.

Cut the shelf member (1) and two end panels (2) from 18mm (¾in) MDF. Make these components large enough to enclose the radiator and both valves. Cut a notch near the base of each end panel to fit the profile of the skirtings.

Glue the panels to the shelf with dowels joints, and dowel a 50 x 25mm (2 x 1in)

tie rail (3) between the sides at skirting level. Cut a new skirting moulding (4) to fit along the base of the cabinet, but first cut away the bottom edge of the moulding on the front to form a large vent. Complete the box by applying a decorative moulding (5) around the edge of the shelf.

Cut a front panel (6) from either perforated hardboard, MDF, aluminium sheet or bamboo lattice, and mount it in a rebated MDF frame (7). Make the frame fit the box, leaving a vent along the top edge. Hold the frame in place with magnetic catches.

Paint the cabinet and, when it is dry, attach it to the wall with metal corner brackets or mirror plates.

Floor-standing radiator cabinet
1. Shelf 2. End panel 3. Tie rail 4. Skirting
5. Moulding. 6. Perforated panel 7. Frame

Radiators: controls

The various automatic control systems and devices available for wet central heating can, if used properly, provide savings in running costs by reducing wastage of heat to a minimum.

Three basic devices

Automatic controllers can be divided into three basic types: temperature controllers (thermostats), automatic on-off switches (programmers and timers), and heating-circuit controllers (zone valves). These devices can be used, individually or in combination, to provide a very high level of control.

It must be added that they are really effective with gas or oil-fired boilers only, since these can be switched on and off at will. When they're linked to solid-fuel boilers, which take time to react to controls, automatic control systems are much less effective.

Thermostats

All boilers incorporate thermostats to prevent overheating. An oil-fired or gas boiler will have one that can be set to vary heat output by switching the unit on and off; and some models are also fitted with modulating burners, which adjust flame height to suit heating requirements. On a solid-fuel boiler, the thermostat opens and closes a damper that admits more or less air to the firebed to increase or reduce the rate of burning, as required.

A room thermostat – 'roomstat' for short – is often the only form of central-heating control fitted. It is placed in a room where the temperature usually remains fairly stable, and works on the assumption that any rise or drop in the temperature will be matched by similar variations throughout the house. Roomstats control the temperature by means of simple on-off switching of the boiler – or the pump, if the boiler has to run constantly in order to provide hot water. The main drawback of a roomstat is that it makes no allowance for local temperature changes in other rooms – caused, for example, by the sun shining through a window or a separate heater being switched on. ☞

SEE ALSO
316–7

▲ *A motorized zone-control valve*

More sophisticated temperature control is provided by a thermostatic valve, which can be fitted to a radiator instead of the standard manually operated valve. A temperature sensor opens and closes the valve, varying the heat output to maintain the desired temperature in the individual room. Thermostatic radiator valves need not be fitted in every room. You can use one to reduce the heat in a kitchen or small bathroom, for example, while a roomstat regulates the temperature throughout the rest of the house.

The most sophisticated thermostatic controller is a boiler-energy manager or 'optimizer'. This device collects data from sensors inside and outside the building in order to deduce the optimum running period for the central-heating system, so the boiler is not wastefully switched on and off in rapid cycles.

Timers and programmers

You can cut fuel bills substantially by ensuring that the heating is not on while you are out or asleep. A timer can be set so that the system is switched on to warm the house before you get up and goes off just before you leave for work, then comes on again shortly before you return home and goes off at bedtime. The simpler timers provide two 'on' and two 'off' settings, which are normally repeated every day. A manual override enables you to alter the times for weekends and other changes in routine.

More sophisticated devices, known as programmers, offer a larger number of on-off programs – even a different one for each day of the week – as well as control of domestic hot water.

Zone-control valves

There's very little point in heating rooms that aren't being used. In most households, for example, the bedrooms are unoccupied for the greater part of the day and to heat them continuously would be wasteful.

One way of avoiding such waste is to divide your central-heating system into circuits or 'zones' and to heat the whole house only when necessary. However, if you divide your house into zones, make sure that the unheated areas are adequately ventilated, as otherwise condensation could cause problems. 🖝

Control is provided by motorized valves linked to a timer or programmer that directs the heated water through selected pipes at predetermined times of day. Alternatively, zone valves linked to individual thermostats can be used to provide separate temperature control for each zone.

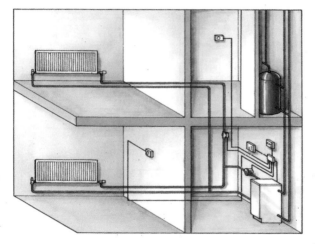

Heating controls
There are a number of ways to control heating: 1. A wiring centre connects the controls in the system; 2. A programmer/timer is used in conjunction with a zone valve to switch the boiler on or off at pre-set times, and run the heating and hot-water systems; 3. Optional boiler-energy manager controls the efficiency of the heating system; 4. Room thermostats are used to control the pump or zone valves to regulate the overall temperature; 5. A non-electrical thermostatic radiator valve controls the temperature of an individual heater.

🖝
SEE ALSO
402–6

Fitting radiator thermostatic valves

Thermostatic valves are useful devices which enable you to regulate the temperature output of individual radiators. They are sometimes fitted in place of a thermostat governing the entire central heating system.

Drain down the system by firstly shutting down the boiler. Leave for a while to allow the water to cool, and then switch off the supply to the expansion tank via the stopcock. Next, slip one end of a length of garden hose over the drain cock, the other end

into the gully. Open the drain cock with a key or adjustable spanner and release all the water. Any water trapped can be removed by opening the bleed valves on all the radiators, starting at the furthest from the drain cock. Pack some dry cloths around the pipe under the old valve. Hold the main body of the valve with a set of grips and, using an adjustable spanner, undo the radiator union nut [A]. Apply the same method removing the cap nut from the bottom of the valve [B]. Carefully lift off the old valve [C].

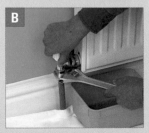

Removing the cap nut and olive could be tricky. If the olive is brass (yellowish) it can be removed with care, freeing the cap nut [D]. A copper olive (the same colour as the pipe) would have compressed onto the pipe when tightened so requires cutting the olive off with pipe cutters. Some thermostatic valves may be longer or shorter than the original, requiring some alteration to the pipe work.

Slide on the cap nut and then the new olive [E]. Older valves might have different

tails from new thermostatic valves, so it is important to compare the originals with the tail supplied with the new valve. If they are different, fit the new tail into the radiator by using a rad valve spanner (a large Allen key).

Don't forget to wrap PTFE tape around the thread half a dozen times or so before fitting in order to make a nice tight joint. Half-tighten the valve to the union first, then the cap nut [F]. Once aligned, tighten the union first, then finish tightening the cap nut [G].

Tools

Adjustable spanner
Plumber's grips/wrench
Radiator valve spanner
Pipe cutter
Dry cloths

Radiators: removing

There are a number of reasons why it may be necessary to remove a radiator – for example, to make decorating the wall behind it easier. You can remove individual radiators without having to drain the whole system.

▲ *1. Close the valve*

▲ *2. Unscrew cap-nut*

Make sure you have plenty of rag to hand for mopping up spilled water, plus a jug and a large bowl. The water in the radiator will be very dirty – so, if possible, roll back the floorcovering before you start.

Shut off both valves, turning the shank of the lockshield valve clockwise with a key or an adjustable spanner (1). Note the number of turns needed to close it, so that later you can reopen it by the same amount.

Unscrew the cap-nut that keeps the handwheel valve or lockshield valve attached to the adaptor in the end of the radiator (2). Hold the jug under the joint and open the bleed valve slowly to let the water drain out. Transfer the water from the jug to the bowl, and continue doing this until no more water can be drained off.

Unscrew the cap-nut that keeps the other valve attached to the radiator, lift the radiator free from

its wall brackets, and drain any remaining water into the bowl (3). If you're going to decorate the wall, unscrew the brackets.

To replace the radiator, screw the brackets back in place, then rehang the radiator and tighten the cap-nuts on both valves. Close the bleed valve and reopen both radiator valves (open the lockshield valve by the same number of turns you used when closing it). Last of all, bleed the air from the radiator.

3. Final draining
Lift radiator from brackets and drain off any remaining water.

Radiators: system support

The efficiency of modern oil-fired and gas boilers depends on their being checked and serviced annually. Because the mechanisms involved are so complex, the work must be done by a qualified engineer. With either type of boiler, you can enter into a contract for regular maintenance with your fuel supplier or the original installer.

Corrosion in the system

Modern boilers and radiators are made from fairly thin materials, and if you fail to take basic anti-corrosion measures, the life of the system can be reduced to 10 years or less. Corrosion may result either from hard-water deposits or from a chemical reaction between the water and the system's metal components. Lime scale, rust and sludge are the main causes of problems.

Reducing corrosion

Drain about half a litre (1 pint) of water from the boiler or a radiator. Orange water denotes rusting, and black the presence of sludge. In either case, treat immediately with corrosion inhibitor.

Adding corrosion inhibitor

You can slow down corrosion by adding a proprietary corrosion inhibitor to the water. Drain off about 20 litres (4 gallons) of water – enough to empty the feed-and-expansion tank and a small amount of pipework – then pour the inhibitor into the tank and restore the water supply, which will carry the inhibitor into the pipes. Finally, switch on the pump to distribute the inhibitor throughout the system.

Reducing scale

You can buy low-voltage coils to create a magnetic field that will prevent the heat exchanger of your boiler becoming coated with scale. However, unless you have soft water in your area, the only way to actually avoid hard water in the system is to install a water softener.

Phosphate balls are sometimes used to prevent the formation of scale in boilers. Before fitting any device to reduce scale, it is essential to seek the boiler manufacturer's advice.

SEE ALSO
310–11

SEE ALSO
40–1

Roofs: flashing maintenance

There are many problems associated with flashings, generally caused by the flashing itself corroding or a breakdown of the joints between the flashing and the house structure. A perished flashing should be stripped out and replaced.

Where flashing is used

Places where flashing is commonly fitted on pitched and flat roofs:
1. Valley
2. Apron
3. Wall abutment
4. Parapet abutment
5. Chimney abutment

Flashing materials

The most common flashing materials are lead, zinc, roofing felt and mortar fillets. Of all these materials, lead is by far the best, because it weathers well and is easily worked (although shaping it is generally a craft skill) and it can be applied in any situation and to any type of roof covering. Zinc is a cheaper substitute for lead.

Injecting caulking compound

Cement fillets often shrink away from wall abutments. If the fillets are otherwise sound, you can simply fill the gap with a gun-applied flexible caulking compound. Choose a colour that matches the fillet. Brush the surfaces to remove any loose material before injecting the mastic.

Applying flashing tape

Prepare the surfaces by removing all loose and organic material. A broken or crumbling cement fillet should be made good with mortar.

Make sure that the surfaces are dry. If necessary, apply a primer – which is supplied with some tapes – about one hour before you use the tape (1). Cut the tape to length, and peel away the protective backing as you press the tape into place. Finally, rub over the

▲ 1. Apply a primer with a 50mm (2in) paintbrush.

▲ 2. Press tape with a pad to exclude air bubbles.

surface of the tape with a cloth pad, applying firm pressure to exclude any air trapped beneath it (2).

Repointing flashing joints

Metal flashings that are tucked into masonry often work loose when the old mortar becomes badly weathered.

If the flashing is otherwise sound, rake out the mortar joint, tuck the lead or zinc back into it, and wedge it there with rolled strips of lead, spaced about 500mm (20in) apart. Then repoint the joint (alternatively, you can apply a mastic sealant).

While you have the roof ladders and scaffolding in place, rake out and repoint all the mortar joints if they are in poor condition.

▶ Rake out joint and repoint with fresh mortar

Patching lead flashing

Lead doesn't readily corrode, but splits can occur where it has buckled through expansion and contraction. Flashing tape can be used to repair lead, and you can mend a split with solder. For a more substantial repair, it is possible to cut away a weak or damaged portion and join on a new piece of lead by 'burning' or welding. However, this is a job for a specialist, not one you should do yourself. ☞

SEE ALSO
339

Roofs: flat-roof construction

Timber-framed flat roofs are often used for rear extensions and outbuildings. Most have joists carrying stiff wooden decking, crossing the shorter span, spaced at 400, 450 or 600mm (1ft 4in, 1ft 6in or 2ft) between centres. Herringbone or solid strutting is required for a span of more than 2.5m (8ft) to prevent joists buckling. Joists may be fixed to wall plates on loadbearing walls or set in metal hangers or recesses in the adjoining masonry wall.

Establishing the fall

The fall of a flat roof should be at least 1:80 for smooth surfaces like metal or plastic, and 1:60 for coarser materials. The fall is designed to shed water – but if the slope is too shallow, puddles will form. Thermal movement of the decking can cause the covering to break down and let standing water through.

Furring methods

1. Tapered furrings fixed in line with joist

2. Furrings strips of decreasing size fitted across the fall

3. Tapered furrings fixed across joists

To achieve a flat ceiling, tapered 'furrings' are nailed to the tops of the joists (1). Alternatively, joists may be set across the line of the fall with parallel furring strips of decreasing thickness nailed to them (2); or tapered strips are fixed across them (3). The latter provides better cross-ventilation. Counterbattens also provide ventilation for an internally insulated roof.

Roof decking

Either exterior WBP (weather-and-boil-proof) plywood or another type of exterior-grade man-made board is fixed to the joists to make a flat base for the roof covering. Older flat roofs were usually decked with tongue-and-groove softwood boards.

The panels – normally 18mm (¾in) thick – are laid

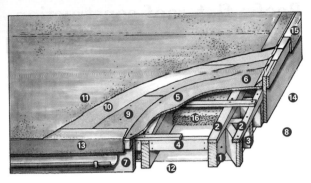

The components of a flat roof

1. Joists 2. Furring 3. Return joist 4. Nogging 5. Counter battens 6. Decking 7. Fascia board 8. Angle fillet 9. First felt layer 10. Second felt layer 11. Cap sheet 12. Eaves drip batten 13. Felt eaves drip 14. Verge drip batten 15. Felt verge drip 16. Insulation

with their longer edges running across the joists; their ends are centred over a joist for support. These joints should be staggered. Noggings may be fitted between the joists to give extra support to the longer edges of the panels, depending on their thickness and the joist spacing.

For a felted roof, you could start with a prefelted decking. This surface-treated board is laid with 3mm (⅛in) gaps between the panels to allow for thermal expansion, and is fixed down with either nails or screws. If you are unable to apply a felt covering

straightaway, this type of decking can be temporarily waterproofed by sealing the gaps between the boards with a cold-bonding mastic and then covering the joints with roof-sealing tape.

Covering the deck

Whatever type of decking is used, it must be fully waterproofed either with asphalt or with two or three layers of roofing felt.

To reflect some of the sun's heat, the roof can be coated with special paint or covered with a layer of pale-coloured chippings 12mm (½in) thick.

SEE ALSO
184–5

Roofs: flat-roof maintenance

The best approach for repairing a flat roof depends not only on its age and general condition, but also on the extent of the damage. You can tackle minor repairs yourself – but if the covering has deteriorated across a wide area, then it may be best to call in a contractor and have the roof re-covered.

Patch repairs

Localized damage such as splits and blisters can be repaired with specialized materials designed for the purpose. Their effectiveness relies on good adhesion, so take care to clean the roof surface thoroughly. Eradicate lichen or moss spores with fungicide before starting the repair work. 🖝

If visible from above, a patched roof can be an eyesore, but you can improve its appearance with a coat of reflective paint or with bitumen and chippings. Work

on a warm day, preferably after a spell of dry weather.

Dealing with splits

You can use most self-adhesive repair tapes to mend splits in all types of roof coverings. First remove any chippings, then clean the split and the surrounding surface. Fill a wide split with a mastic compound before taping. Apply the special primer supplied with the tape over the area to be covered, and leave it for an hour. Even where only a short split has occurred along a joint in the

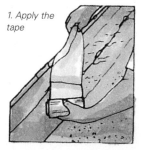

1. Apply the tape

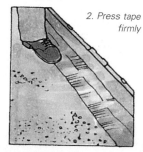

2. Press tape firmly

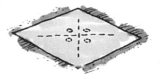

▲ Nail cut edges
*Once the covering is tacky,
nail in down. Then glue a felt
patch over the repair with
bitumen adhesive*

board substrate, prepare the
whole line of the joint for
covering with tape.

Peel back the protective
backing and apply the tape to
the primed surface (1). If you
are repairing short splits, cut
the tape to length first – otherwise, unroll the tape as you
work along the repair. Press it
down firmly and, holding it in
place with your foot, roll it out
and tread it into place as you
go. Cut it off at the end of the
run. Go back and ensure that
the edges are sealed (2).

Dealing with blisters
Any blisters in an asphalt or
felted roof covering are best
left alone unless they contain
water or have been causing
the covering to leak.

To repair a blister in an
asphalt roof, heat the area
with a blowtorch or hot-air
stripper and, when the asphalt

is soft, try to press the blister
flat with a block of wood. If the
blister contains water, cut into
the asphalt to open the blister
up, and let the moisture dry
out. Apply gentle heat before
pressing the asphalt back into
place. Work mastic into the
opening before closing it, then
cover the repair with a patch
of repair tape.

On a felted roof, make two
intersecting cuts across a blister
and peel back the covering.
Heating the felt will make this
easier. Dry and clean out the
opening, apply bitumen
adhesive and, when it's tacky,
nail the covering back into place
with galvanized clout nails.

▼ *There is no alternative but to
replace badly blistered asphalt*

SEE ALSO
342–3

Cover the repair with a patch of roofing felt, bonded on with bitumen adhesive; cut the patch to lap at least 75mm (3in) all round. Alternatively, you can use repair tape.

Treating the whole surface

A roof that has already been patch-repaired and is in poor condition can be given an extra lease of life by means of a liquid waterproofing treatment. However, don't rely too heavily on this treatment if the roof has had numerous patch repairs over a period of time. ☛

One type of treatment uses a cold-applied bitumen-based emulsion that can be reinforced with an open-weave glass-fibre membrane.

▶ Brush on the first coat

First sweep the roof clear of all debris and then treat the surface with a fungicide to kill off any traces of lichen and moss. Following the manufacturer's instructions, apply a coat of primer and leave to cure.

Apply the first coat of waterproofer with a brush or broom (see bottom left), then lay the glass-fibre fabric into the wet material and stipple it with a loaded brush. Overlap the edges of the fabric strips by at least 50mm (2in) and bed them down well with the waterproofer, applying it in liberal amounts.

Allow the first coat of waterproofer to dry thoroughly before brushing on the second, as otherwise the brush strokes will disturb the original coat. When the last coat becomes tacky, cover it with fine chippings. If you plan to apply a solar-reflective coating, let the waterproofer dry thoroughly.

An alternative treatment is to use a resin-based waterproofing compound that incorporates fibres and fillers for extra strength. Only one coat of the compound is necessary, and it can be used over most roofing surfaces.

Roofs: glazed roof repairs

Traditional porches and timber-framed greenhouses and conservatories all tend to suffer from leaks caused by a breakdown of the seal between the glass and glazing bars. Minor leaks should be dealt with promptly because trapped moisture can lead to timber decay and expensive repairs.

Using aluminium tape

You can waterproof glazing bars with self-adhesive aluminium tape.

Clean out the old putty from both sides of the glazing bars and let the wood dry out, then apply wood primer or linseed oil. When the primer is dry, fill the rebates with putty or mastic.

The tape must be wide enough to cover each glazing bar and lap the glass on each side by 18mm (¾in). Start at the eaves and work up the roof, moulding the tape to

▲ Mould the tape over the glazing bar

the shape of each glazing bar and excluding air bubbles.

At a step in the glass, cut the tape and make an overlap. Mould the cut end over the stepped edge, then start a new length, lapping the stuck-down end by 50mm (2in).

At the ridge, either cut the tape to butt against the framework or lap onto it. Cover the ends with tape applied horizontally. Where a lean-to roof has an apron flashing, tuck the tape under it.

The tape can be painted to match the woodwork or left its natural colour. ☛

SEE ALSO
338–9

SEE ALSO
432–3

Roofs: replacing tiles and slates

Roof tiles and slates wear and crack with age, as they are permanently subject to the vagaries of the weather. They should be replaced as soon as they become damaged.

Rebedding ridge tiles

When the old mortar breaks down, a whole row of ridge tiles can be left with practically nothing but their weight holding them in place.

Lift off the ridge tiles, and clear all the crumbling mortar away. Soak the tiles in water before refixing them.

Mix 1 part cement : 3 parts sand, to make a stiff mortar. Dampen the top courses of the roof tiles or slates, and lay a thick bed of mortar on each side of the ridge, following the line left behind by the old mortar (1). Lay mortar for one or two tiles at a time.

▲ 1. Apply bands of bedding mortar on each side

▲ 2. Insert pieces of slate in the jointing mortar

Press each ridge tile firmly into the mortar. Build up a bed of mortar to fill the hollow end of each ridge tile, inserting pieces of tile or slate to prevent the mortar slumping (2). Press the next tile in place, squeezing out enough mortar to fill the narrow end joint flush. Build a similar mortar joint between an end ridge tile and a wall or chimney stack.

▼ Ridge tiles

Replacing a roof tile

Individual tiles can be difficult to remove for two reasons: the retaining nibs on their back edges and their interlocking shape, which holds them together. 🢒

To remove a plain tile that is broken, lift the nibs clear of the batten on which it rests, then pull it out. This is easier if the overlapping tiles are first raised on wooden wedges inserted at both sides of the tile that is to be removed (1). If the tile is also nailed, try rocking it loose. If this fails, you will have to break it out carefully. You may then have to use a slater's ripper to extract or cut any remaining nails.

Use a similar technique for a single-lap interlocking tile, but in this case you will also have to wedge up the tile to the left of the one being removed (2). If the tile has a deep profile, you will have to

Cutting roof tiles with an angle grinder
Follow a scored guide line with the cutting disc

ease up a number of surrounding tiles to achieve the required clearance.

If you are removing tiles in order to put a roof vent in, then you can afford to smash the one you are replacing. Use a hammer to do so, taking care not to damage any of the adjacent tiles. The remaining tiles should be easier to remove once the first is removed.

▼ *1. Lift the overlapping tiles with wedges*

▼ *2. Lift interlocking tiles above and to the left*

🢒
SEE ALSO
384–7

Removing and replacing a slate

A slate may slip out of place because the nails have corroded or because the slate itself has broken. Whatever the cause, slipped or broken slates should be replaced as soon as possible, before a high wind strips them off the roof.

Use a slater's ripper to remove the trapped part of a broken slate. Slip the ripper under the slate and locate its hooked end over one of the fixing nails (1), then pull down hard on the tool to extract or cut through the nail. Remove the second nail in the same way. Even where an aged slate has already slipped out completely, you may have to remove the nails in the same way to allow the replacement slate to be inserted.

You will not be able to nail a new slate in place. Instead, use a copper strip, a plastic clip, or cut a strip of lead, 25mm (1in) wide, to the length of the slate lap plus 25mm (1in). Attach the strip to the batten by driving a nail between the slates of the lower course (2), then slide the new slate into position and turn back the end of the lead strip to secure it (3).

1. Pull out nails

2. Nail strip to batten

3. Fold strip over edge

Cutting slates

You may have to cut a second-hand slate to fit the gap in your roof.

With a sharp point, scratch the required proportion on the back of the slate. Place the slate, bevelled side down, on a bench. Align the cutting line with the edge of the bench, then chop the slate with the edge of a bricklayer's trowel. Work from both edges towards the middle, using the edge of the bench as a guide. Alternatively, use a slate cutter. Either drill nail holes or punch them out with a masonry nail.

▲ *Cut slate with a trowel...*

▲ *... or use a slate cutter*

S

Screws

Screws are manufactured with a small range of head shapes, suited to various purposes, and in a choice of materials and finishes.

Screw fixing

For anything other than rough work, use screws in preference to nails when joining wooden components together or for attaching other materials to wood. ☞

Screw threads

Traditional woodscrews have a plain 'full' shank below the head that acts as a dowel. The shank is about one-third the length of the screw, the remainder being threaded and ending with a gimlet point.

More modern screws have a modified thread that may be single or double. They have a sharp point that makes starting easier, and a shank that's smaller in diameter than the thread – so that the smaller screws, at least, don't require a pilot hole to be drilled. Some screws are threaded along their entire length and so can be driven in quickly using a power screwdriver.

▼ *Parts of a screw*
It may help avoid confusion if you use the accepted terminology when ordering screws.

Head

Shank
diameter
(gauge)

Length

Thread

Screwheads

There are six basic head shapes:

Countersunk head
For work where the screw must be recessed, either flush with the surface or below it.

Roundhead
(sometimes called domed)
Usually used with sheet material that is too thin for countersinking.

Raised head
A combination of domed and countersunk, often used for attaching metal items, such as door furniture, to wood.

Mirror screws, countersunk screws with a threaded centre hole for attaching a decorative dome, are used for fixing wall mirrors and the like in place.

Pan head and flange head
Similar to roundhead but mainly found on self-tapping screws used for joining sheet metal.

Countersunk

Roundhead

Raised head

Mirror screw

Pan head

Flange head

Slotted head   *Cross-head*

A further subdivision of all these screws is between those with slotted heads and those with cross-slotted heads.

Sizes and gauges

All screws are described in terms of their length (given in millimetres or inches) and their shank diameter, or gauge (swg), which is expressed as a simple number from 1 to 20. The thicker the screw, the higher its gauge number. The gauges in most general use are 4, 6, 8 and 10.

Types and uses

The machine-made gimlet-point woodscrew has changed little since it was developed in the last century. However, since the introduction of man-made boards and electric screwdrivers, manufacturers have produced new thread and head forms.

Unhardened woodscrews
The traditional woodscrew, with its single-helix thread, is made in the widest range of sizes, head types and materials. It is suitable for most woods and is particularly suited for fixing metal fittings such as hinges, locks and catches. This type of screw requires a pilot hole and shank-clearance hole to be drilled prior to fitting.

Length: 9 to 150mm (⅜ to 6in). Diameter/gauge: 2 to 18swg.

Hardened-steel woodscrews
Countersunk or roundhead screws are available with twin steep-pitch threads for fast insertion. They can

▶ *Hardened-steel woodscrews*

SEE ALSO
422–5

▲ *Chipboard screw*

▼ *Coach screw*

be used with all types of solid wood and man-made boards. The hardened metal makes it possible to drive into a range of relatively soft materials without the need for pilot holes.

Length: 12 to 100mm (½ to 4in). Diameter/gauge: 3 to 12swg.

Chipboard screws

These hardened-steel screws are primarily used for chip-board, but are also suitable as general-purpose wood-screws.

Although pilot holes are required for most materials, you can drive small-diameter screws directly into softwoods or low-density man-made boards.

Length: 12 to 100mm (½ to 4in). Diameter/gauge: 3 to 6mm ⅛ to ¼in).

Carcass screws

These hardened-steel screws with a coarse single-helix thread are designed to be driven into the edge of chipboard without splitting it. Although not always necessary, drilling a pilot hole makes for easy installation.

Length: 45mm (1¾in). Diameter/gauge: 8swg.

▶ *Security screw*

Dry-wall screws

A special range of hardened screws with twin threads are made for fixing plasterboard or fibreboard to wooden or metal furring strips or studs. Each screw has a sharp point for drilling its own hole and a bugle-shaped countersunk head that enables it to bed down into the board material.

Length: 25 to 75mm (1 to 3in). Diameter/gauge: 3.5 and 4.2mm (¼ and ⁵⁄₃₂in).

Security screws

The heads of these countersunk screws have special slots that permit the screw to be driven into the work but reject the tip of the screwdriver when the action is reversed.

Length: 18 to 50mm (¾ to 2in). Diameter/gauge: 6 to 12swg.

Coach screws

Coach screws are made from unhardened steel, and

▶ *Masonry screw*

are used for heavy-duty applications such as building a workbench. They have a square head and are driven into the work with a spanner.

Length: 25 to 150mm (1 to 6in). Diameter/gauge: 6 to 12mm (¼ to ½in).

Self-tapping screws

Self-tapping screws are designed to cut their own thread in materials such as plastics and thin sheet metal. They are made from case-hardened steel and are normally available in four head forms, countersunk, raised head, pan head and flange head.

Length: 6 to 63mm (¼ to 2½in). Diameter/gauge: 4 to 14swg.

Masonry screws

These extra-hard screws with a special dual thread can be driven directly into all types of masonry without the need for wallplugs.

Length: 57 to 100mm (2¼ to 4in). Diameter/gauge: 4.8 and 6.4mm (³⁄₁₆ and ¼in).

Screw hooks and eyes

Made of steel, screw hooks and eyes have a conventional woodscrew thread for fixing to a wall or panel.

SCREWING TIPS

Driving a screw into a wall or a piece of wood might seem like a straightforward enough task, but there is actually much more skill involved in screwing than you might think. Here are a few useful screwing tips, to be used in conjunction with the advice given on different types of screws in the preceding pages. Following these tips will reduce damage to walls, etc., and will save you time and energy.

Always use the right tool	If you use a screwdriver with a tip that is slightly too big or small, it is likely to slip out of the slot as you turn it, damaging both the screw and the surrounding wood or masonry.
Drill pilot holes to the correct width and depth	Take the trouble to drill a neat, straight pilot hole before attempting to drive in a screw, even if the material you are screwing into seems soft and forgiving. Ensure that the hole is big enough to receive the screw.
Start off slowly with a hand tool	Power screwdrivers are quick and easy to use, but their speed and force mean they are not always the best tool to start off with. An initial few turns with a manual screwdriver will ensure that the screw goes in straight and true.

SEE ALSO
240–2

Sealants

The main purpose for a sealant is to provide a barrier against rain or water seeping between two joining surfaces or edges. This can be inside the home – in the bathroom – or outside, for example, in the abutments of a flat roof or an extension.

Use a flexible silicone sealant to fill gaps up to 3mm (⅛in) wide between a tiled wall and a shower tray, bath or basin: a rigid seal, such as grout, can crack and allow water to seep in. Cartridges of both clear and coloured sealant are available.

Using flexible sealant

With the cartridge fitted into its applicator, trim the tip off the plastic nozzle at an angle (the amount you cut dictates the thickness of the bead).

Clean the surfaces with a cloth and methylated spirit. Then start at one end by pressing the tip into the joint and pull backwards while slowly squeezing the applicator's trigger (1). When the bed is complete, smooth any ripples by dipping your finger into a 50/50 mix of water and washing-up liquid and running it along the joint (2). If you have sensitive skin, use the handle of a wetted teaspoon.

Removing old sealant

Brush a proprietary sealant remover onto a dirty or discoloured joint, and 15 minutes later scrape the sealant off the surface.

1. Pull back slowly to deposit a bead of sealant

2. Smooth out any ripples with your fingertip

Abutments

Leaks can occur wherever a flat roof abuts a house or parapet wall. The roof covering is therefore usually turned up the wall to form a 'skirting', which is either tucked into the mortar bed of the brickwork or covered by flashing for a tight seal.

Parapet walls are particularly prone to damp, being exposed on both sides – so the top edge is usually finished with a brick, stone or tile coping, which should overhang the faces of the wall to throw off rainwater. In addition, a damp-proof course of lead, asphalt or bituminous felt is set in the mortar bedding beneath the coping (1).

Often, a flexible damp-proof course, such as lead or high-performance felt, is set in the bed joint before the roofing is laid and then dressed down to form a flashing over the skirting (2).

Flat-roof coverings

Bitumen-based coverings fall into two types: asphalt and bituminous felt. ☞

Mastic asphalt

This waterproof material, made from either natural or

1. Solid and cavity walls need DPCs under the coping

synthetic bitumen, weathers very well. It is melted in a cauldron and, while hot, spread over the roof. When set, it forms an impervious layer. Laying hot asphalt is a skilled professional job.

Roofing felts

These bitumen-impregnated sheet materials are applied in layers to produce 'built-up' roofing, bonded with hot or cold bitumen. Making a roof of this kind with hot bitumen is best left to professionals.

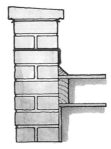

2. Flashing DPC

SEE ALSO
338–9

Sheds: repairing and roofing

Shed roofs are generally cheap and simple in construction and will deteriorate over time. They are relatively easy to repair. Read this in conjunction with the roofing project on pages 342–3.

Dry-laid roof covering

Butyl and EPDM are tough rubber-based roofing materials that can be used for new roofs or to provide a watertight covering over an old felted roof.

To lay either type of covering over old felt, simply brush the surface of the felt clean and cover it with a loose-laid underlay (1). Nail drip battens all round the roof (2). Nail the sheeting to one of the battens, then unfold it and, nail the fixing flaps to the roof (3). Fold the other edges over and nail them to the drip battens. Attach cover trims (4).

Dry-laid roofing
Brush the old roof clean then:
1. Lay a felt underlay.
2. Nail covering to drip battens.
3. Nail down fixing flaps.
4. Attach cover trims

Dealing with wet rot

Once you have eliminated the cause of the damp, cut away and replace wood that is badly damaged, then paint the new and surrounding woodwork with three liberal applications of chemical wet-rot eradicator. Brush the liquid into the joints and end grain well.

Dealing with dry rot

Cut out all infected timber up to at least 450mm (1ft 6in) beyond the last visible sign of rot. Chop plaster from nearby walls, following the wet-rot strands, and continue for another 450mm (1ft 6in) beyond the extent of the growth. Collect all debris in plastic bags and burn it.

Use a chemical dry-rot eradicator to kill any remaining spores. Wire-brush the masonry, then apply three generous brushcoats to all timber, brickwork and plaster within 1.5m (5ft) of the infected area. Alternatively, hire a coarse sprayer and treat the area three times.

Replacing perished felt

Wait for dry weather, then strip off the old felt. Pull out any clout nails, and check the deck for rotten or distorted boards.

Preparing the surfaces

Cut hardboard formers for the eaves and verge drips. Apply special roofing-system primer to all surfaces to be covered.

Applying the underlay

The covering is laid at right angles to the slope of the roof. Measure and cut sufficient lengths of felt to cover the roof. If you need to join pieces end to end, allow a 75mm (3in) overlap where the ends meet. Cut the first strip in half lengthways, so you will be able to stagger the joins when you lay the top layer of felt. Lay one of the half-width lengths flat on the roof, level with the gutter edge. Cut and peel back the release paper and press the underlay onto the roof.

Lay the other strips working up the slope of the roof in a similar way, overlapping the first and subsequent strips by 50mm (2in) along their length (1). Cut and lap internal corners.

Applying the top layer of felt

Before laying the top layer,

prepare and fit the eaves drips. Cut the required number of strips to cover the roof.

Following the procedure used for the underlay, but starting with a full-width strip, lay the plain edge of the first length 50mm (2in) back from the gutter edge (2). Lay the subsequent lengths lapping the one below.

Use special mastic to bond the top sheet where it laps the eaves, to prevent leaking.

▼ *Built-up felt system*
Lap the edges of the felt strips and stagger the joints in alternate layers

1. Lay underlay

2. Lay cap sheet

SEE ALSO
324–6

SEE ALSO
440–2

Erecting a shed

Sheds can be bought ready assembled and delivered to your garden in one piece, but it is far cheaper and more fulfilling to construct one yourself. A wide range of shed kits is available from DIY stores and garden centres.

A concrete screed is often the preferred base for a garden shed, but that can be a laborious and expensive way to create a base. If the shed has a wooden floor, as most of them do, ideally the shed should be slightly elevated off the ground to allow air to circulate underneath, as this prevents rot from setting in. Here we describe a quick, cheap and simple method of creating a shed base support system.

Cut three concrete or breeze blocks (but not lightweight blocks), in half to form six pads. Position these at the four corners of the wooden floor section and two centrally beneath it. Using a spade, dig the pads in so the blocks remain just above the surface. Adjust the pads by packing or excavating to ensure that they are all level, using a spirit level and board. Simply place the 100 x 100mm (4 x 4in) pressure-treated posts across the pads as bearers for the floor section [A].

Lay the floor section across the bearers [B] (no fixings required), and double-check for level.

The walls are next. If you don't have anyone to help you, support the first panel in place with an angled prop, while you screw fix

Tools

Spade
Spirit level
Hammer
Cordless drill/
screwdriver
Tape measure

A

B

through the bottom rail into the base. Position the second section and screw fix through the side rail [C], then do the same through the base rail and remove the prop. Simply attach the remaining panels in the same way. The roof is normally made into easy-fit sections, which slot into a rebate [D]. Screw fix through the rails to secure.

The felt is normally fixed in three sections, with the central ridge piece being fixed last over the two side sections and nailed down with galvanised clout nails to secure the felt [E]. This method ensures a waterproof lap, so take care not to damage the felt during construction.

Fascia boards are fitted to the front and rear elevations to keep the felt in place. The felt can be simply nailed with clout nails on either side, or turned under and fixed with a timber batten along its length (on the underside). You can attach a finial at either end to cover the fascia joints [F], with corner trims nailed to the four vertical corners to finish the job.

Replacing the felt on a shed roof

Shed roofs made of felt will wear out after a few years, especially if the shed is located in an exposed position. However, it is a relatively easy job to repair or replace this material. See more detail on this subject on pages 338–9.

Begin by de-nailing the timber beneath the felt [A] and stripping off the old roof covering [B]. Make sure that you wear safety goggles and gloves when you are doing this, as crumbling old felt gives off a lot of grit and there are bound to be old nails which are difficult to extract. Look for any rotten or distorted timbers and repair or replace them as necessary. At the same time, you could take the opportunity to apply a coat of preservative to the timber roof panels, prior to laying the new roof covering.

Unroll the felt, measure the length required, and then mark and cut it with a craft knife and straightedge [C]. Always allow at least a couple of inches (50mm) overhang at either end. Roll the cut lengths up again and roll out onto each side of the

Tools

Nail bar
Claw hammer
Pinchers
Scraper
Craft knife
Mastic gun
Straight edge
Safety glasses
Protective gloves

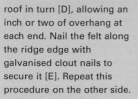

roof in turn [D], allowing an inch or two of overhang at each end. Nail the felt along the ridge edge with galvanised clout nails to secure it [E]. Repeat this procedure on the other side.

Cut the third section to size, once again allowing a minimum overlap of 50mm (2in) either side. This is called the ridge capping piece. The ridge piece can be attached with clout nails or a mastic sealer adhesive. The latter will help make the joint tighter and waterproof. Apply the mastic beads with a mastic gun [F]. Roll out the piece of capping felt and press it into place, working from the middle out [G].

Finally, nail all around the overhung edges to secure the felt covering from blowing off in the wind [H].

Soundproofing

Noise generated by road and air traffic, industrial activity or thoughtless neighbours can make life distinctly unpleasant, if not intolerable. Although it's difficult to block out unwelcome sounds completely, it is possible to reduce intrusive noise levels in almost any house or flat.

Sound is produced as a vibration that sets up pressure waves. These are transmitted to different elements in a house, which in turn resonate, making the noise 'echo' through the building.

The materials that make up the house react differently to sound waves. Carpets and curtains, for example, act as insulators – whereas hard surfaces such as ceramic tiles and plastered walls reflect sound, and thin materials offer little resistance. In addition, loose-fitting doors and windows, holes in the roof, and gaps between the floorboards and under skirtings all contribute to the problem of penetrating noise.

▼ *Detached insulated lining*
1 Head plate
2 Sole plate
3 Studs
4 Insulating blanket
5 Nogging
6 First layer of plasterboard
7 Second layer of plasterboard
8 Electrical fitting

Party and partition walls
Noise can easily penetrate a shared wall between houses.

Filling gaps
Sealing gaps in the party wall is one obvious way to reduce airborne noise. If necessary, remove skirtings and floorboards close to the party wall so you can repoint poor mortar joints and fill any

gaps around joists that are built into the masonry. After replacing the skirting and floorboards, seal any gaps between them with a flexible mastic. It may also be worth repointing the wall in the loft and plastering it to add mass.

Cladding a partition wall
To reduce the noise that passes from room to room in your own home, line both sides of existing stud partitions with plasterboard 12.5mm (½in) thick; then fill and tape the joints and refix the skirting. If you are building a new stud partition, clad it with two layers of plasterboard and include insulation.

Soundproofing doors

To muffle noise from outside, draughtproof exterior doors and fit secondary double glazing to porch or entrance-hall windows, perhaps incorporating toughened glass to improve security. The joints between the surrounding doorframe and the masonry should be sealed with mastic.

Draughtproofing your interior doors will have a similarly beneficial effect; and replacing lightweight hollow-core doors with heavy solid doors may help to reduce sound transmission between neighbouring flats.

Soundproofing windows

It is very likely that outside noise will penetrate through traditional single-glazed windows. Not only does sound find its way through gaps around the sashes (good draughtproofing is needed in order to make them airtight), but it also passes directly through the thin panes of glass. Double glazing will improve matters, but there must be a gap of at least 100mm (4in) between the panes for satisfactory sound insulation. This can be achieved by installing an airtight secondary-glazing system, but triple glazing (which includes a sealed unit) provides the optimum solution. 🠒

If the window is the only source of ventilation, install a ventilator elsewhere in the room – preferably not connected directly to the outside. If that is not feasible, make sure the ventilator has a baffle that interrupts incoming sound.

SEE ALSO
429

If you opt for a mechanical fan, choose one with a shutter that closes automatically when the fan is switched off; if possible, mount it away from the outside wall, connecting it with ducting.

Soundprofing floors and ceilings

Resilient floorcoverings – such as cork tiling and carpet with underlay – are normally sufficient to deaden noise transmission between the floors of a house. However, more drastic measures may be needed when a building has been converted into flats.

Sand pugging
In older houses where the dimensions of the building's

components are fairly generous, a layer of sand can be laid beneath the floorboards to soundproof the room below. However, adding sand across a wide area imposes quite a lot of extra weight on the floor joists; the structure must therefore be checked by a surveyor beforehand.

Nail softwood battens to the sides of the floor joists to support strips of stiff plywood, then staple polythene between the joists to contain a 50mm (2in) layer of dry sand poured on top.

Insulated floating floor
You can buy manufactured systems for soundproofing a suspended wooden floor. The systems include a mineral-fibre insulating blanket, 100mm (4in) thick, which is laid under the floor. The insulation does not significantly increase the floor's weight.

Typically, a metal channel with an integral resilient strip clips over the floor joists to support strips of plasterboard, 19mm (¾in) thick, fitted on each side; the floorboards are screwed on top. To provide additional acoustic insulation, you can fit a second layer of plasterboard, supported by

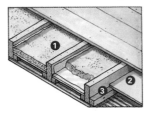

▲ *Sand pugging*
1. Dry sand provides soundproofing
2. Stiff-plywood platform lined with polythene
3. Supporting batten, screwed to joist

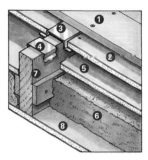

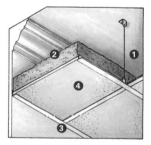

◀ **Insulated floating floor**
1. Floorboards screwed through plasterboard to metal channel
2. Plasterboard rests on metal flanges
3. Metal channel rests on resilient strip
4. Clip locates channel on joist
5. Additional layer of plasterboard supported by battens screwed to joists
6. Insulating blanket
7. Floor joist
8. Existing plaster ceiling

battens screwed to the sides of the joists.

Independent ceilings
If you are unable to gain access to the floor above, you may want to consider introducing soundproofing in the form of a lowered ceiling. It's worth getting expert advice about the most suitable method to adopt. Often, it's possible to recreate a moulded-plaster cornice and central rose on the new ceiling.

A proprietary suspended-grid system with acoustic panels is one relatively simple solution. Insulate the new ceiling with fibre blanket 150mm (6in) thick.

Another alternative is to construct an independent timber frame below the original ceiling. Provide new joists fixed to hangers, or to battens screwed to the walls. Lay insulation

▲ **Suspended ceiling insulated with blanket**
1 Grid hangs from cables attached to original ceiling
2 Lightweight insulating blanket
3 Proprietary metal-channel system
4 Loose-laid acoustic panels

across the joists, then nail two layers of plasterboard over a polythene vapour barrier stapled to the framework. Fill and tape all joints in the plasterboard.

SEE ALSO
187

Stains and dyes

Unlike paint, which after the initial priming coat rests on the surface of timber, a dye penetrates the wood. Its main advantage is to enhance the natural colour of the woodwork or to unify the slight variation in colour found in even the same species.

Wood dyes

Unlike paint, which after the initial priming coat rests on the surface of timber, a dye penetrates the wood. Its main advantage is to enhance the natural colour of the woodwork or to unify the slight variation in colour found in even the same species.

Water-based and oil-based dyes are available ready for use. You can also buy powdered pigments for mixing with methylated spirit. None of these dyes will actually protect the timber, and you will have to seal them with a clear varnish or polish.

Protective wood stains

The natural colour of wood can be enhanced with protective wood stains. Being moisture-vapour permeable, they allow the wood to breathe while providing a weather-resistant satin finish that resists flaking and peeling. Opaque colours are also available.

Protective wood stains are invariably brushed onto the wood. Some wood-stain manufacturers recommend two to three coats, while others offer a one-coat finish. Some ranges include a clear finish for redecorating previously stained woodwork without darkening the existing colour. Water-based stains generally tend to dry faster than those thinned with a spirit solvent. ☞

▼ *The range of stains and dyes can be baffling*

▲ *Coloured wood preservers can be used to decorate wood when paint would look unattractive. From left to right: clear; coloured; green*

Coloured preservers

Sawn timber fencing, wall cladding and outbuildings can look particularly unattractive when painted, yet these wooden structures still need protection and often benefit from decoration.

Use a wood preserver, which penetrates deeply into the timber to prevent both rot and insect attack. There are clear preservers, plus a range of natural-wood colours and green shades that are traditionally used on horticultural timbers.

You can buy preservers that will protect sound exterior timbers against fungal and insect attack, while staining the wood and making it look more attractive at the same time.

Traditional preservers have a strong, unpleasant smell and are unfortunately harmful to plants, whereas most modern low-odour solvent-based and water-based preservers are perfectly safe, even for greenhouses and propagators. These are widely available.

SEE ALSO
429

Stains and dyes: techniques

Unless the wood is perfectly clean and free from grease, wood dye will be rejected, producing an uneven, patchy appearance. Strip any previous finish, and sand the wood with progressively finer abrasive papers. Always sand in the direction of the grain, as any scratches made across the grain will be emphasized by the dye.

Making a test strip

The final colour is affected by the nature of the timber, the number of coats, and the overlying clear finish. You can also mix compatible dyes to alter the colour, or dilute them with the appropriate thinner.

Make a test strip, so that you will have an accurate guide from which you can choose the depth of colour to suit the job in hand. Use a piece of timber from the same batch you are staining, or one that resembles it closely.

Paint the strip with one coat of dye. Allow the dye to be absorbed, then apply a second coat, leaving a strip of the first application showing. It is rarely necessary to apply more than two coats of dye – but for the experiment add a third coat, and even a fourth, always leaving a strip of the previous application for comparison.

When the dye has dried completely, paint a band of clear varnish along the strip. Some polyurethane varnishes react unfavourably with oil-based dyes, so it is advisable to use products made by the same manufacturer.

Working with wood dyes

When you wet a piece of timber, water is absorbed by the wood, raising a mass of tiny fibres across the surface. Applying a water-based dye does the same – which is potentially ruinous for the

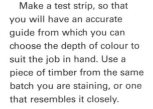

▼ Brushes, pads and rubbers are all useful for applying wood dye

final finish. Avoid the problem by sanding the wood until perfectly smooth, then dampen the whole surface with a wet rag. Leave it to dry out, then sand the raised grain with very fine abrasive paper before you apply the dye. If you are using an oil-based dye, this preliminary process is unnecessary.

If you want to fill the grain, first apply a seal coat of clear finish over the dye. Choose a grain filler that matches the dye, adjusting the colour by adding a little dye to it – but make sure that the dye and filler are compatible. An oil-based dye will not mix with a water-based filler, and vice versa; so check before you buy either.

▲ *Using a wood dye rubber*
Wearing gloves to protect your skin, pour some wood dye into a shallow dish, saturate the rubber with dye, and then squeeze some out so that it is not dripping but is still wet enough to apply a liberal coat of dye to the surface

How to apply wood dye

Use a 100mm (4in) paintbrush to apply dyes over a wide, flat surface. Don't brush out a dye as you would paint, but apply it liberally and evenly, always in the direction of the grain.

It is essential to blend wet edges of wood dye, so work fairly quickly and don't take a break until you have completed the job. If you have applied a water-based dye with a brush, it is sometimes advantageous to wipe over the wet surface with a soft cloth and remove excess dye.

Using a paint pad is one of the most effective ways to achieve an even coverage over a flat surface. However, you may find that you still need to use a paintbrush for staining mouldings and to get the wood dye right into awkward corners.

Because dyes are so fluid, it's often easier to apply them with a wad of soft lint-free rag, called a rubber. This will enable you to control runs on a vertical panel; it's also the best way to stain turned wood and rails. ☞

SEE ALSO
400–1

Staining a flat panel

Whenever possible, set up a panel horizontally for staining, either on trestles or raised on softwood blocks. Shake the container before use; and pour the dye into a flat dish, so that you are able to load your applicator properly.

Apply the dye, working swiftly and evenly along the grain. Stain the edges at the same time as the top surface. The first application may have a slightly patchy appearance as it dries, because some parts of the wood will absorb more dye than others. The second coat normally evens out the colour without difficulty. If powdery deposits are left on the surface of the dry wood dye, wipe them off with a coarse, dry cloth, before applying the second coat in the same way as the first.

Leave the dye to dry overnight, then proceed with the clear finish of your choice to seal the colourant.

Staining floors.

Because a wooden floor is such a large area, it is more difficult to blend the wet edges of the dye.

Work along two or three boards at a time, using a paintbrush and finishing at the edge of a board each time.

Woodblock floors are even trickier; so work with an assistant, to cover the area quickly, blending and overlapping sections with a soft cloth.

Staining a door

So that it can be laid horizontally, stain a new or stripped door before it is hung. A flush door is stained like any other panel, but use a rubber to colour the edges, so that wood dye does not run underneath and spoil the other side.

When staining a panelled door, it is essential to follow a sequence that will allow you to pick up the wet edges before they dry. Use a combination of brush and rubber to apply the dye, and follow the sequence on the top of the next page.

Unlike the order adopted when painting a panelled door, it's best to stain the mouldings last – in order to prevent any overlapping showing on the flat surfaces. Stain the mouldings with a narrow brush, and blend in the colour with a rubber. 🖝

▼ **Pads for mouldings**
It is relatively easy to apply wood dye to a moulding using a narrow paintbrush. Alternatively, you could use a small paint pad intended for painting glazing bars

◀ Method for staining a panelled door

Follow this sequence, using a combination of paintbrush or paint pad and rubber to apply the dye evenly to the various parts of the door. Start with the inset panels, then continue with half of the vertical muntin, the bottom cross rail and half the stiles. Pick up the wet edges with the other half of the muntin and the stiles. Stain the central cross rail, then repeat the procedure for the second half of the door. Finish with the mouldings, using a narrow brush and rubber

Exterior wood stains

Standard wood dyes are not suitable for exterior use. They do not have any protective properties and tend to fade in direct sunlight. For planed joinery and weatherboarding, use a protective wood stain that is moisture-vapour permeable. For sawn timber, use a coloured wood preserver.

Protective wood stain

Make sure the surface is clean, dry and sanded. All previous paint or varnish must be stripped off. For extra protection, treat the timber with a clear wood preserver before staining.

Apply the required number of coats, making sure that the coverage is even.

Stain wall cladding one board at a time (treating the lower edge first).

SEE ALSO
116

Staircase repairs

With an old softwood staircase, the tread is likely to be the first to show damage. Wear on the nosing (the overlap on the tread) is usually concentrated around the centre of the step, and you may be able to repair it without having to renew the entire tread.

Renewing a nosing

Mark three cutting lines just outside the worn area, one parallel with the edge of the nosing and the other two at right angles (1). Adjust the blade depth of a circular saw to the thickness of the tread. Pin a batten the required distance from and parallel to the long cutting line to guide the edge of the saw's baseplate.

1. Mark the cutting lines around the worn area

Cutting out the waste
Make the cut by gradually lowering the blade into the wood (2). Try not to overrun the short end lines. Once you've made the cut, remove the guide batten.

Use a tenon saw to make the end cuts at 45 deg to the face of the tread (3).

Cut away the waste with a chisel, working with the grain and avoiding damaging the riser tongue if it has tongue-and-groove joints. Pare away the waste that remains in the uncut corners (4).

Replacing the nosing
Plane a groove in the underside of a new section of nosing to receive the tongue of the riser, and cut the ends of the new section to 45 deg. Check it fits, then apply wood adhesive and fix in place. Clamp down with a batten screwed at each end to the

2. Make the cut with a saw guided by a batten

3. Make 45 deg cuts at each end of the area

4. Pare away the waste from the corners

5. Clamp new section of nosing with a batten

tread (5). Place a packing strip of hardboard under the batten to concentrate the pressure.

Drill and insert glued dowels, 6mm (¼in) in diameter, into the edge of the nosing to reinforce the butt joint; then when the adhesive has set, plane and sand the repair flush.

Repairing a riser

Risers take much less wear and tear than treads, and rarely have to be replaced. Should a riser become weak through woodworm infestation, it can be reinforced from behind or replaced altogether.

Closed-string staircase

Remove the tread below the damaged riser, then saw through the tongue at the top of the riser. Knock the wedges out of the riser housings, and prise out the riser itself (1).

Measure the distance between the strings and from the underside of one tread to the top of the other. Cut a new riser to fit. It is easier to join it to the treads with glued butt joints (2).

Glue and wedge the new riser into the string housings (3), then glue and screw the upper tread to its top edge.

Refit the tread, but note that

1. Prise out the riser *2. Cut the riser to fit*

you need pack out only the front sawcut, as the new riser has been made to fit. Glue and screw the tread to the lower edge of the new riser.

Open-string staircase

Remove the scotia moulding, then saw through the tongues at the top and bottom of the riser, and remove the wedge from its wall-string housing.

Knock apart the mitred joint between the end of the riser and the outer string. Once free, pull the inner end of the riser out of its housing.

Make a riser to fit between treads, mitring its outer end to match the joint in the string.

Apply adhesive and fit the riser from the front. Re-wedge the inner housing joint, screw treads to riser, nail the mitred end, and replace scotia moulding.

3. Wedge the riser

SEE ALSO
68–9

Replacing treads

Most stairs have tongue-and-groove joints between their risers and treads. In some cases, the tops of the risers are housed in the undersides of the treads; and in others, simple butt joints are secured with nails or screws. A butt joint will allow a thin knife blade to pass through, while a housed or tongue-and-groove joint will obstruct it.

Dismantling a butt joint

First take out the nails or screws, then prise it up with a chisel. Remove the triangular glued blocks in a similar way.

Cutting a tongue

Work from the front of the step when cutting the tongue of a riser jointed into the underside of a tread. Where the riser's tongue is jointed into the top of the tread below, it must be cut from the rear.

1. Chop out the wedges

Before cutting a tongue, remove any screws, nails and glued blocks, then drill two or three 3mm (⅛in) holes just below the shoulder of the joint, so you can insert the blade of a padsaw. Begin the sawcut, then continue with a panel

2. Drive out the tread

saw, using the underside of the tread to guide the blade.

Removing the tread from a closed-string staircase

To continue with the repair, work from the underside of the stair and chisel out the retaining wedges from the string housings at the ends of the tread (1). Free the joints by giving the tread a sharp tap from above with a hammer and block.

Drive the tread backwards and out of its two housings by alternately tapping one end and then the other (2).

Next, make a replacement tread to fit, shaping its front edge to match the nosing of the other steps, and cut a new pair of wedges. Slide the new tread and wedges into place from below. Measure the gaps left by the sawcuts at its front and back (3), and cut wooden packing strips or pieces of veneer to fill them.

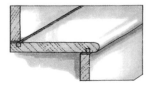

3. Pack out the sawcuts at front and back

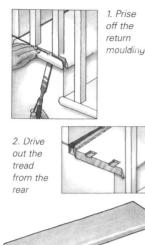

1. Prise off the return moulding

2. Drive out the tread from the rear

3. Cut the baluster housings in the new tread

Remove the tread and apply wood adhesive; then replace it, along with the wedges and packing pieces. Secure the tread with 38mm (1½in) countersunk woodscrews, screwed into both risers.

Removing the tread from an open-string staircase

This type of staircase requires a different approach. Use a chisel to prise off the return moulding (which covers the end of the tread), taking care not to split it (1); and then carefully remove the two balusters.

Chisel the wedge out of the wall-string housing, to free the inner end of the tread. Then drive the tread out from the rear of the stair (2), using a hammer and a wood block on its back edge. You will have to cut through or extract any nails that fix the tread to the outer string before it can be pulled completely clear.

Making use of the original tread as a template, mark its shape on a new board, then cut the board accurately to size. Take care to preserve the exact shape of the nosing, which must be the same as the return moulding prised from the end of the old tread.

Mark out and cut a pair of housings for the balusters (3), and make a new hardwood wedge for the inner-tread housing. Treat all the new wood with a chemical preserver.

Fit the tread from the front, insert packing strips, then glue and screw it, following the method described opposite.

Apply adhesive to the balusters and replace them. Finally, pin and glue the return moulding to the end of the tread and replace any scotia moulding.

SEE ALSO
68–9

Curing creaking stairs

Wood invariably shrinks when it dries out, loosening joints and making them creak when anyone mounts the stairs.

How you set about curing this depends on whether you have access to the back of the treads. A better repair can be carried out from the back – from below the stairs – but if you will have to cut into a plastered soffit, it's probably best to work from above.

Working from below

If it's possible to get to the underside of the stairs, have someone walk slowly up the steps, counting them out loud.

1. Prise out the old wedge with a chisel

2. Apply glue to the joint and drive in the wedge

3. Prise open the joint and inject adhesive

4. Rub-joint glued blocks into the angle

From under the staircase, note any loose steps and mark them with chalk. Get your assistant to step on and off the treads while you discover the source of the creaking.

Loose housing joints

If the tread or riser has become loose in its string housing, the glued wedge may have worked loose. Remove the wedge (1), clean it up and apply PVA wood adhesive; then rewedge the joint (2). If the wedge is damaged, make a new one from hardwood.

Loose blocks

Check the triangular blocks that fit in the angle between the tread and riser. If the adhesive has failed on any of the faces, remove the blocks and clean off the old adhesive. Before replacing the blocks, prise the shoulder of the tread-to-riser joint slightly open, using a chisel, then apply adhesive to the joint (3) and rub-joint the glued blocks into the angle (4).

If suction alone proves insufficient, use panel pins to hold the blocks in place while the adhesive sets (try to avoid treading on the repaired steps in the meantime).

If blocks are missing, make new ones from a length of 50 x 50mm (2 x 2in) softwood.

Working from above

Remove the stair carpet and walk slowly up the stairs. When you reach a creaking tread, walk on it to discover which part is moving and mark it with chalk.

Loose nosing joint

Drill clearance holes for 38mm (1½in) countersunk screws into the tread, centring on the thickness of the riser. Put PVA wood adhesive into the holes and work the joint a little to encourage the adhesive to spread into it, then pull the joint up tight with the screws.

If the screws cannot be concealed by stair carpet, counterbore the holes so as to set the screw heads below the surface of the tread, and then plug the holes with matching wood (1).

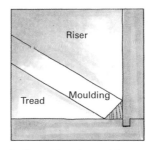

2. Glue a triangular moulding into the angle

Loose riser joint

A loose joint at the back of the tread is tricky to repair from above. You can try working water-thinned PVA wood adhesive into the joint, but you cannot use woodscrews to pull the joint together.

Alternatively, try reinforcing the joint by gluing a section of 12 x 12mm (½ x ½in) triangular moulding into the angle between the tread and the riser (2). This is viable only if it does not make the remaining width of the tread less than the minimum Building Regulation specification of 220mm (8¾in).

Unless the stair carpet covers the full width of the treads, cut the moulding slightly shorter than the width of the carpet; or glue a similar moulding to each step and dye or paint to unify the colour.

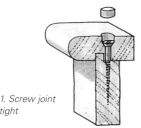

1. Screw joint tight

SEE ALSO
12–15

Steps: building garden steps

Designing a garden for a sloping site offers plenty of possibilities for creating attractive changes of level – by terracing areas of paving or holding planting beds in place with retaining walls. However, people will need to use steps to get to the different levels safely.

Designing steps

In a large garden with a gradual slope, a series of steps with wide treads and low risers can look impressive. For a steep slope, avoid a staircase appearance by building a flight of steps with a few treads interposed with wide, flat landings, at which points the flight can change direction to add further interest and offer a different view of the garden.

For steps to be both comfortable and safe to use, the proportion of tread (the part you stand on) to riser (the vertical part of the step) is important. As a rough guide, build steps so that the depth of the tread (from front to back) plus twice the height of the riser equals 650mm (2ft 2in). For example, match 300mm (1ft) treads with 175mm (7in) risers; 350mm (1ft 2in) treads with 150mm (6in) risers; and so on. Never make treads less than 300mm (1ft) deep, or risers higher than 175mm (7in).

Using concrete slabs

Concrete paving slabs are ideal for making firm, flat treads for garden steps. Construct the risers from concrete blocks or bricks, allowing the treads to overhang by 25 to 50mm (1 to 2in) in order to cast an attractive shadow line to define the edge of the step.

So you can gauge the number of steps required,

1. Cut the shape of the steps in the soil

2. Dig the footing for the first riser

3. Build a brick riser and level it

4. Lay the tread on mortar

5. Mark the position of the next riser

measure the difference in height from the top of the slope to the bottom. Next, mark the position of the risers with pegs, and roughly shape the steps in the soil as confirmation (1).

Either lay concrete slabs, bedded in sand, flush with the ground at the foot of the slope or dig a trench for hardcore and a 100 to 150mm (4 to 6in) concrete base to support the first riser (2). When set, build the riser from two courses of mortared bricks, checking with a spirit level (3). Fill behind the riser with compacted hardcore until it is level, then lay the tread on a bed of mortar (4). Using a spirit level as a guide, tap down the tread until it slopes very slightly towards its front edge, so as to shed rainwater and prevent ice forming in cold weather.

Measure from the front edge of the tread to mark the position of the next riser on the slabs (5), then build the next step in the same way. Set the final tread flush with the paved area or lawn at the top of the steps.

Landscaping each side
It is usually possible to landscape the slope at each side of the steps and to turf or plant it to prevent soil washing down onto them. Another solution is to retain the soil with large stones, perhaps extending into a rockery. Eventually, spreading plants will soften the hard-edge look of the paving, but cut back overhanging growth that could cause someone to stumble.

SEE ALSO
261

Building log steps

You can use sawn lengths of timber to build attractive steps that suit an informal garden. It's best to construct risers that are more or less the same height, otherwise someone may stumble if they are forced to break step.

As it's not always possible to obtain uniform-shaped logs, you may have to make up the height of the riser with two or more slimmer logs. Alternatively, you can buy purpose-made pressure-treated logs, machined with a flat surface on two faces. Soak your own timber in a chemical preserver overnight.

Remove any turf and cut a regular slope in the earth bank, then compact the soil by treading it down. Sharpen stakes cut from logs 75mm (3in) in diameter and drive

1. Drive a stake at each end of a step

2. Place a log behind the stakes

3. Fill behind the log with hardcore

them into the ground, one at each end of a step (1).

Place a heavy log behind the stakes, bedding it down in the soil until it is level (2), and pack broken-brick hardcore behind it to construct the tread of the step (3). To finish the step, shovel a layer of gravel on top of the hardcore, then rake the gravel level with the top of the log riser.

▼ Log steps

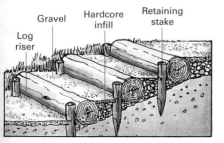

Gravel

Hardcore infill

Retaining stake

Log riser

4. Make up a riser with two slim logs

If you are unable to obtain large logs, you can build a step from two or three straight slimmer logs, holding them against the stakes with hardcore as you construct the riser (4).

Finish by laying a gravel path at the top and bottom of the flight of steps.

Making curved steps

To build a series of curved steps, choose materials that will make construction as easy as possible. One option is to use tapered concrete slabs for the treads, designing the circumference of the steps to suit the proportions of the slabs.

Alternatively, use bricks laid flat or on edge to build the risers. Set the bricks to radiate out from the centre of the curve, and fill the slightly tapered joints with mortar.

Use a length of string attached to a peg driven into the ground as an improvised compass to mark out the curve of each step.

After roughly shaping the soil, lay a concrete foundation for the bottom riser. Build the risers and treads as for regular paving-slab steps (*see* pp360–361), using the improvised string compass as a guide.

▼ *Mark the edge with an improvised compass*

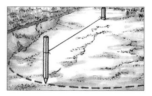

▼ **Building circular landings**
To construct a circular landing, build the front edge with bricks and paving, as for a curved step. When the mortar has set, fill the area of the landing with compacted hardcore and lay gravel up to the level of the tread

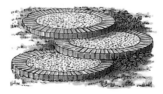

◄
SEE ALSO
256–7

Repairing concrete steps

Casting new steps in concrete requires such complicated formwork that the end result hardly justifies the effort involved, especially when it's possible to construct better-looking steps from cast-concrete slabs and blocks. Nevertheless, if you have a flight of concrete steps in your garden, you will want to keep them in good condition.

Like other forms of masonry, concrete suffers from 'spalling' – frost breaks down the surface of the material and fragments flake off. Spalling frequently occurs along the front edges of steps where a lot of foot traffic adds to the problem. Repair broken edges as soon as you can – not only are they ugly, but damaged steps are not as safe as they might be.

1. Prop a board against the riser

2. Fill the front edge with concrete

3. Run an edging float against the board

Building up broken edges

Wearing safety goggles, chip away concrete around the damaged area and provide a good grip for fresh concrete. Cut a board to the height of the riser and prop it against the step with bricks (1).

Mix up a small batch of general purpose concrete, adding a little PVA bonding agent to help it adhere to the step. Dilute some bonding agent with water (for example, 3 parts water to 1 part bonding agent) and brush it onto the damaged area, stippling it into the crevices.

When the surface becomes tacky, fill the hole with concrete mix flush with the edge of the board (2). Radius the front edge slightly with a home-made edging float, running it against the board (3).

Surface preparation

Preparing any surface before decorating is a very important step. It becomes essential when the plaster surface has minor defects in it.

Filling cracks and holes

Special flexible emulsions and textured paints are designed to cover hairline cracks – but larger cracks, dents and holes will reappear in a short time if they are not filled adequately.

Rake loose material from a crack, using a wallpaper scraper (1). Undercut the edges of larger cracks to provide a key for the filling.

Use a paintbrush to dampen the crack, then press in cellulose filler with a filling

1. Rake out loose material

2. Press filler into crack

Gaps behind skirtings
Large gaps can open up between skirting boards and the wall plaster. Cellulose fillers simply fall into the cavity behind, so bridge the gap with a flexible acrylic filler or inject expanding polyurethane foam.

knife. Drag the blade across the crack (2) to force the filler in, then draw it along the crack to smooth the filler. Leave the filler standing slightly proud of the surface, ready for rubbing down with abrasive paper.

Fill shallow cracks in one go. But in deep cracks build up the filler in stages, letting each application set before adding more. Alternatively, switch to a deep-repair filler.

Fill and rub down small holes and dents in the same way.

SEE ALSO
276–7

Stripping walls and ceilings

BEGINNER

Before you begin stripping any walls or ceilings, remove the carpets and underlay, roll them up, tie them with string and store them away.

Stripping wallpaper

Score the walls with the edge of your scraper or a wallpaper scorer [A], and soak the paper with warm soapy water and a sponge. The more you soak the paper, the easier it will be to strip off. Work a rotation system – in between stripping one wall, soak another.

Ceilings are more difficult to strip. Buy or hire a steam stripper, as they're also useful for walls [B]. Follow the instructions and safety advice carefully. Don't hold the steamer in one place for too long or you may loosen the plaster finish on old walls. Plaster damage can occur by using the scraper forcefully on paper that has not been soaked thoroughly [C].

When stripping wallpaper directly above a socket or light switch, turn off the power supply, and loosen off the socket and switch faces to allow for the paper to be completely removed.

Tools

Steps
Trestles
Steam stripper
Club hammer
Bolster chisel
Scrapers
Wallpaper scorer
Wire brush
Gloves and goggles
Sponge
Paddle brush

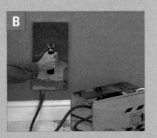

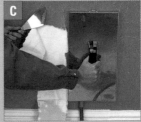

Some wallpapers allow you to strip off the face of the paper leaving just the backing paper as the lining. This can be left on to save time and energy.

To remove backing paper, soak with soapy water [D]; apply at least two soakings and allow 20 minutes to soak through. Remove paper with a scraper [E], then wash the walls down with a warm water and mild detergent solution.

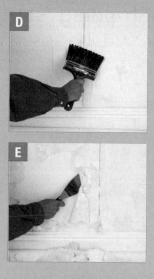

Removing ceramic tiles

Goggles and gloves are essential, as sharp splinters can be created when removing tiles, and broken edges can be as sharp as a razor. Break out one tile first [F]. This will allow you to get the bolster chisel behind the next tile more easily. Use the bolster and hammer to remove the old adhesive as you go. Clean the walls and clear the floor as you go also.

Very old, pre-Edwardian wall tiling was generally fixed with a sharp sand and cement mix. This is extremely tough to remove and will require re-plastering of the walls.

STRIPPING CEILINGS

Use a steam stripper. Most importantly, set up a safe platform to work from, NOT a mere stepladder! Use trestles and a platform at a comfortable height. You will only be able to work for short spells at a time. Working overhead, your arms will feel like lead, so work at a steady pace across the ceiling and take frequent breaks.

Patching a lath-and-plaster wall

If the laths are intact, just fill any holes in the plaster with cellulose filler or repair plaster. If some laths are broken, reinforce the repair with a piece of fine expanded-metal mesh.

Rake out loose plaster, and undercut the edge of the hole with a bolster chisel. Use tinsnips to cut the metal mesh to the shape of the hole, but a little larger (1). The mesh is flexible, so you can easily bend it in order to tuck the edge behind the sound plaster all round (2).

1. Cut with tinsnips
2. Tuck mesh into hole

3. Staple mesh to stud.
4. Trowel on plaster

Flatten the mesh against the laths with light taps from a hammer; if possible, staple the mesh to a wall stud to hold it in place (3). For papering and tiling, patch the hole with one-coat repair plaster (4). If you want a smoother surface for painting, finish the surface with a thin coat of skimming repair plaster.

Filling small holes in plasterboard

Use plasterer's glass-fibre patching tape when mending holes up to 75mm (3in) across. Stick on the self-adhesive strips in a star shape over the hole, then apply cellulose filler and feather the edges (1).

Alternatively, use an offcut of plasterboard just larger than the hole yet narrow enough to slot through it. Bore a hole in the middle, thread a length of string

1. Fill and feather the patch

2. Fix string to offcut

3. Pull on string

through, and tie a nail to one end of the string (2). Butter the ends of the offcut with filler, then feed it into the hole. Pull on the string (3) to force it against the back of the cladding, then press filler into the hole so that it is not quite flush with the surface. When the filler is hard, cut off the string and apply a thin coat of filler for a flush finish.

Patching larger holes in plasterboard

A large hole punched through a plasterboard wall or ceiling cannot be patched with wet plaster only. Using a sharp craft knife and a straightedge, cut back the damaged board to the nearest studs or joists at each side of the hole (1). Cut a panel of plasterboard to fit snugly within the hole and nail it to the joists or studs, using galvanized plasterboard

Large holes cannot be patched with wet plaster alone

nails. Brush on a coat of skimming repair plaster and smooth it with a plastic spreader or a steel plasterer's trowel (2).

1. Cut back the damaged panel to nearest supports

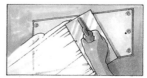

2. Nail on the new panel and coat with plaster

SEE ALSO
278–9

Preparing woodwork

Wooden joinery often needs redecorating long before any other part of the house, particularly window and door exteriors, bargeboards and fascias. The main cause is that wood tends to swell when it becomes moist, then shrinks again when the sun or central heating dries it out.

Paint won't adhere for long under these conditions, nor will any other finish. Wood is also vulnerable to woodworm and various forms of rot caused by damp, so preparation is essential to preserve most types of timber. ☞

Preparing new joinery

New joinery is often primed at the factory, but check that the primer is in good condition before you start. If the primer is satisfactory, rub it down lightly with fine-grade abrasive paper, dust it off, then apply a second coat of wood primer to areas that will be inaccessible after installation. Don't leave the timber uncovered outside, as primer is not sufficient protection against prolonged exposure to the weather.

Ensure unprimed timber is dry, then sand the surface in the direction of the grain, using fine-grade sandpaper. Wrap it round a wood block for flat surfaces and round a piece of dowel or a pencil for moulded sections.

Once you have removed all raised grain and lightly

▼ *Sand along the grain with abrasive paper*

rounded any sharp edges, dust the wood down.

Rub it over with a tack rag (an impregnated cloth to which dust will stick) or a rag moistened with white spirit.

Paint bare softwood with a solvent-based wood primer or a quick-drying water-thinned acrylic primer. Apply either primer liberally, working it well into the joints and, particularly, into the end grain.

Wash oily hardwoods with white spirit before priming with an aluminium primer. Use standard wood primers for other hardwoods, thinning them slightly to encourage penetration into the grain.

When the primer is dry, fill open-grained timber with a fine surface filler. Use a piece of coarse cloth to rub it well into the wood, making circular strokes followed by parallel strokes in the direction of the grain. When the filler is dry, rub it down with a fine abrasive paper to a smooth finish.

Fill larger holes, open joints, cracks and similar imperfections with flexible interior or exterior wood filler. Press the filler into the holes with a filling knife, leaving it slightly proud of the surface so that it can be sanded flush with fine-grade abrasive paper once it has set. Dust down ready for painting.

If, just before starting to apply the undercoat, you find a hole that you've missed, fill it with fast-setting filler.

Sealing knots with shellac knotting

Knots and other resinous areas of the wood must be treated to prevent them staining subsequent layers of paint.

Pick off any hardened resin, then seal the knots by painting them with two coats of shellac knotting. If you are going to paint with relatively dark colours, you can seal the knots and prime the timber in one operation, using aluminium wood primer.

▲ *Seal resinous knots with shellac knotting*

SEE ALSO
442–3

SEE ALSO
293–4

Preparing walls and ceilings for decoration

BEGINNER

Most professional decorators would advocate that the finished job is only as good as the preparation gone into it – and this should also be true for your decorating.

If you have rushed the preparation work before you begin decorating, every time you walk in the room, the areas that you are not happy with because you cut corners will really stand out. So take your time and prepare properly. Even the roughest of walls can be improved immeasurably with a little patience and a modicum of hard work.

In your decorating kit, there should be at least a couple of filling knives, both broad and narrow bladed. These look exactly the same as scrapers, but are much more flexible to enable the filling process to

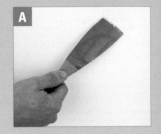

A

be carried out more effectively than if you used a scraper.

In older properties, when the paper is removed, areas of finish plaster (the top coat) quite often come away from the base coat. Ensure that the topcoat edges are stable, but do not insert your scraper

Tools

Scrapers
Filler knives
Sponges
Mastic gun
Mastic
Hammer
Batten
Sandpaper
Craft knife

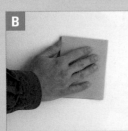

B

C

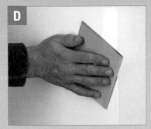

under the finish or you will take off more and more of the surface.

In preparation of plaster damage, always cut and scrape towards the centre from the sides. Prepare the entire wall, and apply a solution of PVA adhesive and water to the dry damaged areas with a paintbrush.

Make up a quantity of filler by adding water to the powder, and apply it to the damaged sections. To areas where there is a crack, cut out the crack to form a 'V' shape using the corner of the scraper. Apply the PVA and water solution, and fill [A].

Allow the filler to harden and dry out, then sand the area smooth. When sanding down, you'll probably only need fine grade paper. Fold the paper and rub lightly over the filled surface until it is smooth to the touch [B].

Quite often corners get damaged, as they are far more vulnerable to getting knocked. Pin a temporary batten to the wall to make a straight edge and fill in the gaps to rectify this, making a perfect corner [C].

Leave it overnight to cure, then remove the batten and fill in the pinholes. When dry, sand the surface [D].

When the room is sanded down and the dust swept up or vacuumed, use clean water and a sponge to rinse over the walls and remove any residue or debris before redecorating [E].

There are lots of new decorating aids available on the market today. One of these, decorator's caulk, is extremely useful. This is mastic in a tube, which you apply with a mastic gun.

When you buy mastic, ensure that you buy the

correct one for the job. There is a wide range available to do a variety of jobs. For decorating, you need a water-soluble decorator's caulk (NOT silicone). This caulk is wonderful for flexible filling between the walls and skirtings or around door and window architraves.

You may well find you have different size cracks to fill, so start by cutting off just the tip of the caulk nozzle applicator with a craft knife and fill all the narrow cracks [F]. To fill the broader cracks, cut off more of the nozzle to create a wider bead.

Using these mastic guns effectively takes a bit of practice. It is recommended that you start at the top, along a straight edge, and in a smooth flowing motion, apply the bead in a steady line along the crack [G]. Remember to release the trigger to cut off the mastic flow at the end of the run, or the caulk will ooze out everywhere.

Smooth off the caulk with a damp sponge, regularly rinsing out the sponge to avoid any mess [H].

T

Taps and valves: draining the system

Rather than calling out a plumber straightaway, it is worth trying to fix the more common faults yourself. Draining the plumbing system is your starting point.

Draining the system

You will have to drain at least part of any plumbing system before you can work on it; and if you detect a leak, you will have to drain the relevant section quickly. So find out where the valves, stopcock and draincocks are situated, before you're faced with an emergency. ☛

Draining cold water taps and pipes

- Turn off the main stopcock on the rising main to cut off the supply to the kitchen tap (and to all the other cold taps on a direct system).
- Open the tap until the flow ceases.
- To isolate the bathroom taps, close the valve on the cold-feed pipe from the storage tank and open all taps on that section. If you can't find a valve, rest a wooden batten across the tank and tie the arm of the float valve to it. This shuts off the supply to the tank, so you can empty it by running all the cold taps in the bathroom. Alternatively, turn off the main stopcock, then run the cold taps.

Draining hot water taps and pipes

- Turn off the immersion heater or boiler.
- Close the valve on the cold-feed pipe to the cylinder and run the hot taps. Even when the water stops flowing, the cylinder will still be full.
- If there's no valve on the cold-feed pipe, tie up the float-valve arm, then turn on

---

SEALED CENTRAL-HEATING SYSTEMS

A sealed system does not have a feed-and-expansion tank – the radiators are filled from the mains via a flexible hose known as a filling loop. The indirect coil in the hot water cylinder is drained as described right, though you might have to open a vent pipe that is fitted to the cylinder before the water will flow.

▶ Closing a float valve
Cut off the supply of water to a storage tank by tying the float arm to a batten.

the cold taps in the bathroom to empty the tank. (If you run the hot taps first, the water in the tank will flush out all your hot water from the cylinder.) When the cold taps run dry, open the hot taps. Run the hot and cold taps together to clear the pipes as quickly as possible in an emergency.

Draining a WC cistern
• To empty the WC cistern, tie up its float-valve arm and flush the WC.
• To empty the pipe that supplies the cistern, either turn off the main stopcock or close the valve on the cold feed from the storage tank. Alternatively, shut off the supply to the storage tank and empty it through the cold taps.

Draining the cold water storage tank
• To drain the storage tank in the roof space, close the main stopcock on the rising main, then open all the taps in the bathroom (hot taps on

a direct system). Bail out the residue of water left at the bottom of the tank.

Draining the hot water cylinder
• If the hot water cylinder leaks, turn off the immersion heater and boiler; shut off the cold feed to the cylinder from the storage tank (or drain the cold water storage tank). Run hot water from taps.
• Locate a draincock to drain the water left in the cylinder. Attach a hose and run it to a sink lower than the cylinder. Turn the square-headed spindle on the draincock till you hear water flowing.
• Water can't be drained if the washer is baked onto the draincock seating; disconnect the vent pipe and insert a hosepipe to siphon cylinder.

SEE ALSO
378–9

Clearing airlocks

There are two main reasons for airlocks occurring in the hot water supply. Firstly, the plumbing may have been constructed with too many bends in the pipework. The more common cause, however, is too great a demand on the reservoir (water tank) system in your home.

A spluttering or hissing tap means there is an airlock and the air needs to be forced out. The best place to start is the kitchen sink. With a piece of rubber hose, slip one end over the spout of the kitchen mixer tap [A], and the other over the spout of the bathroom basin hot tap [B]. Turn the cold tap on the kitchen tap wide open [C], then turn the hot tap on the basin wide open [D]. This forces the air through the bathroom hot tap by using mains pressure until the water flows freely.

To clear the bath taps, repeat this process by closing the basin tap, and if necessary the tank supply, forcing air bubbles into the tank. The whole line is now clear.

If you have a mixer tap in the kitchen, remove the spout and hold your hand tightly over the opening. Fully open the hot tap and slowly open the cold, forcing air up through the open bath tap.

Tools

Piece of
rubber hose
Radiator
valve key
Dry cloth

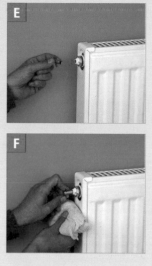

A common cause is if the water mains supply is turned off and the tank is emptied. This allows air into the system. Fix in the same way as above.

Air trapped in a radiator is easily detected – if only half the radiator is hot, there is probably an air pocket. There is a small bleed valve on the top left or right corner of the radiator. You will need a radiator key to open this valve. Push the key onto the valve [E] and turn it gently to release the trapped air (a hissing sound), until water squirts out. Immediately shut off the bleed valve. Have some old rags to soak up any spillage [F].

Check the water pressure indicator on your combi boiler. (Your boiler should have information on the panel regarding the level of pressure required.) If the pressure is low and needs topping up, open up the screw on the valve in the filling loop at the bottom of the boiler [G], using a screwdriver if necessary. Watch the water pressure indicator and shut off the feed immediately by turning back the valve screw when the correct pressure has been reached.

Fitting a garden tap

A bib tap situated on an outside wall is convenient for attaching a hose for a lawn sprinkler, watering down the far end of the garden or for washing the car.

▶ *A suitably robust bib tap for use outdoors*

To comply with the Water Regulations, a double-seal non-return (check) valve must be incorporated in the plumbing to prevent contaminated water being drawn back into the system. Provide a means of shutting off the water and draining the pipework during winter, and keep the outside pipe run as short as possible.

Turn off and drain the mains supply. Fit a T-joint (1) to run the supply to the tap. Run a short length of pipe to a convenient position for another stopcock (2) or miniature valve, and for the non-return valve (3) if the tap doesn't include one, making sure that the arrows marked on both fittings point in the direction of flow.

Fit a draincock (4) after this point. Run a pipe through the wall inside a length of plastic overflow (5), so that any leaks will be detected quickly and will not soak the masonry. Wrap PTFE tape around the bib-tap thread, then screw it into a wall plate attached to the masonry outside (6).

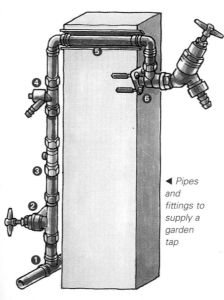

◀ *Pipes and fittings to supply a garden tap*

Repairing a leaking tap

A tap may leak for a number of reasons – none of them difficult to deal with. When water drips from a spout, for example, it is usually the result of a faulty washer; and if the tap is old, the seat against which the washer is compressed may be worn, too. If water leaks from beneath the head of the tap when it's in use, the gland packing or O-ring needs replacing. When you are working on a tap, lay a towel in the bottom of the washbasin, bath or sink to catch small objects.

Replacing a washer

To replace the washer in a traditional bib or pillar tap, first drain the supply pipe, then open the valve as far as possible before you begin dismantling either kind of tap.

If the tap has a metal cover, unscrew it by hand or use a wrench, taping the jaws to protect the chrome finish.

Lift the cover to reveal the headgear nut above the body of the tap. Slip a narrow spanner onto the nut and unscrew (1) until you can lift out the headgear assembly.

The jumper to which the washer is fixed fits into the bottom of the headgear. In some taps the jumper comes off with the headgear (2), but in other types it will be lying inside the tap body.

The washer may be pressed over a small button in the centre of the jumper (3) – prise it off with a screwdriver. If the washer is held in place by a nut, it can be difficult to remove. Soften any corrosion with penetrating oil; then, holding the jumper with pliers, unscrew the nut with a spanner (4). Fit a new washer and retaining nut, then reassemble the tap.

1. Loosen headgear nut

2. Lift out headgear

3. Prise off washer

4. Or undo fixing nut

SEE ALSO
24–5

Curing a dripping ceramic tap

In theory ceramic-disc taps are maintenance free, but faults can still occur. Since there's no washer to replace, you have to replace the whole inner cartridge when the tap leaks. However, before you proceed, make sure that the lower seal is not damaged, as this can be the cause of a dripping tap.

1. Unscrew the cartridge

Turn off the water at the stopcock and remove the headgear from the tap body by turning it anticlockwise with a spanner (1).

2. Lift out and examine

Remove the cartridge and examine it for wear or damage (2). Simply cleaning any debris off the ceramic discs might be all that is required; but if a disc is cracked, then you will need a new cartridge. Cartridges are handed – left (hot) and right (cold) – so be sure to order the correct one.

At the same time, have a look at the rubber seal on the bottom of the cartridge. If this is worn or damaged, it will cause the tap to drip. If needs be, replace the seal with a new one (3), which you can buy at any good hardware shop or DIY store.

3. Replace worn rubber seal

▲ *Plastic push-fit stopcock*

Stopcocks

Stopcocks are simply taps which can shut off the pipes the supply of water to your plumbing system.

A stopcock can also be used to isolate parts of the supply system; for example, having a stopcock fitted on the supply to a shower system means that you can shut off the water supply just to the shower if you need to fix a problem with the shower unit.

Because they are rarely used, stopcocks often fail to work just when they are most needed, in an emergency; so make sure they operate smoothly by closing and opening them from time to time. If their spindles are rather stiff, lubricate them with a little penetrating oil.

Tiles

Tiling allows you to cover a surface with relatively small regular units that can be cut and fitted into awkward shapes far more easily than sheet materials. With an almost inexhaustible range of colours, textures and patterns to choose from, tiling is one of the most popular methods of decorating walls and floors.

Carpet tiles

These have advantages over wall-to-wall carpeting. An error is less crucial when cutting a single tile to fit; and being loose-laid, worn, burnt or stained tiles can be replaced instantly. However, you can't substitute a brand-new tile several years later, because the colour won't match. It's worth buying several spares initially and swap them around regularly to even out the wear and colour change. Most types of carpet are available as tiles, including cord, loop and twist piles, both in wool and a range of man-made fibres. Carpet tiles come mostly in plain colours or small patterns. Some have an integral rubber underlay.

▼ *Carpet tiles can be replaced instantly if one or a small area gets damaged*

SEE ALSO
66–7

Ceramic floor tiles

Floor tiles are generally larger and thicker than wall tiles, so that they can withstand the weight of furniture and foot traffic. As with wall tiling, square and rectangular tiles are the most economical ones to buy and lay, but hexagonal and octagonal floor tiles are also available and are often used in combination with small shaped inserts to create regular patterns.

Tiles with interlocking curved edges require careful setting out in order to achieve a satisfactory result. Choose non-slip ceramic tiles for bathrooms and other areas

▲ *Designs go far beyond standard square or rectangle tiles these days...*

where the floor is likely to become wet.

Small unglazed, encaustic tiles are laid individually to produce intricate patterns that re-create the styles of Victorian and Edwardian tiled floors. They are manufactured in a range of plain colours and with patterns that are fired deep into the tiles.

Quarry tiles

Thick unglazed quarry tiles are ceramic tiles with a mellow appearance. The colours are limited to browns, reds, black and white. Hand-made quarries are uneven in colour, producing a beautiful mottled effect.

Round-edge 'bullnose'

▼ *Ceramic tiles come in all shapes and sizes, allowing you to create many patterns*

Quarry tiles for the floor are extremely hardwearing and come in various shapes. They are limited in colour choice to browns ▶, shades of red such as orangey-red ▼, and black and white.

Ceramic wall tiles
Most ceramic wall tiles are coated with a thick layer of glaze that makes them durable, waterproof and fairly easy to cut. Unglazed tiles are generally more subtle in colour and may need to be sealed to stop them absorbing grease and dirt.

quarry tiles can be used as treads for steps; and shaped tiles are available for creating a skirting around a quarry-tile floor.

▼ *Recreate Victorian-style floors with modern quarry tiles*

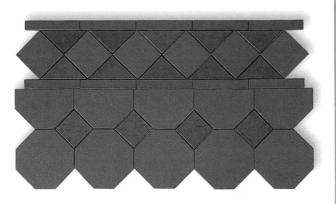

SEE ALSO
12

◄ *Plastic tiles*

Machine-produced tiles are perfectly regular in shapes and colour, and are therefore simple to match. Hand-made tiles have more variation in shape, colour and texture, but this sometimes adds to their appeal.

Patterned tiles can be used for decorative friezes or individual inserts; and some are sold as sets for creating pictorial murals, mostly for cooker and basin splashbacks.

Mosaic tiles

These are small versions of the standard ceramic tiles. To lay them individually would be incredibly fiddly and time-consuming, and lead to inaccuracy. The small squares or irregular shapes are therefore usually joined, either by a paper covering or a mesh backing, into larger panels.

Square tiles are common, but rectangular, hexagonal and round mosaics can be used on curved surfaces and fit irregular shapes better than large ceramic tiles do. ◄

Plastic tiles

Insulated plastic wall tiles inhibit condensation. Provided you don't use abrasive cleaners on them, they are quite durable; but will melt if subjected to direct heat. A special grout is applied to fill the 'joints' moulded across the 300mm (1ft) square tiles.

Rubber tiles

These were originally made for use in shops and offices – but being hardwearing yet soft and quiet to walk on, they

▼ *Rubber tiles*

also make ideal domestic floorcoverings. Rubber tiles are usually studded or textured to improve the grip.

Stone and slate flooring

A floor laid with natural stone or slate tiles will be exquisite but expensive. Sizes and thicknesses vary according to the manufacturer – some will even cut to measure. These materials are so costly that you should consider hiring a professional to lay them.

Other tiles

Cork is a popular covering for walls and floors; mirror tiles, polystyrene tiles and mineral-fibre tiles are also often used.

▲ Stone and slate tiles are best laid by an expert

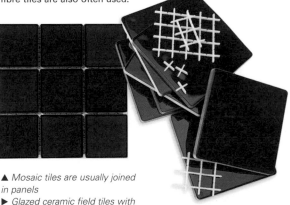

▲ Mosaic tiles are usually joined in panels
▶ Glazed ceramic field tiles with cross-shaped plastic spacers to maintain regular gaps between tiles

SEE ALSO
366–7

Vinyl tiles

Vinyl can be cut easily with a sharp trimming knife. Provided the tiles are firmly glued with good butt joints between them, the floor will be waterproof. They are also among the cheapest and easiest floorcoverings to lay. A standard coated tile has a printed pattern sandwiched between a vinyl backing and a harder, clear-vinyl surface. Solid-vinyl tiles are made entirely of hardwearing plastic.

▲ Vinyl tiles can simulate other flooring materials

Some vinyl tiles have a high proportion of mineral filler. As a result, they are stiff and must be laid on a perfectly flat base. Unlike standard vinyl tiles, they will resist some rising damp in a concrete subfloor.

Most tiles are square or rectangular, but there are interlocking shapes and hexagons. There are many patterns and colours to choose from, including embossed textures that simulate wood, ceramic, brick or stone tiling. ☞

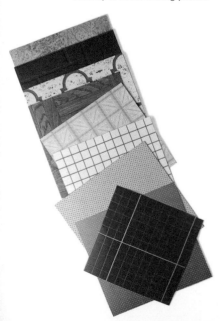

◄ Soft tiles come in relatively large sizes, so you can cover the floor fairly quickly

Tiling: ceilings, floors, walls

**There are two types of tiles you can use on a ceiling –
expanded polystyrene and mineral fibre. Polystyrene
tiles are the most popular, as they are inexpensive, easy
to cut and can be stuck to the ceiling without difficulty.**

For a more luxurious finish on
the ceiling, mineral-fibre tiles
can be used. They can be glued
directly to the ceiling, but
those with tongued-and-
grooved edges are best stapled
to a timber framework, which
is nailed across the ceiling.

Stapling mineral–fibre tiles

These tiles are stapled to softwood battens nailed to the
ceiling joists. Check the
direction of the joists by
examining the floor above. If
it's possible to gain access to
the joists from above, mark
their positions by poking a
bradawl through the plaster on
each side of one or two joists.

If lifting floorboards is too
inconvenient, locate the joists
from below by tapping the
ceiling and listening for a dull
thud that indicates the position
of a joist. Poke with the
bradawl to locate the rough
centre of a couple of joists,
then measure from these
points – they will be anything
from 300 to 450mm (1 to

1ft 6in) apart – and mark their
centres on the ceiling plaster.

Marking out the tiles
Start by marking two bisecting
lines across the ceiling, so you
can work out the spacing of
the tiles in order to create
even margins.

1. Making a tile spacer
*Set out the ceiling strips, using
a simple jig to gauge tile width*

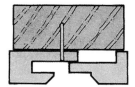

2. Securing the tiles
*Staple through each grooved
edge, then slot in the tongue
of the next tile*

SEE ALSO
408–9

Nailing up the battens
Nail parallel strips of 50 x 25mm (2 x 1in) timber across the ceiling at right angles to the joists; make the distance between batten centres one tile-width. Use a tile spacer – two softwood strips nailed together (1) – to make it easier.

Stapling the tiles
Begin with the margins. Measure the margin tiles and cut off their tongued edges. Starting in the corner, fix two adjacent rows of margin tiles by stapling through the grooved edges into the battens. Fix their other edges by driving panel pins through their faces.

Proceed diagonally across the ceiling. Slide the tongues of each tile into the grooves of its neighbours, then staple it through its own grooved edge (2).

▶ **Fixing ceiling tiles**
1 Space the battens to match the width of the tiles. Arrange the battens to leave even margins.
2 First, fix two rows of margin tiles, starting with the one in the corner.
3 Staple the remaining tiles to the battens, working diagonally across the ceiling

Polystyrene tiles
Polystyrene tiles can be used in most rooms except in a kitchen, where they would be directly over a source of heat.

Setting out the ceiling
Snap two chalked lines crossing each other at right angles in the centre of the ceiling. Align the first rows of tiles with the chalked lines.

Applying the tiles
Use a heavy-duty wallpaper paste or a non-flammable contact adhesive recommended for gluing expanded polystyrene. Brush the adhesive evenly across the back of the tile and onto the ceiling. When touch-dry, align one edge and corner of the first tile with one of the right angles formed by the marked lines, then press the tile against the ceiling; use the flat of your hand to do this, as fingertip pressure can crush polystyrene. Complete one half of the ceiling, then the other.

Cutting the tiles
Mark the margin tiles, then cut them with a single stroke, using a sharp trimming knife with a long blade. Mark out curves with a card template.

Laying vinyl floor tiles

Mark out the floor by finding the mid-point of two opposite walls and snapping a chalk string between them to mark a centre line across the floor.

If the tiles have a directional pattern, make sure you lay them the correct way.

Remove the protective paper backing from the first tile, then press its edge against a guide batten, aligning one corner with the centre line. Gradually lower the tile onto the floor and press down.

Lay the next tile on the other side of the line, butting against the first tile. Form a square with two more tiles. Lay tiles around the square to form a pyramid. Continue in this way, filling one half of the room, then remove the batten and tile the other half. 🢂

▼ *Peel paper backing from self-adhesive tiles*

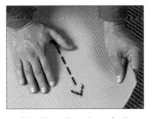

▲ *Checking direction of pile*
Some carpet tiles have arrows on the back to indicate the direction they should be laid

Other soft floor tiles

The methods for laying floor tiles made from carpet, cork and rubber are slightly different.

Carpet tiles
Set out centre lines on the floor, but don't fit a guide batten. Stick down every third row of tiles using double-sided carpet tape, and tape all squares under heavy traffic.

Cork tiles
Use a contact adhesive: thixotropic adhesives allow a degree of movement as you position the tiles.

Rubber tiles
Bed rubber floor tiles onto latex flooring adhesive. Place one edge and corner against its neighbouring tiles before lowering it onto the adhesive.

SEE ALSO
410–11

Laying ceramic floor tiles

ADVANCED

The ideal surface on which to lay ceramic floor tiles is a level and flat screeded floor. If you have floorboards or an uneven surface, a sub-floor may have to be fitted first.

Lay a sub-floor of 12mm (½in) or 18mm (¾in) plywood, screwed down every 305mm (12in). Apply a sealing coat of PVA adhesive mixed with water over the plywood surface.

Tools

Screwdriver
Measuring tape
Hammer
Pencil
Serrated edge trowel
Rubber float
Sponge
Tile cutter
Straight edge

Mark the centre of all four walls and dissect the floor into quarters with a chalk line. Lay the tiles out dry in one quarter, then mark the floor for fixing two wooden battens. The battens must be perfectly square before securing them. Apply the adhesive about a square yard (metre) at a time with a serrated trowel [A]. Press tiles into the adhesive, building out from the corner. Fit equal spacers between the tiles to form equal size joints [B]. Use a spirit level to check

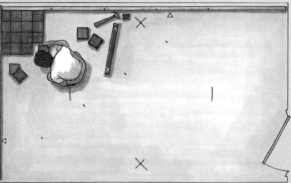

▶ Mark out the floor for tiling with chalk and a tape measure and then set out the field with battens

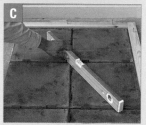

tile for cutting [D]. Allow for spacers and use a tile cutter [E]. Paste the back of the tile with adhesive and slot into place. Check with a spirit level.

Grout the floor using a rubber float, small sections at a time, wiping off excess grout with a damp sponge [F]. Rub over the joints with a shaped piece of timber to compress and shape the joints. Once the grouting has cured, give it a final clean and polish with a soft cloth.

Apply a silicone mastic joint between the floor and the walls as a seal.

the tiles are in line [C]. Clean off any excess adhesive. Repeat until the whole floor area is covered. Leave for 24 hours, then carefully remove the battens to cut in the edges.

Measure the tile space and transfer the dimensions to a

Laying quarry tiles

Lay quarry tiles on a dry concrete surface or replace floorboards with 18 or 22mm (¾ or ⅞in) exterior-grade plywood to provide a sufficiently flat and rigid base.

Setting out for tiling

Set out two guide battens at right angles to each other in a corner of the room, as for ceramic floor tiles (p392-393). The depth of the battens should be about twice the thickness of the tiles, to allow for the mortar bed. The level of the battens is vital, so check with a spirit level. Mark tile-widths along each batten, leaving 3mm (⅛in) gaps between them for grouting.

Dry-lay a square of 16 tiles in the angle, then nail a third batten to the floor, butting against the tiles and parallel with one of the other battens.

Laying the tiles

Lay on a bed of mortar made from 1 part cement to 3 parts builder's sand. When water is added, mortar should be stiff enough to hold an impression when squeezed.

Soak quarry tiles in water before laying to prevent them absorbing water from the

▼ Grouting materials for ceramic floor tiles

mortar. Cut a stout board with notches at each end to span the parallel battens: this will be used to level the mortar bed and tiles.

Spread the mortar about 12mm (½in) deep to cover the area of 16 tiles. Level the mortar by dragging the notched side of the board across it.

Dust dry cement on the mortar, then lay the tiles along three sides of the square against the battens. Fill in the square; tamp tiles down with the unnotched side of the board until they are level. If the mortar is too stiff, brush water into the joints. Wipe off before it hardens.

Fill in between the battens, then move one batten back to form another bay of the same size. Level it to match the first section.

Setting out wall tiles

Having prepared the wall surfaces for tiling, the next stage is to measure each wall.

Setting out a plain wall
Use the gauge stick to plan horizontal rows of tiles, starting at skirting level. If you are left with a narrow strip at the top, move the rows up half a tile-width to create a wider margin. Then mark the bottom of the lowest row of whole tiles.

Temporarily nail a perfectly horizontal guide batten to the wall aligned with the mark (1).

Mark the centre of the wall (2), then use the gauge stick to set out vertical rows on each side of the line. If the margin tiles measure less than half a width, reposition the rows sideways by half a tile. Use a spirit level to position a guide

batten against the last vertical line, and nail it to the wall (3).

Plotting a half-tiled wall.
If tiling part of a wall – up to a dado rail, for example – set out the tiles to leave a row of tiles at the top (4). If skirting tiles or border tiles are to be used, plan their positions first, using them as starting points.

Arranging around a window
For nicely balanced tiling, always use a window as your starting point, so that the tiles surrounding it are equal in size but not too narrow. If possible, begin a row of whole tiles at sill level (5) and position cut tiles at the back of the window reveal (6).

If necessary, fix a batten over a window to support a row of tiles temporarily (7).

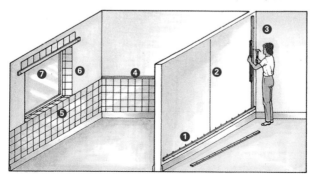

SEE ALSO
72–3

Fixing ceramic wall tiles

Start by tiling the main areas with whole tiles, leaving the narrow gaps around the edges to be filled with cut tiles later.

Applying whole tiles

A serrated plastic spreader is normally supplied with tubs of adhesive, but if you are tiling a relatively large area it pays to buy a notched metal trowel.

Use the straight edge of the trowel to spread enough adhesive to cover about 1m (3ft) square; then turn the tool around and drag the notched edge through the adhesive to form horizontal ridges (1).

Press the first tile into the angle formed by the setting-out battens (2). Press the next tile into place, using plastic spacers to form the grout lines between the tiles. Lay additional tiles to build up three or four rows at a time; wipe excess adhesive using a clean damp sponge.

Continue to tile along the batten until the first rows of whole tiles are complete.

When the entire wall is complete, scrape adhesive from the margins and allow the rest to set firm before removing the battens.

Fitting margin tiles

Cut tiles one at a time to fit the gaps between the field tiles and the adjacent walls. Mark each margin tile by placing it face down over its neighbour with one edge against the adjacent wall (3). Spread adhesive onto the back of each tile (4) and press it into the margin.

Grouting the tiles

Leave the tile adhesive to harden for 24 hours, then use a rubber-bladed spreader or a tiler's rubber float to press grout into the joints (5).

1. Form ridges with a notched spreader

2. Fix the first tile against the setting-out battens

3. Mark the back of a margin tile

4. Butter adhesive onto the back of a cut tile

5. Press grout into the joints with a rubber spreader

V

Varnishes and polishes

Although paint is the most common finish for woodwork around the home, varnishes, lacquers and polishes give an attractive, durable finish to joinery, enhancing – and protecting – the colour of woodwork without obliterating the beauty of its grain.

When choosing a particular finish, bear in mind the location of the woodwork and the amount of wear and tear it is likely to get. This will determine whether you decide on a finish that is tough and durable or simply decorative.

Varnishes

Varnish is a clear protective coating for timber. Most modern varnishes are made with polyurethane resins to provide a waterproof, scratchproof and heat-resistant finish. They come in high-gloss, satin or matt finishes.

Exterior-grade varnishes are more weather-resistant; and some of them, including yacht varnish, are tough enough to cope with polluted urban environments and coastal climates.

Some varnishes are designed to provide a clear finish with a hint of colour; they are available in the normal wood shades and some strong colours.

Unlike a wood dye, a coloured varnish does not sink into the timber – so there may be loss of colour in areas of heavy wear or abrasion unless you apply additional coats of clear varnish.

Fast-drying acrylic varnishes have an opaque

▼ *The effect of different varnishes on the same species of wood*

milky appearance when applied, but are clear and transparent when dry.

Cold-cure lacquer

This plastic coating is mixed with a hardener just before it is used. It is extremely durable (even on floors) and is resistant to heat and alcohol. The standard type dries to a high gloss, which can be burnished to a lacquer-like finish if required. There is also a matt-finish grade, though a smoother matt surface can be obtained by rubbing down the gloss coating with fine steel wool dipped in wax. Black, white and clear varieties of cold-cure lacquer are available.

Finishing oil

Oil is a subtle finish that soaks into the wood, leaving a mellow sheen on the surface. Traditional linseed oil remains sticky for hours, whereas a modern oil will dry in about an hour and provides a tougher, more durable finish. Oil can be used on softwood as well as open-grained oily hardwoods such as teak or afrormosia. It is suitable for interior and exterior woodwork.

FRENCH POLISH

French polish is a specialized wood finish made by dissolving shellac in alcohol. It is easily scratched, and alcohol or water will etch the surface, leaving white stains. Consequently, it can be used only on furniture unlikely to receive normal wear and tear.

There are several varieties. Reddish-brown button polish is the best quality standard polish. It is bleached to make white polish for light-coloured woods, and if the natural wax is removed from the shellac a transparent polish is produced. For mahogany, choose a dark-red garnet polish.

Thick gelled oil is applied like a wax polish, and can be used on bare wood or over varnish and lacquer.

Wax polishes

Wax can be employed to preserve and maintain another finish or as a finish itself. A good wax should be a blend of beeswax and a hard polishing wax such as carnauba. Some contain silicones to make it easier to achieve a high gloss.

Wax polish may be white or tinted various shades of brown to darken the wood. Although very attractive looking, it is not a durable finish and should be used indoors only.

SEE ALSO
158–9

Varnish and polishes: varnishing woodwork

Varnish serves two main purposes: to protect the wood from knocks, stains and other marks, and to give it a sheen that accentuates the grain pattern. Some varnishes can be used to change the colour of the wood or to give it a fresh look with a choice of bright colours.

Apply varnish like paint, using a range of paintbrushes: 12, 25 and 50mm (½, 1 and 2in) are the most useful widths. For varnishing a floor, use a 100mm (4in) brush to achieve fast, even coverage.

Keep your brushes spotlessly clean; any remaining traces of paint on them may spoil the finish.

Load a brush with varnish by dipping the first third of the bristles into the liquid,

Dealing with dust particles

Minor imperfections and particles of dust stuck to the varnished surface can be rubbed down with fine abrasive paper between coats. If your top coat is to be a high-gloss finish, take even more care to ensure that your brush is perfectly clean.

If you are not satisfied with your final finish, wait until dry, then dip very fine wire wool in wax polish and rub the varnish with parallel strokes in the direction of the grain. Buff

the surface with a soft duster. This treatment removes a high gloss, but it leaves a pleasant sheen on the surface with no obvious imperfections.

▶ *Produce a soft sheen with wire wool and wax*

then touch off the excess on the inside of the container. Don't scrape the brush across the rim of the container – this creates bubbles in the varnish, which can spoil the final finish if transferred to the wood.

You can use a soft cloth pad, or rubber, to rub a sealer coat of varnish into the grain. Also, you'll find that a rubber is convenient for varnishing shaped or turned pieces of wood.

Applying the varnish

Thin the first sealer coat of varnish by 10 per cent, and rub it into the wood in the direction of the grain, using a cloth pad. Where a rubber is difficult to use, brush on the sealer coat, instead.

Apply a second coat of varnish within the stipulated time. If more than 24 hours have elapsed, lightly key the surface of solvent-based gloss varnish with fine abrasive paper.

Wipe the surface with a cloth dampened with white spirit to remove dust and grease, then brush on a full coat of varnish. Apply a third coat if the surface is likely to take hard wear. 🖝

French polishing

The art of French polishing has always been considered the province of the expert. It's true that a professional will make a better job of the polishing and will be able to work much faster than an amateur, but there's no reason why anyone cannot produce a satisfactory finish with a little practice.

Making a rubber

Traditionally, shellac – French polish – is applied with a soft pad known as a rubber. To make one, take a handful of cotton wool and squeeze it roughly egg-shaped, then place in the centre of a 300mm (1ft) square of white linen. Fold the fabric over the cotton wool, gathering the loose material in the palm of your hand. Smooth any wrinkles that form across the sole of the pad.

SEE ALSO
438–9

Ventilation

Perforated openings known as airbricks are built into the external walls of a house to ventilate the space below suspended wooden floors. Check their condition regularly, as blocked airbricks can cause dry rot.

▲ *Single ceramic brick*

▲ *Double-size plastic airbrick*

There ought to be an airbrick every 2m (6ft) along an external wall, but often there is less than this. Yet sufficient airflow is more important than the actual number of openings in the wall.

Floor joists that span a wide room are supported at intervals by low sleeper walls made of brick. Sometimes these are perforated to facilitate an even airflow throughout the space – but in other cases there are just gaps left by the builder between sections of solid wall. This

method can lead to pockets of still air in corners where draughts never reach. If you suspect there are 'dead' areas under your floor – particularly if there are signs of damp or mould – fit an additional airbrick in a wall nearby.

Replacing an airbrick

Old ceramic airbricks sometimes get broken. Use a masonry drill and a cold chisel to chop out the brick itself. Spread mortar on the base of the hole, and along the top and both sides of the new airbrick. Push it into the opening, keeping it flush with the face of the brickwork, then repoint the mortar to match the surrounding wall.

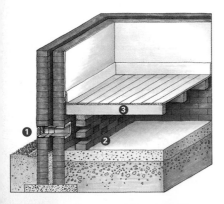

◀ *A cross section through a typical cavity-wall structure, with a wooden floor suspended over a concrete base. 1 Airbrick fitted with telescopic sleeve. 2 Sleeper wall built with staggered bricks to allow air to circulate. 3 Joists and floorboards are susceptible to dry rot from poor ventilation.*

Extractor fans

As kitchens and bathrooms are prone to condensation, it's important to have some means of expelling moisture-laden air. An electrically driven extractor fan freshens a room quickly, without creating draughts.

Types of extractor fans

Many fans have an integral switch. If not, a switched connection unit can be wired into the circuit. Axial fans can be installed in a window; and with the addition of a duct, some models will extract air through a solid or cavity wall.

▼ Window-mounted axial fan

1. Inner casing
2. Motor assembly
3. Interior clamping plate
4. Glass
5. Grille-clamping plate
6. Exterior grille

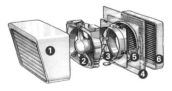

Fitting window fans

If you plan to install an extractor fan in a hermetically sealed double-glazing system, ask the manufacturer to supply a special unit with a precut hole, which is sealed around the edges, to receive the fan.

Cutting the glass

Every window-mounted fan requires a round hole to be cut in the glass. It is possible to cut a hole in an existing window, but stresses in the glass will sometimes cause it to crack. All things considered, it is generally better to fit a new pane, which will be easier to cut and can be installed as soon as the old one has been removed. Cutting a hole in glass is not easy, and you may find it's more economical to have it cut by a glazier – in which case, you will need to provide exact dimensions, including the size and position of the hole. Order 4mm (⅝in) glass that matches the existing glazing.

◄ Wall-mounted axial fan

1 Motor assembly
2 Interior backplate
3 Duct
4 Exterior grille

SEE ALSO
152

Installing the fan

Take out the existing windowpane and clean up the frame; then fit the new pane with the precut hole.

Fit the exterior grille by locating its circular flange in the hole (1). Attach the plate on the inside, to clamp the grille to the glass (2). Tighten the fixing screws in rotation to achieve a good seal. Screw the motor assembly to the clamping plate (3). Wire up the fan, then fit the inner casing over the motor assembly (4).

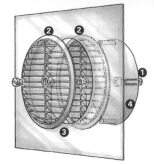

▲ *The components of a fixed window vent*
1. *Fixing bolt*
2. *Louvred grille*
3. *Hole in the glass*
4. *Windshield*

1. Place the grille in the hole from outside

2. Clamp the inner and outer plates together

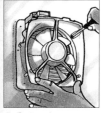

3. Screw the motor assembly to the plate

4. Attach the inner casing to cover the assembly

Fixed window vent

You can provide continuous ventilation by installing an inexpensive fixed vent. Well-designed ventilators of this kind usually have a windshield on the outside – which allows a free flow of air without causing draughts – and are reliable, as there are no moving parts to break down or create the irritating squeaks associated with wind-driven fans.

Have a glazier cut the recommended size of hole in the glass. Then fit one of the vent's louvred grilles on each side of the window (clamping them together with the central fixing bolt), and bolt the plastic windshield to the outer grille.

Whole-house ventilation

If you are prepared to make the necessary investment, you can have a simple system installed to extract moisture-laden air and stale odours from the entire house. It works on the principle that natural convection draws the relatively warm air inside the house via ducts to the roof where it escapes through ridge vents.

This type of system is self-regulating and, since there are no electrical connections, it costs nothing to run. However, for the system to work efficiently, you have to fit effective draughtproofing throughout your home.

Passive stack ventilation
Extraction vents are fitted in rooms where there is likely to be the greatest concentration of moist odour-laden air – usually the kitchen and bathroom. A single duct runs from each vent by the most direct route to the roof ridge, where wind blowing across

COMBUSTION AIR

Rooms containing open-flued heating appliances must be ventilated permanently. Suitable vents can be installed as part of passive-vent systems.

NOISE POLLUTION

Because there are no fans running, passive stack ventilation is perfectly quiet. If there is a possibility of noise penetrating from outside, make sure the air-inlet vents are fitted with acoustic baffles.

the roof creates a suction effect that helps to draw the warm air through the duct, just like smoke being carried up a chimney.

The stale air in neighbouring 'dry' rooms, such as living rooms and bedrooms, moves naturally towards the vented rooms where extraction takes place. Trickle vents, fitted in the windows or exterior walls of the dry rooms, provide a flow of fresh air.

Ventilation by demand
The inlet and extraction vents in each room are operated by humidity-sensitive controls, so that their flaps or louvres open and close progressively to admit or extract air as necessary, to maintain a perfect balance.

Unobtrusive installation
Provided they are fitted with care, the system's slim external vents should be

SEE ALSO
98–9

unobtrusive. Internally, ducting is normally sited within fitted cupboards or can be run through stud partitions up to the roof space, where it must be insulated to prevent condensation forming inside the duct.

▼ Passive-vent system

This type of system is designed to ventilate the entire house without using electrically driven fans.
1. Stale moist air escapes through roof vents.
2. Ducting takes the shortest route from 'wet' rooms to the roof. Air is drawn through the vents by convection.
3. Extractor vents in the kitchen and bathroom draw air from surrounding rooms.
4. Trickle vents mounted in windows or exterior walls admit fresh air but without causing draughts

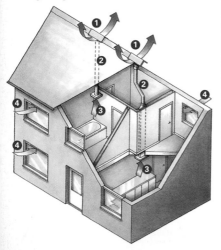

Extracting radon

Radon is an odourless radioactive inert gas, arising from the disintegration of radium, which can seep into buildings from below ground.

In most localities radon levels are so low that they are in fact harmless, but there are places where the gas is sufficiently concentrated to constitute a health risk.

When building new houses and large extensions in these susceptible areas of the country, contractors are obliged to take precautions to prevent radon gas from entering the house or building.

In some cases, this is accomplished by incorporating a continuous gas-impermeable membrane in a solid concrete base.

Below a suspended floor, efficient cross-ventilation is usually sufficient to disperse the gas; however, where there are high concentrations of radon gas, it is often necessary to install below ground a radon-collection sump that is vented to the roof, removing the radon gas by convection.

◄ **Ventilating the eaves**
1. Fit plastic vents in the soffit
board.
2. Push eaves vents between the
rafters and joists to stop
insulation blocking the flow of air

Ventilating the roof space

When loft insulation first
became popular as an energy-
saving measure, householders
were recommended to tuck
insulant right into the eaves to
keep out draughts. However, a
free flow of air is necessary in
the roof space to prevent
moisture-laden air from below
condensing on the structure.

Wet rot can develop in the
roof timbers, so efficient
ventilation of the roof space is
essential in every home. ◄

Ventilating the eaves

Regulations governing new
housing insist on ventilation
equivalent to continuous
openings of 10mm (⅜in) along
two opposite sides of a roof
with a slope of 15 deg or more.
If the pitch is less than 15 deg
or the roof space is habitable,
ventilation must be equivalent
to continuous openings of
25mm (1in). Adopt similar
standards when refurbishing a
house of any age.

The simplest method of
ventilating a standard pitched
roof is to fit soffit vents made
with integral insect screens.
Space the vents evenly along
the roof. Push the vents into
openings cut with a jigsaw.

If the opening at the eaves is
likely to be restricted by
insulation, insert a plastic or
cardboard eaves vent between
each pair of joists.

Slate and tile vents

Certain types of roofs do not
lend themselves to ventilation
from the eaves only, but the
structure can be ventilated by
strategically replacing tiles or
slates with specially designed
roof vents.

◄ *Slate
vent*

SEE ALSO
184–5

Vinyl floorcoverings

Sheet vinyl makes an ideal wall-to-wall floorcovering for kitchens, utility rooms and bathrooms, where you are bound to spill water from time to time. It is straightforward to lay, provided you follow a systematic procedure.

There are a great many sheet-vinyl floorcoverings to choose from. Make your selection according to durability, colour, pattern and, of course, cost.

Unbacked vinyl
Sheet vinyl is made by sandwiching the printed pattern between a base of PVC and a clear protective PVC covering. All vinyls are relatively hardwearing, but some have a thicker, reinforced protective layer to increase their durability; ask the supplier which type will suit your needs best.

Vinyl floorcovering comes in a vast range of colours, patterns and textures.

Backed vinyl
Backed vinyl has similar properties to the unbacked type, with the addition of a resilient underlay to make it warmer and softer to walk on. The backing is usually a cushion of foamed PVC.

▼ *Left to right:*
1. Unbacked vinyl
2. Backed vinyl
3. Vinyl carpet

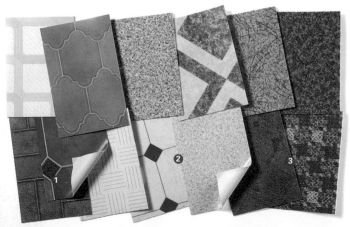

Vinyl carpet

Vinyl carpet – a cross between carpet and sheet vinyl – was originally developed for contract use but is now available for the wider market. It has a velvet-like pile of fine nylon fibres embedded in a waterproof expanded-PVC base, and is popular for kitchens as spillages are washed off easily with water and a mild detergent. It comes in 2m (6ft 7in) wide rolls.

Laying sheet vinyl

Leave the vinyl sheet in a room for 24 to 48 hours before laying, preferably opened flat – or at least stood on end, loosely rolled. Make a scribing gauge by driving a nail through a wooden lath about 50mm (2in) from one end. You will use this gauge for fitting the sheet against the skirtings.

Fitting and cutting sheet vinyl

Assuming there are no seams, start by fitting the sheet against the longest wall. Pull the vinyl away from the wall by approximately 35mm (1¼in); make sure it is parallel with the wall or the main axis of the room. Use the scribing gauge to score a line that

1. Fit to first wall by scribing with a nailed strip

2. Press the folded edge to the skirting and cut

follows the skirting (1). Cut the vinyl with a knife or scissors, then slide the sheet up against the wall.

To get the rest of the sheet to lie as flat as possible, cut a triangular notch at each corner. At external corners, make a straight cut down to the floor. Remove as much waste as possible, leaving 50 to 75mm (2 to 3in) turned up all round.

Using a bolster, press the vinyl into the angle between the skirting and the floor. Align a metal straightedge with the crease and run a sharp knife along it, held at a slight angle to the skirting (2). If your trimming is less than perfect, nail a cover strip of quadrant moulding to the skirting.

SEE ALSO
388

Fixing vinyl floor tiles

As with other types of floorcoverings, makes sure that the floor surface is flat and dry. If the floor is concrete, screed out any unevenness or board a wooden one.

In the case of a conventional boarded wooden floor, overlay the floor either with hardboard or 6mm (¼in) plywood. Fix the plywood or hardboard with 25mm (1in) ring nails.

Vinyl tiles are normally self-adhesive, but if you store them in the room for a couple of days they will become acclimatized to the room temperature.

Mark the centre of two opposite walls and snap a chalk line or string between the two points [A]. Do the same on the opposite two walls and you'll have a centre point. Lay out some tiles at

this centre point, without removing the protective backing, to work out the most effective way of fixing them with minimum wastage and balanced cut edges.

Mark your starting position. Lift the tiles and give the floor a final vacuum. Peel the backing off the first tile [B]

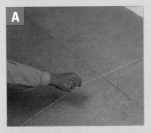

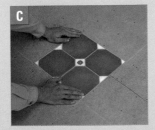

Tools

Hammer
Chalk line
Straight edge
Craft knife
Measuring
tape

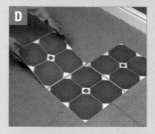

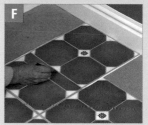

and carefully place to the marks, applying smoothing pressure with your hands [C]. Repeat the process, concentrating on one half of the floor and steadily laying a pyramid shape, carefully butting the tiles together [D].

For trimming in the edges, lay a tile against the wall over the last full tile [E] (without removing the backing) and mark the fixed tile [F]. Transfer the marks onto a tile for cutting with a sharp craft knife and straight edge [G]. Peel the back off and stick the cut tile firmly into place.

In a kitchen or bathroom, make sure that the floor and bottoms of the surrounding walls are absolutely dry and clean before you lay the tiles. Also, use silicone sealant around the edges of tiles to give a fully watertight finish.

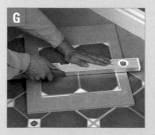

3. Make triangular cuts around a curve

a threshold bar over the edge of the sheet.

Sticking/joining sheet vinyl
Modern sheet-vinyl floorcoverings can be loose-laid, but you may prefer to glue the edges, especially across a door opening.

Peel back the edge and spread a band of the recommended flooring adhesive, using a toothed spreader; or apply double-sided adhesive tape, 50mm (2in) wide, to the floor.

If you have to join widths, then overlap the free edge with the second sheet until the pattern matches. Cut through both pieces with a knife, then remove the waste strips.

Without moving the sheets, fold back both cut edges, apply tape or adhesive, then press the join together.

Cutting around a toilet
To fit around a WC pan or basin pedestal, fold back the sheet and pierce it with a knife just above floor level; draw the blade up towards the edge of the sheet. Make triangular cuts around the base, gradually working around the curve until the sheet can lie flat on the floor (3). Crease, and cut off the waste.

Trimming to fit a doorway
Fit the vinyl around the doorframe by creasing it against the floor and trimming off the waste. Make a straight cut across the opening, and fit

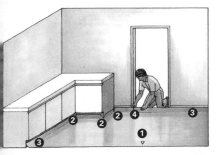

◀ ***Positioning sheet vinyl***
Lay the vinyl on the floor so that it laps the skirting all round, then:
1 Start by fitting the sheet to the longest, uninterrupted wall.
2 Cut notches at each corner, so the sheet will lie flat.
3 Allow folds of about 75mm (3in) all round for scribing to fit.
4 Make a straight cut across the door opening, and fit a threshold bar

W

Wallcoverings

There is a huge range of paper-backed fabrics, from exotic silks to coarse hessians. Plastics have widened the choice of wallcoverings still further: there are paper-backed or cotton-backed vinyls, and plain or patterned foamed plastics.

Printed wallpapers

One advantage of wallpaper is the superb range of printed colours and patterns, which is much wider than for any other wallcovering. Most cheaper papers are machine-printed.

The more costly hand-printed papers are prone to tearing when wet, and the inks have a tendency to run if you smear paste on the surface. They are not really suitable for walls exposed to wear or condensation.

Relief papers

Wallpapers with deeply embossed patterns hide minor imperfections. Reliefs are invariably painted with emulsion, satin-finish oil paints or water-based acrylics.

Washable papers

These are printed papers with a thin impervious glaze of PVA to make a spongeable surface. Washables are suitable for bathrooms and kitchens.

Vinyl wallcoverings

A base paper, or sometimes a cotton backing, is coated with a layer of vinyl on which the design is printed. Many vinyls are sold ready-pasted for easy application.

Foamed-plastic covering

This is a lightweight wallcovering made solely of

▼ 1. Hand-printed
2. Machine-printed

❶ ❷

foamed polyethylene with no backing paper. You paste the wall instead of the covering.

Flock wallcoverings

Flock papers have the major pattern elements picked out with a fine pile produced by gluing synthetic or natural fibres (such as silk or wool) to the backing paper. Flock papers are difficult to hang, as contact with paste will ruin the pile.

Grass cloth

Natural grasses are woven into a mat and glued to a paper backing.

Cork-faced paper

This is surfaced with thin sheets of coloured or natural cork.

Paper-backed fabrics

Finely woven cotton, linen or silk on a paper backing has to be applied to a flat surface.

Unbacked fabrics

Upholstery-width fabric – typically hessian – can be wrapped around panels, which are then glued or pinned to the wall.

▼ *Left to right:*
1. *Washable papers*
2. *Textured and patterned vinyls*
3. *Foamed polyethylene*
4. *Flock papers*
5. *Paper-backed fabric*
6. *Grass-cloth mats*
7. *Cork-faced paper*

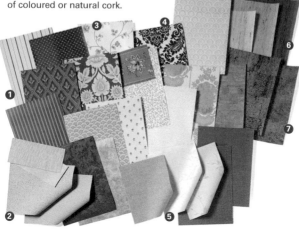

SEE ALSO
304–5

Lining a wall

Lining a wall before papering is only necessary if you are hanging embossed or luxury wallcoverings, or if the wall has imperfections that might show through a thin wallpaper.

Mark a horizontal line on the wall one roll-width from the ceiling. Start at the top right-hand corner, aligning the bottom edge with the marked line. Smooth onto the wall, working from the centre towards the edges of the paper. Work along the wall, unfolding the length as you go. Lightly mark the corner, peel back the paper and trim to the line. Brush the paper back in place. Work down the wall, butting each strip against the last.

Leave the lining paper to dry out for 24 hours before covering.

▼ **Hanging lining paper horizontally**
Hold the concertina-folded paper in one hand and smooth it onto the wall, starting top right. Butt the strips of paper together or leave a slight gap.

▲ *Centre a large motif over a fireplace*

▲ *Butt two lengths between windows*

Papering a wall

Don't apply a wallcovering until all the woodwork in the room has been painted or varnished, and the ceiling painted or papered.

Where to start

The traditional method is to hang the first length next to a window close to a corner, then work in both directions away from the light. But it may be easier to paper the longest uninterrupted wall first to get used to the techniques before

trying corners or obstructions. If your wallcovering has a regular motif, centre the first length over the fireplace for symmetry.

Hanging on a straight wall
The walls of a room are rarely truly square, so use a plumb line to mark a vertical guide against which to hang the first length of wallcovering. Start at one end of the wall and mark the vertical line one roll-width away from the corner minus 12mm (½in), so the first length will overlap the adjacent wall.

Allowing enough for trimming at the ceiling, unfold the top section of the pasted length and hold it against the plumbed line. Brush the paper gently onto the wall, working from the centre in all directions to squeeze out any trapped air.

When the paper is positioned, draw the point of your scissors along the ceiling line, peel back the top edge and cut along the crease. Smooth the paper back. Unpeel the lower fold of the paper, smooth

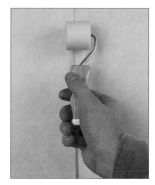

▲ *Sticking down the edges*
Ensure that the edges of the paper adhere firmly by running a seam roller along the butt joints

it onto the wall with the brush, then tap it into the corner. Crease the bottom edge against the skirting, trim and brush back against the wall.

Hang the next length in the same manner. Continue to the other side of the wall, allowing the last drop to overlap the adjoining wall by 12mm (½in).

▶ *Losing air bubbles*
If a blister remains, inject a little paste through it and roll it flat. Alternatively, cut across it in two directions, peel back the triangular flaps, and paste them down.

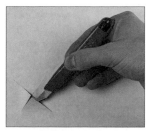

SEE ALSO
372–4

Wallpapering tips

INTERMEDIATE

A general rule for hanging wallpaper is if you are right-handed, work from right to left of the door, and vice versa. Alternatively, start between two windows or the centre of a chimneybreast, especially if the paper has a large pattern.

Once you've chosen your starting position, mark a vertical level line on the wall using either a plumb line and bob, or a long spirit level, rotating the level as you mark.

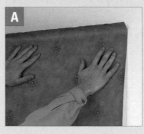

Offer the end of the wallpaper to the ceiling [A]. Ensure there is surplus paper for trimming on the top and bottom. Pre-cut enough lengths to cover at least one wall. Check that you have allowed enough paper to enable a match on paper with well spaced repeating patterns. These lengths of paper are known as 'drops'.

Roll out all the drops that you have pre-cut face down on

Tools

Pasting bench
Paste brush
Craft knife
Seam roller
Paper shears
Paper brush
Sponge
Oilstone
Plumb bob
Spirit level

▲ *To paper around an internal corner, cut a piece so that it covers the overlap on the first wall. If the piece you trimmed off at the corner is wide enough, use it as your first length on the new wall.*

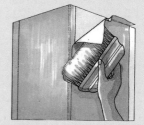

▲ *To paper around an external corner, trim the last length so that it wraps around the corner, overlapping by about 25mm (1in). Hang the last strip with its edge about 12mm (½in) from the corner.*

a pasting table. Cover the whole table surface so that you do not get any paste onto the face of the paper. Put the paste on with a large pasting brush, pasting away from the centre. Fold the pasted paper in a concertina shape, paste-to-paste and face-to-face. Next, apply a coat of watery paste to the walls. This is called sizing, and will make hanging the paper much easier and also prevent the plaster soaking up the paste from the paper.

Offer the first pasted drop up to the ceiling and move the drop parallel to the marked line, allowing for trimming. Brush from the centre out towards the edges, moving any trapped air bubbles [B]. Continue down the whole length of the drop. Using a thin straight edge, tuck the paper into the ceiling joint and trim with a sharp craft knife or scissors [C]. Repeat at skirting level.

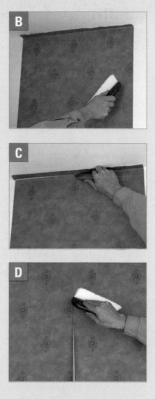

Take the next drop and repeat the process, ensuring that the pattern matches and the edges butt, as you brush out any air bubbles [D]. Use a damp sponge to wipe off any excess paste on the paper, ceiling and woodwork surfaces as you go [E].

Pasting wallcoverings

Use any wipe-clean table for pasting, but a fold-up pasting table is a good idea if you are doing a lot of decorating. Lay several cut lengths of paper face down on the table. To stop the paper rolling up while you are pasting, tuck the ends under a length of string tied loosely round the table legs.

Applying the paste

Use a large, soft wall brush or pasting brush to apply the paste. Mix the paste in a plastic bucket; tie string across the rim to support the brush, keeping its handle clean.

Align the wallcovering with the far edge of the table, to avoid pasting the table. Apply paste by brushing away from the centre. You can also use a short-pile paint roller. Pour the paste into a roller tray and roll it onto the wallcovering in one direction only, towards the end of the paper.

Pull the wallcovering to the front edge of the table and paste the other half. Fold the pasted end over and slide the length along the table to expose an unpasted section.

Paste the other end, then fold it over to almost meet the first cut end. The second fold is invariably deeper than the first – a handy way to tell which is the bottom of patterned wallcoverings. Fold long drops concertina-fashion.

Hang vinyls and lightweight papers immediately; drape other wallcoverings over a

1. Lay several drops face down on the pasting table, their ends retained with string ties

2. Align wall-covering with edge of table and apply paste by brushing away from the centre, covering the edges well

3. Pull wallcovering to front of table, paste the other half, and then fold over. Slide the wall-covering along, and paste as before

4. For long drops, as in a stairwell, fold the paper in a concertina-style and leave to soak. Carry the drop draped over your arm

▲ *Allowing for patterned wallcoverings*
You may have to allow extra on alternate lengths of patterned wallcoverings to match patterns.

broom handle across two chair backs, and leave to soak. Some heavy or embossed coverings need to soak for 15 minutes. 🐦

Pasting the wall
Instead of pasting the back of exotic wallcoverings, paste the wall, to reduce the risk of marking their delicate faces. Apply a band of paste just wider than the length of wallcovering, so you won't have to paste right up to its edge for the next length.

Ready-pasted wallcoverings
Many wallcoverings come precoated with adhesive, activated by soaking a length in a trough of cold water. Plastic troughs are sold for this.

Trimming and cutting
Most wallpapers are machine-trimmed to width to join adjacent lengths accurately. Some hand-printed papers are left untrimmed. These are usually expensive coverings, so don't attempt to trim them yourself: ask your supplier.

Cutting plain wallcoverings
Measure the height of the wall where you will hang the first 'drop'. Add an extra 100mm (4in) for trimming top and bottom. Cut several pieces and mark the top of each one.

Trimming around switches
Turn off electricity. Hang the wallcovering over the switch or socket and make diagonal cuts from the centre to each corner. Trim; loosen faceplate, tuck the margin behind; retighten plate.

▼ *Trim off the waste paper, leaving about 6mm (¼in) all round the object*

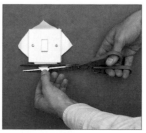

SEE ALSO
15

Wall fixings

To make secure fixings to anything other than solid wood or man-made boards involves using fixing aids. These range from simple plugs that take a woodscrew in a hole drilled in brick or masonry to elaborate heavy-duty devices complete with bolts. There are also special products for making fixings to hollow walls.

Wallplugs

These relatively simple fixings anchor a variety of screws.

Moulded plastic

Extruded plastic

Locking pin (extra security for use with some threaded plugs)

Threaded plug

Clothesline fixing

Moulded-plastic wallplugs
These are lightweight to medium-duty wallplugs that take a range of standard gauge woodscrews, generally from No 4 to No 14. Some are colour-coded for easy recognition.

A wallplug is pushed into a drilled hole, and then the screw is driven into the plug, which expands to grip the sides of the hole tightly.

Extruded-plastic plugs
These are straight fluted tubes that fit only the thread of the screw, so have to be cut shorter than the hole depth. Cheaper than moulded plugs, but less convenient.

Fibre plugs
Traditional fibre plugs come in set sizes.

Threaded plugs
These are for use in walls of crumbly material like aerated

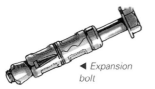

◄ *Expansion bolt*

concrete blocks. These plugs have a coarse thread on the outside and are screwed into the soft material to provide a socket for screws.

One plastic type uses a locking pin for extra security. Another sort is supplied with a universal drill bit for making the hole, fitting the plug and driving the screw. There is also an all-metal plug with a coarse thread and a sharp point that cuts its own hole in a plasterboard wall.

Heavy-duty nylon wallplugs
These come complete with coach screws or with screw hooks (for use as clothesline attachments, for example).

Expansion bolts

These are for making very rugged fixings. There are various designs, but all work on the same basic principle: a bolt is screwed into a segmental metal or plastic shell and engages the thread of an expander. As the bolt is tightened, the expander forces the segments apart to grip the sides of the hole. Hooks and eyes that employ a similar principle are also available.

Nailable plugs

These can be used in place of wallplugs and screws. There are two types: one comprises a flanged expansion sleeve with a masonry nail; the other consists of a ready-assembled wallplug and 'hammer screw'. Both types are hammered into a drilled hole, but only the hammer screw can be removed, using a screwdriver. These plugs are often used for fixing frames, battens, wall linings and skirting boards. 🖝

Nailable plug

Nailable plug for plasterboard

Hammer screw

🖝
SEE ALSO
240–2

Plastic frame fixing

Metal-sleeved frame fixing

Frame fixings

These are designed to speed up screw fixings in wood, plastic or metal door and window frames by eliminating the need to mark out and predrill the fixing holes.

Supplied with a plated screw or bolt, these long fittings are available with plastic plugs or split metal expanding sleeves.

The item to be fixed is first set in position and a clearance hole drilled through it into the wall. The frame fixing is then fitted and the screw tightened.

Fixings for hollow walls

There are all sorts of variations on the different devices for making fixings to hollow walls of plasterboard on studs, lath and plaster, and so on. Most of them operate on the principle of opening out behind the panel and gripping it in some way.

Special wallplugs, plastic toggles and collapsible

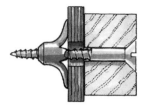

Nylon anchor

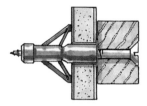

Toggle cavity anchor

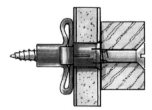

Plastic collapsible anchor

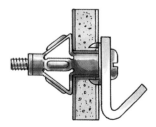

Metal collapsible anchor

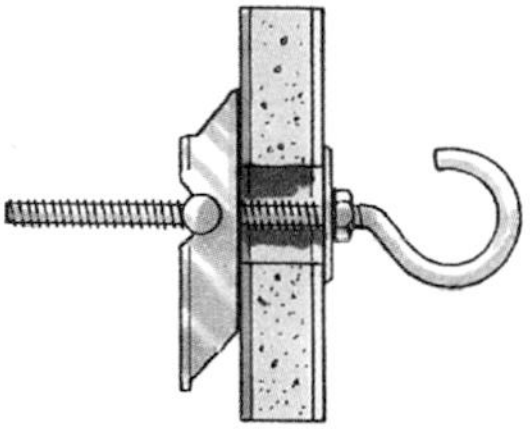

Gravity toggle

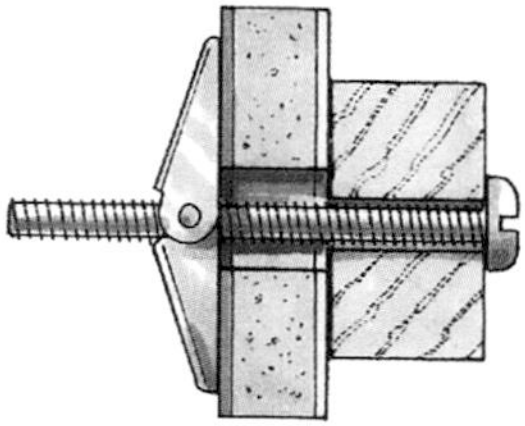

Spring toggle

anchors all have segments that open out or fold up against the inside face of the wallboard or panel.

A rubber anchor has a steel bolt which, when tightened, draws up an internal nut that makes the rubber sleeve bulge out behind the panel.

Metal gravity toggles and spring toggles have arms that open out inside the cavity. A gravity toggle has a single arm, pivoted near one end so that its own weight causes it to drop. A spring toggle has two spring-loaded arms that fly open when clear of the hole and a bolt that draws them tight up against the panel.

A nylon strap toggle has an arm that is held firmly behind the panel by a thin plastic strap while the screw is driven into its pilot hole. The strap is cut off after installation.

Some types of anchor remain in the hole if the screw has to be removed. Others, such as nylon anchors and spring toggles, will be lost in the cavity. A rubber anchor can be removed and then used again.

None of these devices should be used for fixings meant to take a heavy load. Instead, locate the timber wall studs and fix directly into them. On lath-and-plaster walls, even for moderate loads use the larger spring and gravity toggles, rather than plug-type fixing devices.

Nylon strap toggle

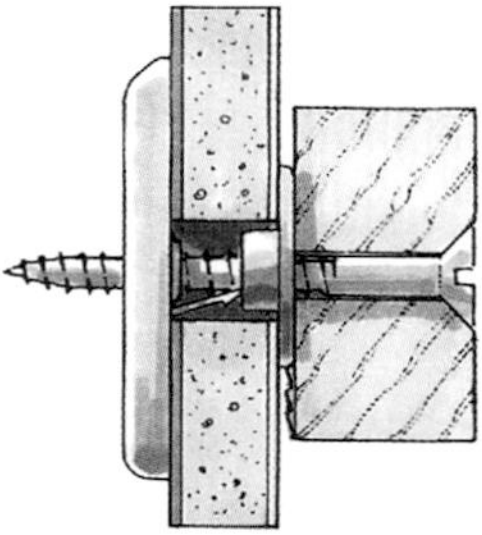

SEE ALSO
332–5

Windows

Traditionally windows have been referred to as 'lights', and the term 'fixed light' is still used to describe a window or part of one that does not open.

Casement windows

Of all the various types of window, the simple hinged or 'casement' window (1) is the most widely used.

Traditional casement window frames made of wood are constructed in much the same fashion as a doorframe. A vertical jamb at each side of the frame is joined by means of mortise-and-tenon joints to the head member at the top and a sill at the bottom.

Glazing bars – relatively lightweight moulded strips of wood – are often employed to divide the glazed areas of a window into smaller panes (2).

Mild-steel casement windows (3) have relatively slim welded frames and sashes. They are strong and durable, but will rust unless protected by galvanized plating or a suitable primer.

Sash windows

Vertically sliding windows are usually known as sash windows. When both the top and the bottom sash can be opened, they are referred to as double-hung sash windows.

Traditional wooden sash windows are constructed with a 'box frame' in which the jambs are made up from three boards – the pulley stile, and the inner and outer lining. A back lining completes the box, which houses the sash counterweights. The head is made up in a similar way but without the back lining, and the sill is cut from solid wood. The pulley stiles are jointed into the sill, and the linings are set in a rebate.

The sashes of a double-hung window are held in tracks formed by the outer lining, a parting bead and an inner staff bead. Both beads can be removed to service the

1. Casement windows

2. Glazing bars

3. Steel casement

WINDOW FRAMES

Most frames and sashes are made up from moulded sections of solid wood. However, mild steel, aluminium and rigid plastic are also used, though such frames are often fixed to the masonry by means of wooden subframes.

Spiral balances

Frame stile

▲ Spiral balances
The exposed balances are fixed to the frame stiles and are set in grooves cut in the sash stiles.

sash mechanism. Each sash is counterbalanced by two cast-iron or lead weights, attached by strong cords or chains that pass over pulleys in the stiles.

Spiral balances
Modern wooden, aluminium or plastic sliding sashes have spring-assisted spiral balances. The balances are fixed to the faces of the stiles.

Pivot windows
Wooden-framed pivot windows are constructed in a similar way to casement windows, but the special hinge mechanism allows the

sash to be rotated so that both sides of the glass can be cleaned from inside. Using the built-in safety catch, the sash can be locked when ajar or when fully reversed.

Louvre windows
A louvre window is a specialized pivot window. The louvres are unframed strips of glass, 6mm (¼in) thick, capped at each end by a moulded plastic carrier. These carriers pivot on metal uprights screwed to the window frame. The louvres are linked by a mechanism that allows them to be opened or closed simultaneously.

Louvre windows provide excellent ventilation, but offer minimal security unless fitted with bonded blade locks. ◄█

▼ *Use two sets of louvres for a wide opening*

SEE ALSO
345

Curtain poles and rails

Window dressings play an important part in interior design. Although the size and shape of the window cannot easily be altered, you can emphasize or modify its proportions by careful dressing with curtains or blinds.

As well as providing privacy, curtains help insulate the room from the sun, cold, draughts and noise. Both the choice of material and the method used for hanging them contribute to the decorative style.

Curtain rails

Modern curtain rails are made from plastic, aluminium or painted steel. They come in various styles and lengths, complete with fixing brackets and glider rings or hooks. Some are supplied ready-corded, which makes drawing curtains easier and minimizes soiling due to handling.

Although typically used in straight lengths, most can be shaped to fit a bay window. Depending on the tightness of the radius, you'll probably need more brackets to support a plastic rail in a bay than a metal one. Plastic bends more easily when warm.

Curtain poles

Curtain poles, once a feature of heavily draped Victorian interiors, are a popular alternative to modern track systems. Curtain poles come in a range of plated, painted or polished finishes.

Traditional-type poles are supported on decoratively shaped brackets, and fitted with end-stop finials and large curtain rings. Some modern ones conceal corded tracks, providing up-to-date mechanisms while retaining old-world charm.

A pair of wall-mounted decorative brackets are normally used to support curtain poles, but a central bracket may be required to support heavy fabrics. Lightweight slim poles are also made for sheer or net curtains. These are fitted with side-fixing or face-fixing sockets.

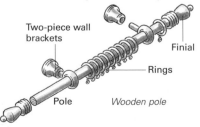

Two-piece wall brackets

Finial

Rings

Pole   *Wooden pole*

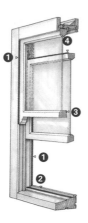

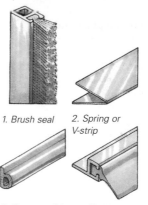

1. Brush seal   2. Spring or
                   V-strip

3. Compressible   4. Blade-seal
strip   strip

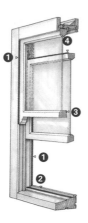

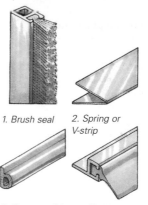

1. Brush seal   2. Spring or
                   V-strip

3. Compressible   4. Blade-seal
strip   strip

Draughtproofing windows

Hinged casement windows are straightforward to seal, using flexible foam and vinyl draughtproofing strips, which are easy to cut into lengths and apply around the window seal. Draughtproofing a sliding-sash window, however, presents a more complex problem. The devices above are similar to those excluders used for a door. ➡

Sealing a sash window

The top and bottom closing rails of a sash window can be sealed with any form of compressible excluder. The sliding edges admit fewer draughts, but they can be sealed with a brush seal (1) fixed to the frame – inside for the lower sash, outside for the top one.

To seal the gap between the sloping faces of the central meeting rails of a traditional sash window, use a springy V-strip (2) or a compressible plastic strip (3). For square faces, use a blade seal (4).

Sealing a pivot window

When you close a pivot window, the movable frame comes to rest against fixed stops. Fitting excluders to these stops will seal off the worst draughts. Provided they are weatherproof, you can use either compressible spring, V-strip or good quality flexible-tube draughtproofing.

SEE ALSO
186

Draughtproofing windows and doors

Efficient and good quality draughtproofing for your house will easily pay for itself in fuel savings in the first year. It will also make for a much cosier home, blocking out those icy blasts through the windows in the winter.

Windows

Most hinged casement windows made of wood will eventually warp and become ill-fitting, causing draughts in your rooms. This can easily be fixed using a soft plastic, self-adhesive moulded draught excluder.

Draught excluder usually comes in a double width roll, which must be split into two single strips for windows [A]. Starting at one end, peel off the backing paper of the strip to reveal the adhesive side [B]. This will be stuck to the outside of the fixed frames, which the opening casement will press against when closed.

Working from the top right hand corner, and ensuring the surfaces of the frame are clean, carefully press the end of the excluder into place, leaving a 25mm (1in) trimming edge [C].

Work anti-clockwise around the edge of the frame. Cut the ends of each length at a 45 deg angle to join neatly at each corner. Close the window and secure it firmly in place to enable the excluder to stick properly.

Tools

Small screwdriver
Bradawl
Scissors
Saw (optional)

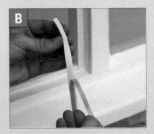

Doors

Doorframes can be draughtproofed using the double draught excluder applied as described above.

Another source of draughts in doors is the keyhole. This can be overcome by fixing what is known as an escutcheon cover plate over the keyhole [D].

Another place which is vulnerable to draughts is the front door letterbox opening. You can purchase ready-made brush draught excluders, but make sure you have the dimensions of your letterbox

with you when you go to buy it. A little oversize is fine, but undersize is no good at all.

Before you begin, remove the inside flap of the letterbox if you have one, as the brush excluder will be replacing this.

Place the brush frame over the letterbox, opening on the inside of the door. Make sure the frame is squarely over the opening, mark the holes with the bradawl and then screw the draught excluder securely to the door [E].

It really is worthwhile spending some time and money to draughtproof your home properly. You might not give this matter much thought during a warm summer, but if you wait until the autumn and winter nights close in, and the wind gets up, you'll realize there is no substitute for cosy, draughtproof windows and doors.

Securing windows

Since windows are particularly vulnerable, it's worth making sure they're adequately secured. There are all sorts of locks for wooden and metal windows, including some that lock automatically when you close the window.

How windows are locked

The type of lock suitable for a window depends on how the window opens. Sliding sashes are normally secured by locking the sashes together, whereas casements – which open like doors – should be fastened to the outer frame or locked by rendering the catches and stays immovable.

Window locks must be strong enough to resist forcing and situated correctly for optimum security. On a small window, for example, fit a single lock as close as possible to the centre of the meeting rail or vertical stile; on larger windows, you will need two locks, spaced apart.

▲ *Using a paint shield*
A plastic or metal shield enables you to paint a straight edge up to glass

Painting window frames

Like doors, window frames need to be painted in sequence so that the various components will be coated evenly – and also so you can close the windows at night.

Painting a casement window

Remove the stay and catch before you paint – but so that you can still operate the window without touching wet paint, drive a nail into the underside of the bottom rail and use as a handle.

First paint the glazing bars, cutting into the glass on both sides. Then the top and bottom horizontal rails, followed by the vertical stiles. Finish with the edges; then paint the frame.

▼ *Where to place window locks*
The black dots indicate the best positions for bolts or locks

Removing cracked glass

In wooden window frames, the glass is set into a rebate cut in the frame's moulding and is then bedded in putty. Small wedge-shaped nails, known as sprigs, are also used to hold the glass in place.

If the glass in a windowpane has shattered, leaving jagged pieces set in the putty, grip each piece separately and try to work it loose. Old putty will usually give way, but it may have to be cut out using a hacking knife and a hammer (1). Work along to remove the putty and glass. Pull out the sprigs with pincers (2).

If the glass is just cracked, run a glass cutter round the perimeter of the pane about 25mm (1in) from the frame, scoring the glass (3). Fasten strips of self-adhesive tape across the cracks, then tap each piece until it breaks free (4). Carefully remove individual pieces of glass, working from the centre of the pane.

Clean remnants of old putty out of the rebates, then seal wood with primer. Measure the opening to the inside the rebates, and have your new glass cut 3mm (⅛in) smaller on each dimension to provide a tolerance for fitting.

1. Cut away old putty

2. Pull out the old sprigs

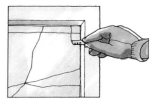

3. Score glass before removing a cracked plane

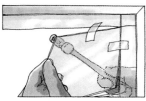

4. Tap the glass to break it free

SEE ALSO
244–5

Repairing/overhauling windows

In most houses, the original window design is the best one suited to the building, so to keep these as long as possible it is worthwhile keeping up basic maintenance.

The most commonly used window in this country is the casement window. These are particularly vulnerable to the weather as they are normally face-fixed (flush with the brickwork) and so have no protection from the elements. The opening sash often distorts slightly with the

temperature, causing it to rattle and become draughty. A solution may be to move the catch plate of the lever fastener to pull the sash tighter into the frame, preventing the rattle.

Undo the catch plate from its original position on the mullion or transom and move it slightly away from the sash [A]. Hold the catch plate in its new position, use a bradawl to start off the new fixing holes [B] and secure. Having moved the catch plate slightly, this should stop the rattle.

Sticking windows can be a problem if they are left undecorated. A window will quickly let in moisture, which

will make the timber swell, in turn making the window difficult to open and close. When a window sticks, a lot of people force the window either open or shut, which can cause problems with the mortice and tenon joints in the sash construction.

Try using candle wax on both the sash window edge and the mullion or transom edge [C]. If that doesn't work, try planing the edge of the sash to help the window open properly [D]. Keep opening and closing the window while planing, so you remove only the minimum amount.

After planing the edge, you must prime, undercoat and topcoat the raw edge of the sash as soon as possible [E]. Allow the paint to dry fully between coats, and then rub up with wax.

Refitting window sashes:
1. Mark the cord grooves
2. Pull the cord through
3. Cut the cords at mark
4. Nail the cord to the sash

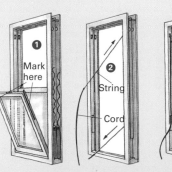

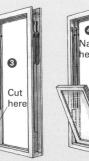

Wood

Timber is classified into two main groups, softwood and hardwood, according to the type of tree it comes from. Softwoods are from evergreen coniferous trees such as firs and pines, whereas hardwoods are from deciduous broad-leaved trees. Most softwoods are in fact softer than most hardwoods, but that is not invariably the case.

Softwoods

Most of the wood you see in a timber yard is softwood, as it is much cheaper than hardwoods and is more widely used for structural house timbers, floorboards, stairs and the simpler kinds of domestic furniture. Softwoods can also be referred to as whitewood, pine, or redwood.

▲ *Knots*
Knots can look attractive in pine boards, but they must be 'live' knots – glossy brown. Black 'dead' knots will shrink and may drop out, weakening the wood.

▲ *Warping*
Distorted timber is another common problem. Look along the edges of each board to check it is not bowed or twisted.

Buying softwood

Most softwood is available in rough and smooth versions called, respectively, sawn and planed. The rough, unplaned surface of sawn timber means that it is suitable only for jobs where it will be out of sight.

Wherever appearance is important, you need planed wood. Having been through a planing machine, this will be relatively smooth. But here, confusion can arise. Planed timber – or PAR (planed all round) – is always slightly thinner and narrower than its nominal dimensions. Machine planing takes about 4 to 6mm (⁵⁄₃₂ to ¼in) off the width and thickness of the wood, but the loss is not uniform, so PAR is generally referred to in terms of its nominal size (the size before planing). You usually need to take this into account

▲ End shakes
Splits at the ends of boards caused by rapid drying; should be regarded as waste.

▲ Heart shakes
Splits that occur along radial lines in the log; when combined at the centre of the tree, they are known as star shakes.

when planning jobs involving planed wood; prepacked planed wood in DIY stores, however, is now sometimes labelled in finished sizes.

Timber yards use the metric system, but most assistants are experts at instant conversion and will advise you if you think and work with imperial dimensions.

▲ Cup shakes
These occur parallel to the tree's annual 'rings'; a board cut from the centre of the tree may have the central ring split away from the other ones along its length.

Hardwoods

Hardwoods are much more expensive than softwoods, and usually have to be bought from specialist timber merchants. They are often coated with clear finishes to display their attractive grain.

Ordering hardwoods

Some hardwoods – for example, oak and meranti – are stocked by timber yards, but a wider range is available from specialist suppliers.

Like softwoods, commonly stocked hardwoods are listed in nominal sizes. Specialist timber merchants will machine the wood to a finished size; or sell you whole planks as cut from the log, ready seasoned for you to convert into smaller sizes with the necessary machinery.

Hardwoods are relatively knot-free, but can suffer from warping, shakes and checks. The figure and colour of the wood may vary from tree to tree of the same species, and also depend on the way it is cut from the log. So ask to see a sample before having a large section of wood machined for you.

If you need to match a hardwood with one already

SEE ALSO
36–8

used in your home, check it carefully, as woods are not always what they seem. Wood dyes are often used to improve the colour of the timber or change its appearance to resemble another species – light-coloured beech, for example, is commonly stained darker to simulate mahogany.

Working with hardwoods

In order to work hardwoods, which are generally somewhat harder than softwoods, tools need to be sharpened more frequently and honed to a fine cutting edge.

▼ Wood is a very versatile material

Screw fixings require drilled pilot holes. If you are screwing into oak, use brass or plated screws; because of the acidic nature of the wood, steel screws will stain it black.

The dust that's created when machining hardwoods can be unpleasant if inhaled. It is therefore advisable to wear a suitable face mask or respirator when working with these woods.

Hardwoods such as teak are naturally oily, and joints need to be glued with a synthetic-resin adhesive to give best results.

Hardwood veneers

Veneers are thin slices of wood cut from the log in various ways. For centuries, expensive hardwoods have been used in veneer form to cover cheaper timber. Today, a wide range of veneers is available for laying onto man-made boards in order to create a luxurious-looking material that is far more stable than solid wood.

Veneers can be bought either as single leaves or in bundles. Pre-veneered boards are also available, but only in a limited range of hardwoods.

Types of parquet flooring

Parquet flooring is a relatively thin covering of decorative timber laid in panels or narrow strips. Hardwoods such as oak, birch and cherry are used for their attractive grain patterns and rich colouring, further highlighted by applying one of the many floor waxes, polishes and varnishes available.

Strip flooring

Wood floors can be made from tongue-and-groove (T&G) or square-edged strips or tiles, machined from solid timber or veneered plywood. Fix either as parallel strips or arrange to make herringbone or woven patterns.

Hardwood panels

Perhaps the most common form of hardwood flooring consists of panels 450mm (1ft 6in) square made by gluing 8mm (⅜in) solid-wood fingers into herringbone or basket-weave patterns. The panels are pre-sanded and sometimes pre-finished.

Timber-faced cork

Not a conventional parquet flooring; made of composite tiles from a layer of cork backed with vinyl and surfaced with a natural or stained hardwood veneer.

1. **Strip flooring**
This is available as plywood or solid-wood strips, and some are prefinished
2. **Hardwood parquet panels**
Solid-wood strips made into flat panels for gluing to the subfloor.
3. **Timber-faced cork**
This type of flooring is easy to lay. Cut to fit with a sharp knife

SEE ALSO
150–3

Woodworm

Our homes are sometimes invaded by insect pests. Some of these are quite harmless, although they cause a great deal of annoyance; but certain insects can severely weaken the structure of a building, and often go unnoticed until the damage is done. At the first signs of infestation try to identify and eradicate the pests as quickly as possible – before they seriously damage your home.

Attack by woodworm
Furniture beetle
Woodworm is the term used to describe all kinds of woodboring insects. The most common of these pests is the furniture beetle. The adult insect is a brown beetle about 3mm (⅛in) long, but the damage is caused by its larvae, which feed on the sapwood of most household timbers. The beetle, which is most active in early summer, lays its eggs in the crevices of bare timber.

When the grubs hatch, they burrow into the wood for up to three years, then pupate just below the surface. The new adult emerges by

▲ *Furniture beetle*

chewing its way out, leaving the familiar round flight hole. These tiny holes, about 1 to 2mm (⅟₁₆in) in diameter, are generally the first signs of infestation – but there may be several generations of woodworm active inside the timber.

Other types of woodworm
The furniture beetle is said to inhabit about three-quarters of British homes – and most outbreaks of woodworm are certainly caused by this pest. However, there are other woodboring insects that can create even greater damage.

Both the deathwatch beetle and the house longhorn

▼ *Deathwatch beetle*

beetle bore much larger holes – from 3 to 6mm (⅛ to ¼in) in diameter. The environmental authorities are anxious to control the spread of these rarer insects, so contact your local Environmental Health Department if you suspect their presence in your home.

Another common pest is the weevil, which attacks wood at two stages in its life cycle. Both the adults and the grubs burrow into all types of timber – but only when it is already decaying and in a very moist condition.

▲ *Weevil*

Locating woodworm

Check the unfinished parts of your furniture, particularly plywood drawer bottoms and backs of cabinets – as wood-boring insects have a taste for the glues used in their manufacture. The wooden frames of upholstered furniture are another favourite habitat; so is any form of wickerwork.

▼ *House longhorn beetle*

The structural timbers of your house are the place where woodworm can do most harm. Inspect roof timbers, stairs, floorboards and joists. The unpainted under-sides of doors and skirtings are also common breeding grounds, as is the upper edge of picture rails.

Where the insects' flight holes are dark in colour, it may be that the timber has already been treated – but clean holes, especially when surrounded by the fine pale-coloured dust known as 'frass', are evidence of recent activity. If the signs are extensive, push a knife blade into the infected timbers; if the wood crumbles, the infestation is serious and you need to seek specialist advice immediately. The damaged woodwork will have to be cut away and replaced, then the new and old wood treated with a chemical preserver. ☞

SEE ALSO
442–3

Treating woodworm

If woodworm is spotted by a surveyor when inspecting a house that you are thinking of buying, your mortgage company will insist that you hire a specialist to eradicate the pest – mainly because the work will carry a 30-year guarantee.

Similarly, if you detect woodworm in your present home, have it inspected by a specialist firm who will advise you on the extent of the damage (which may not be obvious to the untrained eye) and quote a price for treating the infested timber.

Hire a specialist contractor to treat woodworm in structural timbers. The contractor will use a spray lance to treat the joists and the undersides of floorboards.

You can treat less serious infestation yourself, using a chemical insecticide. Most of these fluids are flammable; so don't smoke when applying them, and extinguish any naked flames. Wear protective gloves, goggles and a respirator. The initial smell of solvent-based eradicators can be unpleasant, but will gradually fade.

▲ *Inject fluid into the flight holes*

Water-based low-odour woodworm eradicators are solvent-free and non-flammable. This type of eradicator is suitable for use in bat roosts.

Minor outbreaks

Dealing with a minor woodworm outbreak in furniture and other small wooden items is a fairly simple task.

Woodworm fluid

Use either a can with a pointed nozzle or a special aerosol applicator to inject woodworm fluid into the insects' flight holes every 75 to 100mm (3 to 4in). Since the tunnels are connected, the fluid will penetrate deeply into the wood. Continue the treatment by painting all unfinished

▲ *Spray fluid into confined spaces*

timber with two coats of fluid. There's no need to paint fluid onto polished surfaces, although it will not harm them.

Use a pump-action spray can or an aerosol to coat wickerwork and the inside of confined spaces.

Disguising flight holes
After treatment, fill flight holes in painted woodwork with cellulose filler. Use sticks of wax to match the colour of polished or varnished wood. It is possible to use children's wax crayons, but sticks of harder wax are available from specialist wood-finish suppliers. Cut off a piece of wax and put it on top of a radiator to soften. Using a pocket knife, press the wax into the woodworm holes and leave it to harden. Scrape the repair flush with an old plastic phone or credit card, then fold a piece of sandpaper and use the paper backing to burnish the wax filling.

Preventative treatment
To protect new timber from attack, treat it with a chemical preserver. Once the wood is dry, it can be decorated in the usual way.

Furniture can be protected with an insecticidal polish. If you buy an old piece of furniture that shows any signs of infestation, treat it with a chemical preserver to be on the safe side.

▶ **Disguising flight holes**
Fill small holes with sticks of wax that match the colour of the polished or varnished timber

SEE ALSO
82–5

Index

Acknowledgements

The publishers would like to thank the following individuals for producing the materials from which this book was derived:

Illustrators: Brian Craker, David Day, Robin Harris, Michael Parr and Brian Sayers

Photographers: Paul Chave, Peter Higgins, Ben Jennings and Neil Waving

The publishers would also like to acknowledge the generosity of the many companies – too numerous to list here – which supplied samples of their materials and products for artists' reference and photography.